Praise for Dan Jenkins and

JENKINS AT THE MAJORS

"For style, outrageous humor and longevity, it's hard to top Dan Jenkins."
—*Newsday*

"His writing and his ear recall—there is no higher compliment— Ring Lardner, though in different times and different Americas."
—David Halberstam, *The New York Times Book Review*

"Jenkins ranks with the best and most influential sportswriters of the twentieth century."
—Gary Van Sickle, Golf.com

"Jenkins takes us inside the world of golf like no one else."
—*The Sacramento Bee*

"Jenkins is hilarious, providing more laughs per page than any other writer in the 'bidness.'"
—*People*

Dan Jenkins

JENKINS AT THE MAJORS

Dan Jenkins was an award-winning writer for *Sports Illustrated* for more than twenty years. He is the author of nineteen works of fiction and nonfiction, including *Semi-Tough*, *Dead Solid Perfect*, *Baja Oklahoma*, *Life Its Ownself*, *Rude Behavior*, *Fairways and Greens*, *Slim and None*, *The Franchise Babe*, and most recently, *Jenkins at the Majors*. He currently writes a popular column for *Golf Digest* and now lives full-time in his native Fort Worth, Texas.

JENKINS AT THE MAJORS

JENKINS AT THE MAJORS

Sixty Years of the World's Best Golf Writing,
from Hogan to Tiger

DAN JENKINS

Anchor Books
A Division of Random House, Inc.
New York

FIRST ANCHOR BOOKS EDITION, JUNE 2010

Copyright © 2009 by D&J Ventures, Inc.

All rights reserved. Published in the United States by Anchor Books, a division of
Random House, Inc., New York, and in Canada by Random House of Canada Limited,
Toronto. Originally published in hardcover in the United States by Doubleday,
a division of Random House, Inc., New York, in 2009.

Anchor Books and colophon are registered trademarks of Random House, Inc.

The author and publisher gratefully acknowledge *Sports Illustrated* and *Golf Digest* for
the right to reprint material in this book.

Frontispiece: Tony Triolo/*Sports Illustrated*/Getty Images

The Library of Congress has cataloged the Doubleday edition as follows:
Jenkins, Dan.
Jenkins at the Majors : sixty years of the world's best golf writing,
from Hogan to Tiger / by Dan Jenkins.—1st ed.
p. cm.
1. Golf—Tournaments—History. 2. PGA Tour (Association)—History.
I. Title II. Title: Jenkins at the Majors.
GV970.J64 2009
796.352'64—dc22
2008039255

Anchor ISBN: 978-0-7679-2529-7

Book design by Elizabeth Rendfleisch

www.anchorbooks.com

Printed in the United States of America
10 9 8 7 6 5 4 3 2 1

This book is dedicated to all of the excellent editors and reporters
I've had the pleasure of working with over the years. Gentlemen and ladies
on newspapers and magazines who became friends and whose deft work
often made me sound smarter than I am, and who were alert enough on other
occasions to apprehend the line that might draw too much blood,
thereby saving me from myself, and excess sniper fire.

"A golfer's true greatness must always be measured by the number of major championships he wins."

—Herbert Warren Wind, to a young Texas sportswriter
on the Augusta National veranda in 1954

CONTENTS

PART TWO: THE SIXTIES

PART THREE: THE SEVENTIES 77

PART FOUR: THE EIGHTIES   143

PART FIVE: THE NINETIES

PART SIX: THE TWO THOUSANDS

ACKNOWLEDGMENTS

FIRST I HAVE to sing thanks for the memories to two daily newspapers, the *Fort Worth Press* and *Dallas Times Herald*. They no longer exist today, but before anyone can lay the blame on me for this because I once worked in their fun-filled newsrooms, there's proof that I'd left long before the evils of the financial world forced them to become extinct, all too sadly.

A hearty thanks goes to *Sports Illustrated*. It kept me in luxurious comfort on its campus in New York City for 23 wonderful years—when it wasn't sending me all over the country and various parts of the globe.

A mighty salute also goes to *Golf Digest*, which at this writing continues to provide food, shelter, friendship, and help with the dangling modifiers.

It is with the kind permission of both *SI* and *Digest* that I'm able to give another life to the stuff in here they paid me to write for them.

Finally, I'm indebted to Mark Mourer for his assistance with this collection. He's a Texas friend who was attacked by the sportswriting bug at an early age but refuses to go see a doctor and have it cut out.

INTRODUCTION

IF YOU WERE to string all these pieces and fragments of pieces end to end, they would no doubt make the longest par five in the history of journalism, or even golf.

Of course, you wouldn't want to do this. It would probably require getting down on your hands and knees at some point. I have to confess that it was hard enough for me to go back and read about some of our heroes who sometimes found fascinating ways to lose.

There are two main things these essays have in common.

One, they all deal with golf's major championships—the Masters Tournaments, U.S. Opens, British Opens, and PGAs—that I've had the good fortune and pleasure of covering for one publication or another. Two, owing to deadlines, most of them were written in such haste that the nearest tavern wound up having me on its hands for a longer period of time than the pressrooms did on those urgent evenings.

I should mention that about half of these stories were written on typewriters, those quaint machines some of you may remember. A typewriter had an ink ribbon running from one spool to another and sounded like Fred Astaire on a hardwood floor while you were pecking away, trying to keep Hemingway from snatching the Nobel from you again.

The pieces I've chosen to put in here were typed for the *Fort Worth Press*, *Dallas Times Herald*, *Sports Illustrated*, and *Golf Digest*, and there is a certain amount of fresh material included.

It all adds up to 94 holes—uh, stories—a number that corresponds with my score on the golf course these days, if I'm forced to count them all.

It may be irrelevant to readers that I was once a scratch golfer. This was back in my college days and for a few years afterward in Texas amateur circles. But it's not irrelevant to my fond memories. Not that I ever won anything. There were too many guys around named Don January, Billy Maxwell, Don Cherry, Morris Williams Jr., Joe Conrad, Earl Stewart, Jacky Cupit, and Ernie Vossler for the rest of us to think about winning anything.

I hope these particular pieces present a significant history of pro golf as it unfolded from 1951 through 2008.

From Ben Hogan to Tiger Woods, in other words, with Arnold Palmer and Jack Nicklaus in between. Or close to 60 years, to put it another way.

Nearly all of the pieces—game stories, features, columns, or fragments of game stories, features, and columns—have been doctored one way or another. Shortened for sure, smoothed out, tweaked, dated. Such is the privilege of a man doing a collection, unless, like Bogart in *Casablanca*, I was misinformed.

It would not have been possible to include every story of every major that I've covered. Not unless I wanted to go up against *The Oxford English Dictionary* for weight. Recently, I counted up that I've been to exactly 197 of them over these years.

I could add one more if I wanted to include the 1941 U.S. Open at Colonial Country Club in my hometown of Fort Worth. I was only 11 years old at the time, taken out there each day by my golf-nut dad and golf-nut uncle. It was fascinating. But I have to confess I spent most of the time marveling at the snappy beltless slacks the pros were wearing, and the magic of golf balls spinning backward on the lush bent greens.

Those things hadn't made it to my neighborhood.

Or as the Florida waitress said in a catfish joint one night when I asked her for a cappuccino, "Hon, that ain't got here yet."

That 197 number is surely a record of some kind. To which I can only say that if any writer has covered more than 58 consecutive Masters Tournaments, 55 U.S. Opens, 44 PGAs, and 40 British Opens, let him speak now or forever hold his press credential and parking pass.

As for writing on deadline, I can best sum up the task by quoting my first newspaper boss, lifelong friend and guru Blackie Sherrod, who in those quaint days seemed to enjoy saying, "Stop feelin' up that story, and get the damn thing in here."

Finally, I suppose I should pass along the time-honored remark of the sportswriter on the road who has written and filed his or her story to the office, having beaten the deadline yet again. It goes:

"It's a good thing I didn't have more time—I could have really screwed it up."

—Dan Jenkins

PART ONE

The Fifties

•

"Ben Hogan would rather let a black widow spider crawl around inside his shirt than hit a hook."

—CLAUDE HARMON

MONSTER BROUGHT TO ITS KNEES

Ben Hogan at the 1951 U.S. Open at Oakland Hills

BEN HOGAN shot the greatest round of his life—maybe of anyone's life—a stunning three-under 67 in the final round of the U.S. Open championship to win it yet again, this time on the torturous layout of Oakland Hills Country Club near Detroit, but mostly what he wanted to talk about afterward was why people watch golf in the first place. Goodness, don't they have something better to do?

"The golf fan really has my respect," Ben said. "They go out there and get sunburned or rained on, they push each other around, they stand until their backs ache, and I just can't understand how they do it."

He said, "There were probably twenty thousand people out there in the last round, and fifteen thousand of them didn't see anything. There is this couple from Orange, New Jersey, that's followed me for, well, I don't know for how long. They always seem to turn up where I'm playing, and I can always spot them in the crowd."

Interesting to hear this from the man who is supposed to concentrate so deeply that walking from green to tee he's been accused on occasion of failing to recognize his wife, Valerie, when he encountered her.

Hogan went on, "There's a man from Tyler who's been watching me play for more than 10 years. And there's a fellow from Memphis—I don't even know his name—he's always in my gallery. I like to watch college football. You can see everything in reasonable comfort, and it only takes about three hours. But golf . . . I don't know."

Those who watched the golf at Oakland Hills saw the greatest player in the game win on what may have been the toughest Open course ever devised. He did it in the final hours of "Open Saturday," firing the low round of the championship and one of only two scores below 70 over the entire 72 holes. Considering that the average score of the field in the last 18 was 78 strokes, it could be argued that Hogan's closing 67—despite two bogeys—was actually 11 under.

It was Hogan's fourth Open title. That's if you count the '42 "wartime" National Open that he won at Chicago's Ridgemoor Country Club. Next was the record-setting win at Riviera in '48, then last year's comeback triumph in a playoff at Merion, and now this one.

Ben only smiled when reminded that if you ignore the '49 Open at Medinah, the championship he missed because of the near-fatal car wreck, he had actually won three in a row with the Oakland Hills victory.

Even Bobby Jones hadn't done that.

After rounds of 76 and 73, Hogan began the last 36 holes five strokes behind the halfway leader, Bobby Locke, and in a 10-way tie for 16th place.

His 71 in the morning round drew him within striking distance. At this point he was only two back of the co-leaders, Locke and Jimmy Demaret, with Julius Boros and Paul Runyan one ahead of him.

In the afternoon Ben went out directly behind Demaret at a 12-minute interval, and a full hour and a half ahead of Locke, the jowly South African whose putting style resembles a slap but who often makes life uncomfortable for American pros—by beating them on their own tour.

Overlooking the spike marks and divots, and the wear and tear on his body, the golf course Hogan conquered in that final round was a devilish thing that architect Robert Trent Jones had remodeled with orders from the club's membership to "toughen it up and make it memorable."

What Jones did was triple the number of bunkers and relocate them where they were most likely to catch drives off the tee, grow the rough up to eight or 10 inches in most spots, and pinch in the fairways to a sinister 22 yards across.

Sam Snead described the fairways after his one-over 71 led the first round. He said, "I knew it was gonna be tough when I played my first practice round. Three of us walked side by side down the first fairway, and two of us were in the rough."

One of Hogan's trademarks is that he knows how to learn from his mistakes.

At the 380-yard seventh hole in the morning round, Ben's tee shot found a brook that cut into the right side of the fairway. It cost him a bogey five. But in the afternoon he hugged the left side of the fairway from the tee, pitched to two feet of the cup, and made a birdie.

The 392-yard 15th hole featured a bunker squarely in the middle of the fairway. Hogan's drive in the morning round went too far left and became tangled in the deep rough. It cost him a double-bogey six. But in the afternoon he played a beautiful spoon off the tee and the ball sneaked safely into the narrow alley left of the bunker. Then from there, his approach was a deadly shot to within six feet of the flag, and he got another birdie.

Don't tell Ben how to get even with a golf course.

All week long, there was more grumbling and growling than usual on the part of the pros regarding the "unfairness" of Oakland Hills, but Hogan may have said it best at the presentation ceremony.

As he caressed the Open trophy, he said, "I'm glad I was finally able to bring this course, this monster, to its knees."

Actually, he called it something else in private.

SLIPPERY SLOPES

Sam Snead at the 1952 Masters

SAM SNEAD said he grabbed the 1952 Masters on greens "slicker'n the top of my head."

Nobody expresses things better than Sam, usually. But he might have mentioned that the wind had something to do with the tournament—and the greens.

"One or two times, I thought I was on roller skates out there on those greens," said Sam.

The final scores reflected that the wind had never blown harder, gustier, or more continuously over the Augusta National layout than it did during the last two days. Not only did it drive Snead's winning total up to 286—highest in Masters history—it all but swept away such serious challengers as Ben Hogan, Cary Middlecoff, and Tommy Bolt.

Snead and Hogan began the last round in a tie for the lead at 214. Middlecoff was two back. Bolt was three. Ben had shot 70-70-74 while Snead had gone low and high with 70-67-78.

But Hogan's five three-putt greens on Sunday helped drag him to a disastrous 79, the highest score he'd posted in a major championship since his 80 in the last round of the U.S. Open at Philadelphia's Spring Mill in '39—the Open where Snead made his famous eight on the last hole and Byron Nelson eventually won in a playoff over Craig Wood and Denny Shute.

While this was happening, Middlecoff was stumbling to a 78—"I couldn't get comfortable out there," he said—and then there was Bolt. The tempestuous one was two under par and only one back of Snead when he went to the 15th hole, but he three-putted three straight greens, the winds rocking him around in his stance, and came into the clubhouse to preach sermons about the wind, the greens, and pin placements.

Meanwhile, Sam carved out an even-par 72—and there were only three rounds better than Snead's all day. The best one, and the only sub-70 score, was Jackie Burke's 69, which pulled him up into second place. Burke required only 27 putts, or as he put it, "The cup wouldn't get out of the way."

Snead somehow managed only 31 putts in the gusts and gales to win his second Masters and his sixth major championship, while Hogan required a ridiculous 40 putts.

Hogan had no explanation for a collapse that saw him finish in a tie for seventh when he was thought to be the odds-on favorite Sunday.

"I thought I hit the ball as well as I did the first three rounds," Ben said, "but things kept going wrong. It wasn't always the wind. There were some bad bounces out there."

This was the fourth year of the green jacket ceremony, which was introduced in 1949 when Snead won his first Masters. The winner now receives a blazer similar to those worn by Augusta National members.

Hogan slipped the coat on Snead as the winner and defending champion gathered on the 18th green with the Masters tournament committee.

"This one don't fit either," Sam said, "but I'll keep it."

THE HUNGARIAN

Julius Boros at the 1952 U.S. Open at Northwood in Dallas

N U.S. OPENS it's usually Ben Hogan that's "holding the Hungarian," as golfers and other gamblers call it, meaning a sure thing. But this time, somewhat ironically, it was a young pro of Hungarian blood with a golden putting stroke that was holding it. Otherwise, it wouldn't have been possible for the little-known Julius Boros to snatch the 1952 Open away from Hogan in the draining heat and humidity of Northwood Country Club, a new course nestled in a new-rich neighborhood of Dallas.

Boros did it over the final two rounds Saturday even though Hogan knew the course better than anybody, had strongly campaigned for Northwood to host the national championship after the club was opened in 1948, had equaled the 36-hole Open record of 138 with 69s on Thursday and Friday, and had seemed to have the title firmly in his grasp for two and a half of the three days.

But Hogan started losing it in his morning round when a shocking double bogey sent him to a 74, and Boros, who may have smoked more cigarettes than Hogan while "hitting it on the run," as he described his style, started winning it with his putting stroke. Among other things, Boros one-putted seven greens over the last nine holes. This brought him in with a one-over 71 and the 281 total that left him four ahead of Porky Oliver and five ahead of Hogan.

Ben and Porky, who were paired together, looked like a cinch to wind up tied for second until the very last green, where the jolly, wisecracking Oliver holed a 50-foot putt for a birdie.

Northwood's sporty but confining layout was designed by William Diddel, an architect from Indiana, but half the course was revamped for the Open by Fort Worth's Ralph (Rab) Plummer, who was particularly proud of the sixth hole.

"Pecan Narrows" is the affectionate name given by members to the long, dark, 450-yard sixth. The fairway is closed in by trees, the green guarded by deep bunkers, and directly behind the green is a ditch and service road, which is out of bounds.

Hogan bogeyed it the first day when his 2-iron second found a bunker, but it was the double-bogey six on Saturday morning that started his downfall. Ben hit a fine drive and a seemingly wonderful 4-wood to the green. In the air, the shot looked like a two. But it found a hard spot and bounced to the back of the green, and drifted down the slope and was out of bounds—by one foot.

This cost Hogan the Open lead and he would never regain it.

"It was a stupid club selection," Ben said later. "I paid for it. I got what I deserved."

Boros actually started winning it with his Saturday-morning 68 when he took only 11 putts on the last nine holes. This round pushed him two shots ahead of Hogan, and it was his putter that kept saving it for the former staff sergeant in the Army Medical Corps, a man who quit his job as an accountant to take up golf.

"I got tired of working for a living and turned pro," he said.

It was over a four-hole stretch on the last nine of the championship—the 13th through the 16th—that Boros and his putter defied logic.

By then the majority of fans were following him. So were his brother, Ernest, and a fellow North Carolinian, Clayton Heafner, a gruff, burly tour veteran who'd withdrawn earlier. They walked next to Boros every step, keeping up the pep talk, which sounded like chatter from a baseball dugout.

Boros snap-hooked his drive into the rough at the 13th hole, put his second in the bunker, blasted out to eight feet, and awkwardly hit behind the putt. But the ball found the cup to save his par.

At the par-five 14th he was again bunkered but came out to within 10 feet and holed the putt for a birdie.

He was bunkered at the 15th, and his sand shot was a long way from drawing any applause, seeing as how it was 30 feet from the cup. But his putt went in after sliding around the edge.

Boros continued his miracles with an unbelievable par save at the 16th hole, a 210-yard par three. Off the tee he hit a nervous apple-turnover into the tall rough near the green. If that wasn't bad enough he almost whiffed the next one, a look-up pitch that stopped inches shy of the green, about 35 feet from the flag over a tricky contour.

What happened instead of the double bogey he deserved? He rammed home the monster putt to save another par.

In case you're not a Ben Hogan and can do it with fairways and greens, that's how you win a U.S. Open.

4

SLAMMING THE DOOR ON THE SLAMMER

Ben Hogan vs. Sam Snead at the 1953 U.S. Open at Oakmont

THERE WERE those ink-stained wretches on hand who swore they saw Ben Hogan tuck the 1953 U.S. Open under his arm and run off with it after his first-round 67. It's all over, they said. Look, there he goes now, romping through Oakmont's furrowed bunkers and lightning greens like they don't even exist.

Hogan, of course, knew better. In this shady suburb of Pittsburgh he knew he was going to be in a long fight, primarily with Sam Snead, his top rival, and that it wasn't going to be over until late Saturday.

Ben's five-under round on Thursday was the low 18 of the championship, and it did give him a three-shot lead on the field and a five-shot lead on Snead. And Hogan did birdie three of the first four holes on Friday, which sent certain writers to muttering, "It's no contest."

But Snead had some golfing to do himself, and Sam, after all, had won the PGA on this same Oakmont two years earlier. Sam's 69 on Friday picked up three strokes on Ben, and his 72 Saturday morning picked up another stroke. Now Hogan was left with a thin one-stroke advantage going into the final 18, and to make matters worse Ben went off a full hour ahead of Sam.

That's inconvenient for a golfer. Only being able to guess at what those noises behind him mean. The advantage would be Snead's. He'd always know what Hogan was doing up ahead, and what he might need.

Even though Ben led after each round, and his scores of 67-72-73-71 added up to an Oakmont record of 283, giving him a six-shot margin over Snead at the finish, it would be a mistake to say that Hogan won in a cakewalk.

Snead was two strokes ahead of Hogan through five holes of the Saturday-morning round, and Sam was still one stroke ahead of Ben through nine, or 45 holes, with 27 remaining.

When Hogan made up that stroke and one more, however, they broke for lunch with Hogan at 212 and Snead at 213. It was a ball game. And it stayed a ball game throughout the afternoon, right up until Hogan's fantastic finish over Oakmont's last three holes.

On the 16th tee was where Hogan, one over on the round, heard from a friend in the gallery that he was still holding a one-shot lead on Snead. Sam was more than an hour behind now, and had six or seven holes left to play on which he could make up ground.

Hogan clearly needed a big finish, and what a finish it was.

The brassie to the 234-yard 16th was his best shot of the day, Ben insisted. A choked-down, high cut into a crosswind. The ball settled 25 feet from the flag and rewarded him with a two-putt par on a hole that seriously worried him.

Then came the 17th. In three rounds he hadn't tried to drive the green at this unique 292-yard par four. He'd been laying up off the tee, but this time he went for it and drove perfectly onto the green, 25 feet from the flag. His putt for an eagle just missed, but he had a tap-in birdie.

Hogan's monstrous drive at the 462-yard par-four 18th split the fairway, and his 5-iron second stuck within 10 feet of the cup. Then, with practically everyone with a ticket lining the hole from tee to green, he sank the putt for another birdie and the 3-3-3 finish that took care of anything Snead might have in mind behind him.

Later, Ben was reminded of something he said two months ago in Augusta, Georgia, when he set the 72-hole record of 274 in winning his second Masters. "This was the best golf I've ever played," he had said.

So how about the 283, five under par, on rugged old Oakmont with its furrowed bunkers and marble-top greens, a much tougher course?

Hogan said, "I believe I prepared for this Open more than most of the other fellows. I played more practice rounds. I didn't know what to expect from this course. It has quite a reputation."

It was Hogan's fourth "official" U.S. Open, but he doesn't have long to celebrate. He and Valerie sail in 10 days for England and his first try in the British Open at Carnoustie in Scotland.

Fred Corcoran, Ben's former agent-manager and once the director of the PGA Tour, said in Pittsburgh, "If Hogan can win the British Open to go with his Masters and U.S. Open this year, it will give him a Triple Crown, and this will be the greatest golfing achievement since Bobby Jones's Grand Slam."

AUTHOR'S NOTE: I've always regretted that I didn't make an effort to cover Hogan at Carnoustie. I was even traveling around Europe at the time, enjoying a college graduation present from my folks. But I did think about Hogan, Scotland, Carnoustie, and the possible Triple Crown, while I was being unavoidably detained at this sidewalk café in Paris—and I don't even remember her name.

5

TWO IMMORTALS, ONE WINNER

Ben Hogan vs. Sam Snead in a Playoff at the 1954 Masters

MONG THE sweltering crowd of 5,000 there were men who climbed trees and plumpish barefoot women, and they all trudged in and around Augusta National's pines and blossoms for three hours and 32 minutes to find out that perhaps Ben Hogan, the club maker, is not quite as good a golfer as Ben Hogan, the Bantam, Hawk, Wee Icemon.

This was sort of what everyone concluded as they beat through the nettles and thicket and took shortcuts through the trees like natives going deep into gorilla country to watch the 1954 Masters decided in a memorable 18-hole playoff.

The dry leaves crackled and the sun bore down and the Southerners among them let out a howl that traveled from President Dwight Eisenhower's white cottage near the 10th tee to the eastern seaboard when Sam Snead was home in front by a scant stroke, 70 to 71.

Maybe a golden era was over. Both men are in their forties, and it's doubtful they will ever collide again, head to head, in a duel for a major championship.

Here was Sam going for his third Masters in dark blue slacks, yellow shirt, and customary straw hat, more than willing to submit his explosive, long-hitting game to Augusta's daring options.

Then here was Hogan in his customary gray slacks, white shirt, and white cap. Icy and calculating, prepared to play his own steady game and let Sam take the chances. It was not lost on historians that Ben was going for his fourth major in a row, having won the Masters, U.S. Open, and British Open a year ago.

The week gave the American press a chance to talk to Ben about his win at Carnoustie, since none of them had been there. Yes, he'd made headlines by saying he would send Carnoustie some lawn mowers for the course. He spoke of his two ticker-tape parades upon returning—one in Manhattan and one in Fort Worth. He talked of never knowing exactly how he stood until the last four holes of the final round. Communications weren't so wonderful, but then Great Britain was still recovering from the war. Food rationing still existed. One egg a day.

In the final analysis of the playoff, it wasn't Snead's bold shotmaking that brought him victory as much as it was Hogan's old brass-head putter that betrayed him throughout the week, or there would have been no playoff. When a man's mind is elsewhere when he's trying to win a golf tournament, much less a major, it will tell in the putting stroke more than anywhere else.

Actually, there might not have been a playoff at all if a third character in the drama of Sunday's final 18 hadn't been so impulsive. This was the amateur, Billy Joe Patton. The drawling, quick-hitting young guy from North Carolina led the first two rounds, and after surrendering the 54-hole lead to Hogan he reclaimed it with a thunderous hole-in-one at the sixth hole Sunday. He was still leading at the par-five 13th—thanks in part to Hogan's double bogey at the 11th when he pulled a 4-iron into the pond—but that's when Billy Joe drowned his own chances.

"Ah didn't git whur ah am playin' safe," he said to the gallery an instant before he whacked a 4-wood into the creek. Double bogey. Doom.

This gave the Masters back to Snead and Hogan to settle on Monday.

It's an interesting historical note that there have now been only three playoffs in Masters history, and Hogan has lost two of them. The first was in 1935 when Gene Sarazen topped Craig Wood, the second came in 1942 when Byron Nelson narrowly edged Hogan in what some people called "a Fort Worth city championship," and now this one.

Ben and Sam had it out in their own self-styled ways. Hogan was cautious. From tee to green, he was nearer perfection than at any time during the week. He hit 17 greens but took 36 putts. Snead was the opposite. Sam went for everything, and it paid off. He two-putted for three of his birdies after attacking the eighth, 13th, and 15th holes, all par fives.

Snead hit only 14 greens and took 32 putts in comparison, and may well have struck the greatest blow of the day when he chipped in for a birdie from 50 feet with his 7-iron at the long, downhill, picturesque 10th hole, a par four.

Hogan missed at least six decent birdie putts, each time the ball slowly creasing the lip of the cup but refusing to drop. And when he three-putted from 14 feet at the 16th hole to fall two behind, it was all over.

Snead bunkered his second shot to the 18th to give Ben some hope, but Sam blasted out to six feet and two-putted for the bogey he needed when Hogan's birdie putt failed again.

So it ended. A playoff and perhaps a golden era.

DOCTOR MAKES A COURSE CALL

Dr. Cary Middlecoff Wins the 1955 Masters

T'S ENTIRELY possible that Dr. Cary Middlecoff gave up dentistry because people couldn't hold their mouths open that long.

Middlecoff is beyond a doubt the most tedious, fidgety, and methodical golfer that has ever roamed the fairways, and now the tall, 34-year-old ex-dentist from Tennessee, a guy usually seen in a white visor pausing on his backswing long enough for a turkey to be roasted, holds the record for the biggest margin of victory in the history of the Masters.

It's one thing to say that Doc won the 1955 Masters by seven strokes, but it's another to say that he did it by beating Ben Hogan, who was second, and Sam Snead, who was third.

This gives Middlecoff his second major and lifts him into the category of a marquee star in the game. His first major came in the 1949 U.S. Open at Medinah in Chicago, the one Hogan missed because of the car wreck.

If there was any single round that won it for Doc, it was the second. That's when he fired a seven-under-par 65, the second-lowest round ever shot on the Augusta National premises. Lloyd Mangrum's 64 in the opening round in 1940 is still the lowest, although Lloyd couldn't ride it to a win. He finished second that year to Jimmy Demaret.

If there was a single stroke in Middlecoff's 65 that stood out, it was certainly his 80-foot putt for an eagle three at the 13th hole. He had put his second shot on the green with a 4-wood from a downhill lie. A beauty.

He then rapped in the meandering putt that started on the far left side of the green and seemed to take forever, going by way of Macon, Georgia, Milledgeville, Georgia, and Walton Way in downtown Augusta, and finally into the cup.

Middlecoff started the last round with a four-stroke lead on Hogan, and while shooting a 70 to Ben's 73 he found himself in difficulty only once. This was when he stubbed his second shot to the tenth and put it in a bunker and took two to get out. Result: double-bogey six.

It brought back a memory. Middlecoff had been paired with Jim Ferrier in 1950 when Ferrier doubled the 10th and went on a bogey rampage and blew a five-shot lead that allowed Demaret to win.

"That was in the back of my mind," Middlecoff admitted. "But Byron settled me down."

Byron Nelson, he meant. The man with whom Middlecoff was paired in the last round. It seems Byron has a habit of being paired with Masters winners.

Nelson thus accompanied his sixth winner to the Augusta National clubhouse, not counting the two Byron won for himself in '37 and '42.

Middlecoff recalled Byron saying to him more than once, "Come on, Doc. Play golf. You're okay."

UPSET OF THE AGES

1955 U.S. Open at the Olympic Club in San Francisco

WHEN A sportswriter for the *Pittsburgh Press* named Bob Drum called his wife long-distance from the 1955 U.S. Open pressroom at the Olympic Club in San Francisco, the conversation went like this:

"I gotta stay over another day," Bob said.

"Why?" asked Marian Jane Drum.

"To cover the playoff."

"There's no playoff. Ben Hogan won the Open. They said so on TV. What a liar you are! You just want to stay in San Francisco and get drunk another day."

"I can get drunk in Pittsburgh."

"So come home."

"I'm telling you, I've gotta cover the playoff tomorrow between Hogan and Jack Fleck."

"Who?"

"Jack Fleck. He tied Hogan after TV went off."

"*Jack Fleck?* That's the dumbest name you've ever made up."

Ben Hogan had already won this Open, of course. With his pinpoint driving and his finely honed irons for dealing with Olympic's tall, damp, gnarled rough, he had shot a final-round 70, even par, for a total of 287.

That total was five strokes better than Sam Snead, who finished 30 minutes ahead of him, and Tommy Bolt, who finished 30 minutes behind him. They would be tied for second.

Nobody could have played the course better than Hogan for four rounds. Feeling he had won, Ben had even handed the last golf ball he used to Joseph C. Dey Jr., the executive director of the U.S. Golf Association, when he walked off the 72nd green.

"Here, Joe, this is for Golf House," he had said, referring to the USGA museum in New York City.

Moments later, looking sapped and weary from Saturday's labors, Hogan smoked a cigarette and sipped an iced tea on a bench in the Olympic locker room while a half-dozen writers hovered around him.

"Well, Ben, it looks like you finally have your fifth Open," one of the New York journalists said.

"Sixth," Ben said quietly.

To which a Hogan fan explained to the New York writer about Ben winning the wartime Open in '42.

"Oh," the New York man said. "Yes. Of course."

Soon enough, a man pushed into the group and said, "There's a guy named Jack Fleck still on the course. He needs two birdies on the last four holes to tie."

Ben looked around and asked, "What's his name?"

Fleck, he was told. Jack Fleck.

"Huh," said Ben. "I don't know him. But I hope he either makes three birdies or one. I don't want a playoff."

When the news arrived that Jack Fleck had, in fact, birdied the 15th and parred the 16th and 17th holes, every guy with a press badge wandered out to No. 18 to see how the stranger would finish.

Fleck was obviously in an "Open coma" when he drove into the fairway, hit a short iron onto the green, and sank a seven-foot birdie putt for the 67 that tied Ben Hogan.

Sunday's 18-hole playoff was agony for Hogan people.

When Fleck sank birdie putts of 10, 20, and 15 feet for birdies at the eighth, ninth, and 10th holes, seizing a three-stroke lead, it appeared impossible for Hogan to rally.

A faint ray of hope came out of the fog and mist at the 14th when Ben sank a 20-foot birdie putt while Fleck three-putted for a bogey. Now Hogan was only one shot back with four to play.

But Hogan couldn't get another birdie to drop, and when his foot slipped as he tried to launch a big drive on the 18th tee, the ball buried in the brutal rough. It took him two slashes to get out, and the result was a double-bogey six, giving Fleck the playoff—and the Open—with a 69 to Ben's 72.

Some might recall a couple of obscure fellows named Sam Parks Jr. and Tony Manero winning the U.S. Open in the back-to-back years of 1935 and 1936 at Oakmont and Baltusrol.

But at Olympic it was safe to say that a thin, somber man named Jack Fleck of Davenport, Iowa, a pro for only three years, added a new dimension to the word "unknown."

8

THE MAN WHO RUINED A STORY

Jackie Burke Wins the 1956 Masters

JACKIE BURKE'S victory in the 1956 Masters ruined more newspaper leads than a worn-out typewriter ribbon. When the handsome, entertaining, curly-haired ex-Marine came sneaking in with a final-round 71 on a day that wasn't really fit for golf, copy paper came flying out of typewriters like confetti.

"Hey, I was only trying to be low pro," Burke joked.

The army of journalists had been forced to throw away their leads, notes, and paragraphs on amateur Ken Venturi, who'd led for three rounds and 16 holes of the fourth, and was looking like the first amateur to win a major since Johnny Goodman at the U.S. Open in 1933.

It would have been quite a story.

But on a day when cruel blasts of wind sent most scores higher than the Augusta National pines, the engaging amateur and Cary Middlecoff, the defending champion—Venturi's closest challenger at four shots back starting the day—took more gas than the *Hindenburg*.

Without hitting a truly bad shot, the 24-year-old Venturi blew to an

80, and Middlecoff, whose round featured a four-putt green at No. 5, staggered home with a 77.

This left the door open for Burke, who began the day in the impossible position of eight strokes behind Venturi. When it ended, Jackie had proved that he is, in fact, the game's greatest putter today.

Burke, a native Texan who was born in Fort Worth and calls Houston home, required only 29 putts on his one-under round, and the most precious one among them was the birdie on the 71st green. It looked like it came from 1,500 feet away and seemed to take a half hour to reach the cup.

Burke was paired with his good friend Mike Souchak, and it was "Sooch" who plucked the ball out of the cup before Jack or his caddie could get to it. He then hugged Burke as he hollered, "Come on, man, let's go get it—they're all falling apart out here!"

Moments later, while Burke was playing the 18th hole, Venturi came to the 17th still holding the lead. Two pars and the Masters would stunningly belong to an amateur, a San Francisco car salesman, a protégé of Byron Nelson.

But after hitting a fine drive and what he thought was a superb 9-iron second, Venturi bogeyed the hole. This represented a two-stroke swing with Burke, giving the Texan the lead.

"I took the paint off the ball with that 9-iron," Venturi said later, "but it just didn't do what it should have done."

It bounced over the hard rye green, leaving him with a chip shot that he got within five feet of the cup. But once again his short putt for a par lipped out. For the day, it was Venturi's sixth putt of five feet or less that looked in but stayed out.

Meanwhile, Burke hit a nervous 4-iron approach to the 18th and found the big right-hand bunker beside the green. He exploded out nicely enough but faced a testy six-foot putt for par—and the Masters.

Jackie said, "I looked at that thing and said to Willie, my caddie, 'It looks like it goes a little right. What do you think?' "

Willie said, "That's it, Mr. Jack. Just start it out to the left side and let it cruise on in."

Which Jackie did, and it did.

Burke's rounds of 72, 71, 75, and 71 gave him a tie for the highest winning Masters total of 289, but a win is a win.

Venturi, whose sensational six-under 66 on Thursday was one of the highlights of the week—he birdied the first four holes that day—confessed in the aftermath that he had played too defensively, too cautiously, all day on Sunday.

"I played Middlecoff," he said. "I should have played the golf course. I was running from Cary and got hit by Jackie going out the door."

9

OLD TOM

Tommy "Thunder" Bolt at the 1958 U.S. Open at Southern Hills

I T WAS with astonishing ease that Tommy Bolt won the 1958 U.S. Open on a vicious golf course that sent Sam Snead home in two days and wrenched Ben Hogan's wrist.

Old Tom, as he refers to himself, led all the way and was in front by four strokes when the last man had come in from under the blistering Tulsa sun and off of Southern Hills Country Club's 6,907 yards of trial, trouble, and terror, particularly the clawing, calf-high Bermuda rough.

This was a course on which Bolt shot rounds of 71-71-69-72 for a 283 total, while it caused Snead to miss the 36-hole cut after rounds of 75 and 80, and caused Hogan to injure his wrist at the 11th hole on that same Friday while trying to extricate himself from the rough, a rough that made everybody in the field complain—except Bolt. He rarely was in it.

Hogan at least fought off the injury and finished in a tie for 10th. It was the 14th straight Open in which Ben had finished in the top 10 while winning five of them—a record no one else can approach.

This time Hogan did it on a course that he has always liked and had been recommending to the U.S. Golf Association as a possible Open site for more than 10 years. Hogan had once selected his "All American golf course" for *Life* magazine and included the 465-yard 12th hole at Southern Hills, a dogleg left to a green protected by water and sand.

Bolt remembered this and couldn't wait to remind Hogan, a man he respects more than any other—they have a good friendship—that he "whipped up" on this favorite golf hole of Ben's, and the Southern Hills members.

In the four rounds, Bolt birdied the rugged 12th three times on the way to his first major title, most spectacularly in the Saturday-morning round with a soaring 3-iron second that wound up three feet from the flag.

The Saturday-morning 69 was the round that gave Old Tom a three-stroke lead on the field, the margin he needed to carry him through the afternoon when his driver deserted him occasionally.

Bolt was two under going to the 18th Saturday morning, but his tee shot on the demanding 468-yard finishing hole found the rough. While he was forced to pitch out with a wedge, Lloyd Mangrum, from another fairway, called over to him.

"Hey, Tom, they got your score wrong," Mangrum yelled. "You're five under, aren't you? You haven't missed a putt that anybody's heard about."

Bolt hollered back, "Naw, Lloyd, I'm making all these putts for bogeys."

After which Old Tom saved himself with a bogey on the 18th when he sent a screaming 3-wood to the uphill green and got down in two putts from 30 feet for the 69.

Old Tom was on good behavior all week. Far from the scowling, club-breaking tyrant the press has made him out to be, although not without a little help from the man himself.

In each day's interview he spoke in low, cordial, candy-sweet tones, sounding more like Zsa Zsa Gabor than his usual self, or a member of the House Un-American Activities Committee bellowing on TV at a Hollywood personality.

The Bolt of argumentative days surfaced only once. This was on Friday, when he was the halfway leader after two rounds of 71.

He took a moment to chastise a writer from the *Tulsa World* for writing that he'd shot a "49" on the front side of Thursday's round.

"I shot a 36," Bolt reminded the writer in front of everyone.

"I know that, Tommy," the writer replied. "It was a typographical error."

"The hell it was," said Old Tom. "It was a perfect four and a perfect nine."

10

A PUTTER AND A PAUNCH

Billy Casper Wins the 1959 U.S. Open at Winged Foot

ALL THE people who watched Billy Casper win the 1959 U.S. Open in the leafy elegance of Winged Foot Golf Club up in New York's Westchester County will no doubt start eating between meals and throw away 13 of the clubs in their bag. They'll keep the putter.

It became obvious that all you need to do to capture the biggest prize in golf is have a paunch and a magical putting stroke. The 29-year-old Casper, who has a bulging waistline to go along with his trusty mallet-head putter, did everything at Winged Foot but turn a raw egg into a white dove.

For four rounds he escaped from more dangers than Tarzan. The only thing he didn't do was swing from a vine to save a par.

It's doubtful if any golfer ever played more poorly from tee to green and still managed to win a major championship. To post his 282 score over the 72 holes, Casper one-putted 31 greens, came out of the rough 22 times, and dug himself out of 21 bunkers. He birdied only eight holes.

The reticent Casper even stumbled home with a four-over 74 in the final round and won looking out of a clubhouse window at others failing to catch him. In that last round he looked like he was shooting 91. He hit only six greens in regulation—six—and was in the rough nine times off the tee, and forced to play out of seven bunkers.

Casper's record of taking only 114 putts for the four rounds should stand forever.

•

THERE WERE OTHER curiosities regarding this Open. It was held at Winged Foot in Mamaroneck, New York, for only the second time in history—and for the first time since 1929, the year Bobby Jones barely sneaked into the 36-hole playoff but then won easily over Al Espinosa.

That was the Open where Jones holed his famous 12-foot putt on the 72nd green for the 79 that got him into the playoff in the first place. The moment has been memorialized in paintings.

For years, it's been a game around Winged Foot for members and their guests to try to duplicate Jones's curling putt on No. 18.

Casper's Open was the first in which the four rounds were spread over four days, the result of a driving rainstorm early Saturday when play was suspended three times until at least 18 holes were completed.

Much to the discomfort of the competitors, the rain brought on a 50-degree chill and blustery winds for Sunday's final round. So it was that Casper's two most serious challengers at the finish were Mike Souchak and Bob Rosburg, both of whom were wrapped up in Laplander sweaters.

Souchak, once an assistant at Winged Foot, and Rosburg each needed a birdie at the last hole to tie Casper. But as Casper watched from the warmth of the clubhouse, Souchak hit a poor second shot that missed the last green, and his chip shot wasn't even close.

Then came Rosburg. He had holed a chip shot for a birdie at No. 11

and sank a 50-foot putt for another bird at No. 12 to pull into a tie with Casper. But he three-putted for a bogey at No. 13 to fall one back again. He drove well on the final hole and put a 6-iron on the green 30 feet from the cup, but he left the birdie putt short.

●

TWO OLD WARHORSES, both 47 years old, were in the hunt earlier. Ben Hogan started Sunday in second place, three back of Casper, but he never made a birdie putt, and in fact three-putted four times, winding up with a 76 and a tie for eighth place with Sam Snead, who shot a 75.

"I suppose I should be pleased," Ben said. "I'm just a jolly golfer now. I don't put in as much preparation as I once did."

Rosburg took the credit for ending Snead's chances. They were paired together.

"At the 11th hole," Rossy said, "Snead had it two feet from the cup for a birdie. If he makes it, he's in great shape. He's got par in for 282. But I holed it out of the bunker, and Sam was so shook up, he blew the putt and never got over it."

All that helped the guy with the paunch become an Open champion, but nothing helped Billy Casper more than his great escapes from Winged Foot's rough and sand, and his jab stroke with the mallet-head putter.

PART TWO

The Sixties

●

"There ain't a mother geese anywhere who don't cuss
on the golf course, or somewhere."

—TOMMY BOLT

11

WRINGING DESTINY'S NECK

Arnold Palmer at the 1960 Masters

T'S BEGINNING to look like Ken Venturi can't win the Masters and Arnold Palmer can't lose it. For the third time in five years, Venturi seemed to have the 1960 green jacket ready to hang in his closet only to have it snatched away and fitted to someone else. It was in the late-evening shadows on Sunday that Palmer grabbed destiny by the neck and wrung it like a chicken.

Palmer wrestled the Masters away from Venturi the only way that was left for him to do it, on the only two holes left out of 72, and in about as tense a finish as you could imagine.

Arnold, who had held the lead for three rounds, started the last day—a chilly but sunny afternoon—with a one-stroke lead over a group of well-known players that a wit in the press headquarters had named "Sheriff Ben Hogan's posse."

Venturi was in that group along with Hogan, Dow Finsterwald, Billy Casper, and Julius Boros.

Soon enough, the final round became a duel between Venturi and Finsterwald, who were out early and paired together. When Ken birdied the second, third, and sixth holes, he found himself two shots ahead of Palmer but mostly worried about Finsterwald.

Then, when Dow ran home a 20-foot putt for a birdie at the 14th, he was tied with Venturi and it didn't seem to matter what Palmer was doing behind them. Kenny and Dow remained tied until the 18th hole, where Finsterwald's second found the greenside bunker and, although his explosion was a dandy, he missed the six-foot putt for par.

Now Venturi was in with a 70, low round of the day, and a total of 283. Finsterwald was home in 71, second-best score of the day, but his 284 wasn't good enough to tie Venturi, the gabby, sometimes cocky, but likable and talented Californian. Kenny is a sportswriter's dream.

Dow would have tied if he hadn't suffered a two-stroke penalty in the first round on Thursday, a blow that changed his 69 into a 71. Dow reported the crime himself—he unknowingly took an illegal practice putt on the fifth green. He'd thought the tournament was being played under USGA rules rather than the Augusta National's local rules.

Rather than moan about the fact that the penalty had kept him from tying with Venturi, Finsterwald said, "I was lucky they kept me in the tournament."

The "they" he spoke of consisted of a panel of judges, Masters Chairman Clifford Roberts, USGA Executive Director Joe Dey, USGA President John Ames, and PGA Tournament Director Edwin Carter.

The overwhelming unofficial vote among players in the Augusta locker room, however, was that Finsterwald should have been disqualified.

"Everybody else read the rules," said Jackie Burke Jr., the winner in 1956. "Why didn't Dow? He's kind of a 'locker room lawyer' anyhow."

But the incident was just one of the things that made this Masters one of the most fantastic ever. It not only stayed close all the way, it wasn't settled until the very end.

This was after the others in "Hogan's posse" had failed, Ben himself with a 76, Boros with a 75, Casper with a 74.

Venturi, who had lost to Burke in '56 and to Palmer in '58—when Arnold had received a favorable ruling on an "imbedded" ball that allowed him to make a par three at the 12th instead of a double-bogey five—was in the clubhouse chatting with a small cluster of writers as they all watched the television set.

Venturi was making jokes and talking about how much the Masters would mean to him after his two disappointments. And why not joke a little? Hey, he was in the clubhouse with a two-shot lead, and the only guy out there who could catch him had only two holes to play.

When Palmer holed his 35-foot birdie putt on the 17th green to pull within one of Venturi, nearly all of the writers fled the room.

Then, when Palmer laced a good drive on No. 18 and put a 6-iron to within six feet of the flag and sank the winning birdie putt, Venturi could do nothing but shake his head and sit there, dazed.

Palmer had miraculously won his second Masters with a birdie-birdie finish, and Venturi had lost his third Masters in five years.

When Arnold lifted the ball out of the cup, he may as well have been tearing out Venturi's heart at the same time.

12

THE GREATEST DAY

Ben Hogan, Arnold Palmer, and Jack Nicklaus Collide at the
1960 U.S. Open at Cherry Hills

S O IT had come down to this, to the moment when one immortal
would give the 1960 U.S. Open to another, from Ben Hogan to
Arnold Palmer, with best wishes—grudgingly.

It came down to the 71st hole of a gasping three days at Cherry Hills
Country Club in Denver, down to a sad portrait of Ben Hogan with
a pants leg rolled up, standing in a dark pond, holding a wedge in his
hands, an instrument that had betrayed him.

Hogan had plainly lost the Open a few moments earlier when he'd
tried too risky a shot in an effort to make a birdie he felt he needed. He
hit a 50-yard pitch that failed by one foot to clear the moat guarding the
518-yard, par-five 17th hole. Now he'd had to wade in and make what he
could of it, and get out of the way.

While Mike Souchak dominated the championship through three
rounds, setting a couple of scoring records, Hogan had grimly fought to
the front after rounds of 75 and 67 on Thursday and Friday and a 69 on
the morning of Open Saturday. Eventually, Hogan was two under going

to the 71st hole, needing a par-par finish to reach the clubhouse with another 69 and a total of 280. That number would maybe give him the title, which would be his fifth or sixth U.S. Open, depending on whether your math corresponded with his. It would give him no worse than a tie with Palmer.

Arnold had scorched the earth on the outgoing nine of the last round with six birdies in the first seven holes. But Hogan, 48, a man in semi-retirement, had hung on, and after the lead had shifted from one competitor to another, or one group to another, over a matter of hours, he had rammed home a 10-foot birdie on the 69th green to pull into a share of the lead.

This was after all sorts of insanity had taken place during the afternoon. For a long while it was impossible to know what guy was leading, or how many people were tied for the lead.

Souchak didn't actually lose the lead until he bogeyed the ninth hole, and this put Jack Nicklaus, the beefy young amateur, in front. Suddenly, the 21-year-old fat kid was five under and the whole world was four under.

The whole world included Palmer, Souchak, Julius Boros, Jack Fleck, Ted Kroll, Dow Finsterwald, Dutch Harrison, Jerry Barber, and another amateur, Don Cherry.

But then the whole world started losing it. Nicklaus, the crew-cut bull from Ohio, with arms like an interior lineman for the Buckeyes, left it on the greens when he three-putted 13 and 14 for bogeys. Then everybody else left it on the greens or in the bunkers.

And now here was Hogan, who had hit 34 straight greens, in the water on the next-to-last hole. He'd figured he would need one more birdie and a par, for Palmer was back on the tee behind him, steaming hot, taking apart the golf course, surely on his way to a six-under 65.

The pin was up front, only six feet from the water, at the 71st hole. Hogan clipped the 50-yard wedge shot high and directly at the flag. It looked good. In fact, it looked perfect. But then came a horrible noise from the crowd as the ball hit the bank and dribbled back down into water.

Hogan went to the green side of the moat and peered into the pond. He spied the ball and decided he could play it out, although no part of it was showing.

The crowd squealed with approval when Ben removed his shoe and sock and rolled up his right pants leg to the knee and waded in and took his stance. Back behind was the twosome of Boros and Gary Player, waiting, and behind them was the twosome of Palmer and Paul Harney, waiting.

They were all gazing up ahead at this grievous sight, certainly an amazing moment in the history of the Open.

Ben splashed a marvelous shot out of the water, the ball stopping about 15 feet beyond the cup. But his putt to save par curled away. Even Hogan was too human to recover from the shock of the ill-fated pitch shot.

At the last hole, a 470-yard uphill par four, normally a five for members, Hogan went for a big drive that might put him in position for a birdie, but he hooked the tee shot into the lake and was forced to finish slowly and painfully with a triple-bogey seven, dropping him into a tie for ninth place, four strokes out.

It was the most heroic seven you would ever see.

Arnold Palmer then parred the last two holes without incident for his remarkable 65, slung his red visor in the air, and, having added the Open to his Masters victory in April, assumed the giddy platform of the world's greatest player. Among other things, Arnold became only the third player ever to win the Masters and U.S. Open in the same year. Hogan had done it in '51 and '53, and Craig Wood had first done it in 1941.

In the last 18 holes Palmer had shot the lowest final round for a winner in Open history, and he had come from an astounding eight strokes and 14 competitors behind to win. Nobody had ever made so great a comeback in a major championship.

What ignited Palmer was his drive on the 346-yard first hole, a downhill par four, to start the last round Saturday. He'd been trying to drive the green for three rounds and failed, but this time he burned a hole through the rough and two-putted for the birdie that started him toward a front nine of 30.

On his way out of the Cherry Hills locker room after grabbing a quick bite between rounds, Palmer had run into two newspaper friends and talked about the first hole bugging him.

"A man ought to drive that green if he can land it just right. If I drive the green, I can two-putt for a birdie," Arnold said. "If I get started good, I could shoot a 65."

"Go on, boy. Get out of here," Bob Drum of the *Pittsburgh Press* said to him. "Go make your six birdies and six bogeys. Stop bothering us."

Persisting, Palmer said, "A 65 would give me 280. Doesn't 280 always win the Open?"

"Yeah, when Hogan shoots it," I said with a grin.

Palmer laughed and went out the door—to shoot his 65.

Arnold's two-stroke margin was over Nicklaus, who'd made some history himself. Nicklaus's finish was the greatest by an amateur since Johnny Goodman won the Open at Chicago's North Shore in 1933.

Later on, as Hogan tried to relax in the locker room, having a cigarette, having a cocktail, I kept him company for a while and helped out with the smoking.

"I thought it was a good shot," he said wearily, referring to the doomed wedge shot. "A pretty good shot."

I nodded. He paused.

Then he said, "Oh, well. I lost another golf tournament, but I'll tell you something. I played 36 holes today with a kid—this Jack Nicklaus— who could have won this Open by 10 shots if he'd known what he was doing."

13

FOREIGN BODY INFECTS MASTERS

Gary Player Beats Arnold Palmer for the 1961 Masters

GARY PLAYER of South Africa is the 1961 Masters champion because Arnold Palmer was in too big a hurry to win it again.

There's no other way to say it. The 18th hole at Augusta National might as well have been a slab of meat, the way Palmer butchered it.

Here he was at the tail end of a brilliant charge in which he was three under par for the day and had picked up five strokes on Player, the 54-hole leader, who had wobbled to the clubhouse with a disappointing two-over 74. Palmer needed only to par the last hole to wrap up his second Masters in a row, and his third in four years.

His tee shot had been perfect and he was standing in the fairway with nothing but a simple 7-iron to the big green.

That's when he did his shocking imitation of a high-handicap hacker using rented clubs on a public course, and he did it before his adoring gallery of thousands on the premises and millions watching on TV.

First, he pushed his approach shot and it landed in the upper part of the big bunker to the right of the green. The little South African had been there earlier, and Gary had exploded out to four feet and saved his par to secure his total of 280. Arnold would make the same four, no doubt about it.

Hardly. Palmer half-bladed the sand shot and it scooted all the way over the green and down a wicked slope, leaving him with a difficult chip shot just to get up and down for a bogey even to tie.

So what did Arnold do next? He chipped too strongly. The ball raced across the green in the other direction, this time leaving him with a triple-breaking putt of 30 feet. Which he promptly two-putted for a disastrous double-bogey six, thus handing Player the Masters.

It made Gary the first foreigner to win a major championship in the United States since Jim Ferrier, the Australian, took the PGA in 1947 at Plum Hollow in Detroit.

"I was overconfident and played too fast," said Palmer, who was basically humiliated. "It was stupid. That was the first time in my life I ever felt I had a tournament sewed up. I played so good down the stretch. I never gave a thought to losing, even on the last hole, even after I hit the shot in the bunker. I guess that was the problem."

Player had frittered away the lead when he took a double-bogey seven at the par-five 13th and a bogey six at the par-five 15th, two of the five water holes on the back nine that present opportunities for birdie, or catastrophe.

"I don't think I choked," Player said in his interview. "I had bad lies on both of those second shots and didn't pull off the right shot."

He said, "This is a lifelong ambition for me, to win the Masters. Of course, I'm sorry for Arnie—sorry he had to lose the way he did."

Someone asked Gary if he might have been rooting against Palmer as he watched TV with his wife Vivian in the clubhouse.

"I'll put it this way," he said. "If the boss in your office offered a five-hundred-dollar-a-week raise to the best writer, would you root against the other birds?"

14.

THE MACHINE

Gene Littler at the 1961 U.S. Open at Oakland Hills

THE 4-WOOD is to Gene Littler as mustard is to the hot dog.

The 1961 U.S. Open that played out on the celebrated layout of Oakland Hills in a suburb of Detroit was all about Littler and his 4-wood, basically a fairway club that enabled the little man to cut a big course down to size and capture golf's biggest prize.

"The winner is usually the one who scrapes it around the goodliest," Littler said in what was presumed to be San Diego English. "I must have used my 4-wood 20 times in the four rounds."

The new Open champion is known as Gene the Machine, so named by his fellow pros in tribute to his smooth, rhythmic swing. Littler closed with a 68 on Saturday afternoon, and the round swept him past six serious contenders who each looked like the winner in certain moments and brought him from three strokes off the pace in the last round.

There was irony involved as well.

Gene said, "Eight years ago I didn't know what golf was all about. It came easy for me. I just swung at the ball and knocked in a few putts and seemed to win my share. But I remember how this same 4-wood cost me the Open at Baltusrol when I was inexperienced."

Everybody recalls that. Littler came to the last hole in the '54 Open needing a birdie four to tie Ed Furgol in the first major shown in color on TV. His 4-wood shot that time found a bunker, not the green, and he'd had to settle for runner-up.

Oakland Hills was an ex-monster this time. The fairways were wider, the rough thinner and not as deep, and dozens of bunkers had been removed since Ben Hogan brought the monster to its knees in '51.

Proof could be found in the scoring. Ten years ago, there were only two scores below par—Hogan's 67 and Clayton Heafner's 69. This time there were 18. In addition, there were five 67s and they were posted by such unlikely fellows as Doug Sanders, Bob Rosburg, Jacky Cupit, Eric Monti, and Bob Harris.

Yet Oakland Hills was still a long, tough 281 course, which was the one-over total that won for Littler.

There was no better testimony to its length than the fact that Littler was forced to use his 4-wood to reach three of the four par-three holes, and no better testimony to Gene the Machine's talents than the fact that he played those tough par threes in three-under for the championship. No one else came within four shots of that.

Down the stretch, the three main people Littler had to beat were Mike Souchak, Bob Goalby, and Sanders.

It was Souchak who wheeled into the lead starting the last 18. He went three-under through the first four holes, but then he double-bogeyed the fifth and was gone.

Mike said, "I'm winning the Open and I hit a 5-iron 230 yards over the green and make a double. How do you figure that? Nobody can hit a 5-iron that far!"

Goalby played along quietly and steadily and reached the house at 282 and thought it might be good enough. All he could do was wait.

SANDERS WAS THE 54-hole leader at noon Saturday and kindly permit-ted a Texas sportswriter to buy his buffet lunch in the clubhouse, seeing as how Doug was fresh out of script, or so he claimed.

Eating hurriedly, Doug said, "I need 280 to win, but baby, this old putter is acting up. I don't know if I can get there."

For energy, Sanders asked for a jar of honey from a waiter, took four spoonfuls with his lunch, and kept the jar to put in his golf bag.

The Texas writer said, "Now you can win the Open and get sick to your stomach at the same time."

Doug left to meet his destiny. Which was to miss holing out a chip shot, just barely, at the last green that would have tied Littler and led to a playoff. He wound up second with Goalby.

Littler had taken the lead with a birdie at the 13th hole. But the only way he knew it was the crowd.

He said, "When I saw all the people come running, I figured I might be leading."

So the man who scraped it around "the goodliest" at Oakland Hills this time took one more moment to speak of his fondness for the 4-wood.

"It's a dandy little club," Littler said. "A lot of guys out here don't even carry one anymore."

15

THE TEMPESTUOUS ONE

Tommy "Thunder" Bolt at the 1961 PGA at Olympia Fields in Chicago

T**EMPESTUOUS TOMMY** (Thunder) Bolt raised his arms in the Olympia Fields locker room like a dictator on a balcony during the Armed Forces Day parade and said, "There ain't a mother geese anywhere who don't cuss on a golf course, or somewhere."

Out on the golf course on this far south side of Chicago, the 45-year-old Jerry Barber was sinking putts from as far away as the Pump Room downtown to beat the 31-year-old Don January out of the 1961 PGA Championship, but Bolt was creating a greater disturbance indoors.

Tommy had just had his license to play golf revoked for using "vulgar and abusive" language, so suddenly he had become as big a story as the championship itself.

"Man, man," said Tom, who had withdrawn from the competition—twice, in fact—"everybody cusses. I cuss, sure. But I cuss myself, don't you see? I wasn't cussin' nobody in here."

There was no other writer around, so your friendly neighborhood typist was getting a scoop.

The day before, Bolt had quit the tournament on the 13th hole. He'd been complaining of sharp pains in his back. He'd also withdrawn on Friday after six holes, but he was allowed back in since the day's play had been rained out.

He had, therefore, become the first man to withdraw twice from the same tournament. And now he was the PGA Tour's first player to draw an indefinite suspension for using too many Elizabethan words in front of innocent listeners.

Bolt drew his breath, gnawed on a mouthful of chewing gum, and said, "I got hot, sure. My poor old back was killin' me out there. I wanted somebody to find me an osteopath. I needed help. But they didn't nobody do anything, so I picked up and came in here. I was over there packing up my stuff yesterday—and hell yeah, I was cussin'. But I was cussin' myself and nobody else in particular."

He added, "There ain't no sense in them folks making me out to be John Dillinger or Al Capone."

Funny he should mention Al Capone, he was told. It was a part of the lore of the place that back in the Prohibition days Capone and another upstanding gentleman, the honorable "Machine Gun Jack" McGurn, used to play the occasional round of golf at Olympia Fields.

"Well, there you go," Tommy said.

Bolt had no idea who reported his abusive language to the PGA's executive committee, but it didn't matter, he said, because the organization was out to get him anyhow.

The year after he won the '58 U.S. Open, he was fined and placed on probation for withdrawing from two tournaments without an excuse, and it was hardly a secret that he has paid continual fines for club throwing.

He hadn't acquired the nickname Thunder by accident.

"I admit I been wrong in the past," he said, "but I haven't done nothin' wrong this time. If they suspend everybody out here who cusses, they ain't gonna have nobody left on the tour but the folks who do the suspendin'."

Bolt said, "Man, over there at Milwaukee was where Doug Ford took a swing at Doug Sanders in the clubhouse, but I see the two of 'em are still playin' on the tour."

They were for sure, but it's known that Ford is currently on PGA probation for "conduct unbecoming a professional."

Maybe Bolt could take his case to a court, it was suggested.

He said, "Old Tom's gonna go to some kind of court, you can book it. Now, lookie here. See that man over there. He's a priest—and he's a friend of mine. Come over here, Mr. Priest."

A small man with a Polish accent came over.

"How you doin', Father?" Bolt said. "Gosh, you're lookin' good."

Tommy and his character witness chatted for a moment, the priest wandered off, and Bolt said, "See, I can be nice when I have to, but I'm also a human being, don't you see?"

He is that. And there's not another one like him in golf.

16

LET'S HEAR IT FOR GREED

Arnold Palmer at the 1962 Masters

E HATES to be greedy about it, but Arnold Palmer honestly believes he should have won the Masters five years in a row. Arnold got around to saying this yesterday after he had won it for the third time, the 1962 version, with a sizzling 68 in a fascinating 18-hole playoff with Gary Player and Dow Finsterwald.

As Palmer was freshening up in the locker room, having greatly pleased his boisterous army, he said, "You know, the two times I should have won here with ease . . . those were the two I lost."

He flashed back to the two tragedies, the one in 1959 and the one last year. Well, tragedies for him and his army, but glorious occasions for Art Wall Jr. and Gary Player.

Palmer led the '59 Masters after 36, and was the co-leader after 54, and was leading by two strokes with seven holes to go, but that's when he dumped a 7-iron into Rae's Creek at the dangerous, 155-yard 12th hole, which has merely become the most famous par three in the world.

His double-bogey five and eventual 74 opened the door to all sorts of contenders, and it was Art Wall who made the most of it, going five-under over the last four holes for a 66 and a one-shot victory over Cary Middlecoff and two shots over Arnold, who finished third.

Then there was last year, when Arnold shocked himself and the world by making a double-bogey six on the 72nd hole with the Masters in his pocket. Player, of course, was the grateful recipient.

This time, Palmer was again the leader at 36 and 54 holes and quite the dominant figure throughout the week, but to win he needed two of his patented "charges," as the press knows them.

First, in regulation, came the miracles of a curling, 60-foot chip-in for a birdie at the 16th hole and a 10-foot putt for a birdie at the 17th hole. That was just to tie Player and Finsterwald at 280 and slip into the playoff.

It was frustrating for his fans on the first nine holes of the playoff. Player dipped to two under and carried a two-stroke lead over Palmer to the back side. Dow was already bogeying his way out of things.

"I never have much luck getting birdies on Augusta's front nine," Palmer said. "It's not an easy nine for me."

The Augusta National's opening nine is the driest—not a water hazard out there—but it also plays longer and is less inviting than the back side.

When Arnold bagged a birdie three at the difficult 10th as Gary suffered a bogey five, the two-stroke swing sent a signal to his loyal army.

The army then erupted at the treacherous 12th when Palmer stuck an 8-iron to within two feet of the flag for a birdie and another two-shot swing as Player made bogey. Now Arnold suddenly held a one-stroke lead.

Palmer went on to birdie 13, 14, and 16 and fire a stunning 31 on the back nine for his 68 to Player's 71 and Finsterwald's 77.

Just to show there was no partiality in the town, or at the club, the keeper of the huge scoreboard at the 12th hole, after Palmer birdied to take the lead, posted a big message in red letters for all to see. It read:

GO ARNIE.

17

THE NEW GUY

Jack Nicklaus at the 1962 U.S. Open at Oakmont

ARNOLD PALMER'S stranglehold on pro golf may be at an end due to the emergence of a young man named Jack Nicklaus, who can simply overpower him. This thought dawned on everyone who watched the 22-year-old Nicklaus take the 1962 U.S. Open away from Palmer at famed Oakmont Country Club in a suburb of Pittsburgh on Sunday, and do it impudently, right there in Arnold's backyard.

The way Nicklaus did it in their 18-hole playoff was to drive the ball longer and straighter—clean over Oakmont's folklore bunkers in most instances—and put his iron shots closer to the flags, and roll more putts into the cups on Oakmont's undulating, linoleum-slick greens.

The two tied at 283 when Nicklaus fired a three-under 69 to Palmer's one-under 71 in the last round, an afternoon that saw them pull away from Phil Rodgers and Bobby Nichols, the other most steady challengers. Rodgers and Nichols tied for third, two shots back.

All Opens are usually lost by someone before they can be won by someone else. If anyone could be said to have thrown this Open away, it was the short, stocky Phil Rodgers.

Phil made a disastrous eight in the first round on the short, par-four 17th hole, the easiest on the course, when he got tangled up in a small tree near the green. He kept whacking at the ball instead of taking an unplayable penalty. It would have saved him two strokes. He never quite recovered.

When Nicklaus blazed to two under through the first six holes of the playoff, it gave him a four-shot lead and the drama was pretty much taken out of things. Arnold slowly and agonizingly cut Jack's lead to two strokes by the time they reached the 18th tee.

What happened then was Arnold swung at his drive like he was try-ing to make a one on the 462-yard hole, and wound up with a double-bogey six. This prompted the intelligent Nicklaus to play for a safe bogey five out of the rough, which made their playoff scores read Nicklaus 71, Palmer 74.

Of course, the damage had been done earlier. Nicklaus pounding his tee shots from 50 to 100 yards past Palmer on every hole that called for the driver to come out of the bag was a startling sight.

Nicklaus said, "I decided before the tournament that I would try to drive the ball higher than normal, hoping to get it over most of the trou-ble and avoid too much roll that would go into the rough. Fortunately, I had a good driving week, and it was the best golf I've ever played under the circumstances."

This from a very promising golfer who had won two U.S. Amateurs, in '59 and '61, and had finished second and tied for fourth in the past two U.S. Opens before turning pro this year.

Graciously, Nicklaus said, "Arnold is the finest golfer in the world today. If he had putted just normally well, he would have won this cham-pionship so easily it would have been frightening."

You could carve that on a tree trunk.

Palmer played the best golf tee to green during the regulation 72 holes, but he suffered eight three-putt greens in those four rounds and two more in the playoff, while Nicklaus three-putted only once in 90 holes.

"What can I say about it?" Arnold said. "I started losing the tournament on the greens the first day. It was a struggle with the putter all the way. When you miss as many putts as I did, you get to thinking you have to hole out your second shot if you're going to do any good."

On the subject of Nicklaus, Arnold said, "Jack is a great player and you're going to be reading about the tournaments he's won for a lot of years. He's got everything."

One thing Nicklaus's victory did was put a hold, at least temporarily, on all the chatter of a modern professional Grand Slam. Palmer started it in '60 after he won the Masters and U.S. Open and was heading to St. Andrews to enter the British Open.

"The modern slam," he announced, and repeated it often, "would be to win the Masters, the U.S. and British Opens, and the PGA in the same year. Those are our four majors today."

Even after he lost the '60 British Open by one stroke to Kel Nagle, he said he would continue the quest. And when he got off to a good start this year at Augusta, it looked like the Slam was on again as he dominated most of the proceedings at Oakmont—until the end.

Still, Palmer joined a rather illustrious list. A few of the other heroes who've lost U.S. Open playoffs are Ben Hogan, Sam Snead, Byron Nelson, Bobby Jones, Gene Sarazen, and Harry Vardon.

All of which proves that Arnold Palmer does something exceptional even when he loses.

18.

WELCOME TO "PALMERSTON"

Arnold Palmer Wins the 1962 British Open at Troon

ARNOLD PALMER'S cherished Grand Slam slumbers in a shallow grave in Pittsburgh, but you might as well try to tell 20,000 British subjects that the Queen is really Tuesday Weld.

"Palmer the Magnificent," as the British press labeled him, shot a record five-under 67 in the third round of the 1962 British Open Friday morning on Old Troon, then tagged it to a wonderful 69 in the afternoon and won the championship by the approximate width of the English Channel.

It was Palmer's second straight British Open victory—he had conquered Royal Birkdale last year—and his seventh career major, and the British crowd was well aware of it.

Among other things, they wanted to heap their love and affection on this American star who had personally rejuvenated their ancient championship—the oldest professional major, dating back to 1860—when he entered it for the first time in 1960 and came within a single stroke of winning it at St. Andrews.

The fans pushed and shoved and swarmed over the fairways and through the bunkers, shouting and waving flags, imploring higher powers to save Palmer and the Queen, though not necessarily in that order.

They wanted to be as near as they could to the man whose 72-hole score of 276 broke the British Open record by two strokes. Palmer was the only American in the championship, as far as the Brits were concerned.

However, news was smuggled in that Phil Rodgers shot 289 and finished 13 strokes back in a tie for third, and Jack Nicklaus, who had spoiled the Slam quest at Oakmont last month, and was playing in his first British Open, posted a frustrating 305 total and tied for 33rd place.

"Playing over here takes some learning," Nicklaus said.

The stewards' control of the mob completely collapsed during the morning round, when Palmer was firing a course record and taking full command of the competition. They couldn't be kept outside the ropes.

Rounds of 71 and 69 gave Palmer a two-stroke lead through 36 holes. The nearest in pursuit was Kel Nagle, the straight-hitting Australian who had nipped Palmer by a stroke at St. Andrews.

After that 67 in the morning round, Palmer led Nagle by five, but when he came through the front nine in the afternoon's final round, he was up by nine strokes and chomping on Troon like a starving man diving into the meat loaf.

From the start of Friday's 36 holes it was Palmer and Nagle. Then it was Palmer. Then bedlam.

"Kel and I almost got trampled five times," Palmer said.

The 11th hole was where Palmer put his stamp on Troon, a course that was hosting only its second British Open in history. The first was held back in 1923, a year when Walter Hagen didn't win it.

As you stand on the 11th tee at Troon and look at all the ghoulish things that can happen to a golf ball, it's hard not to think of the Frankenstein monster.

The 11th is a 485-yard hole that plays as either a par five or a par four, depending on the winds on the west coast of Scotland. It was considered a par five during the Open.

What you see gazing straight ahead is a narrow stretch of lumps and knobs, which is supposed to be the fairway, and it's bordered on the right by a railway and on the left by endless clusters of shrubs and heather from which some golfers never return. In the predominantly gray light of Scotland, the hole has even more of an evil cast.

On the right, nothing separates the players from the railroad but a small rock wall that's crawling with heather and travels all the way to a bunkered green.

Certain members of the British press chose such colorful names for the hole as Calamity Corner, Hell's Acre, and The Shocker. They also settled on "Palmerston" as the new name for Troon itself.

Clearly, the most thrilling moments of the championship were when Palmer attacked No. 11. He played it with a 1-iron off the tee and a 2-iron to the green. It was the birdie four and eagle three he made there in the first two rounds that went a long way toward his victory.

In each case, his second shot with the 2-iron was a full blast from a hanging lie that started out low and screamed toward the rock wall—and out of bounds. But the shot turned away from the railway at the perfect instant and tailed into the green.

Nobody said it better than a British spectator the second day.

"By Jove," the gentleman said, "you have to like a chap who plays up the brave side."

19

TO HELL AND BACK

Ken Venturi Wins the 1964 U.S. Open at Congressional

WHAT AN improbable thing it was that Ken Venturi won the 1964 U.S. Open at Congressional Country Club, and did it with the second-lowest score in the history of the championship. But on a course not far from the nation's capital, they opened up the coffin and out he crawled.

As most people knew, Venturi had been a dead man for three years.

Those who'd known him since his rise to stardom eight years ago, first as a brash amateur and then as a stylish pro, could have sworn he still looked more battered and bruised from his three heartbreaking losses in the Masters back in his past than he did surviving Congressional's smothering heat and humidity and all the salt tablets he swallowed over the Open's final 36 holes.

It was in the '56 Masters that Ken led all the way as an amateur and didn't really hit a bad shot the last day in a 40-mile-per-hour wind and yet somehow lost by a stroke to Jackie Burke's brilliance with the putter.

It's just as hard to forget Venturi losing the '58 Masters at a moment when he was looking like the player of his era. Like the guy Arnold

Palmer became. That was the Masters where Palmer played the 12th hole twice after receiving the infamous "imbedded ball" ruling that allowed him to turn a double-bogey five into a par three—and Venturi finished those same two strokes back.

Then there was the way Ken lost the '60 Masters while he sat there joshing with the press in the clubhouse in the manner of a winner. Suddenly, Venturi and a half-dozen writers watched on TV as Palmer sank birdie putts on 17 and 18 to beat him by a shot.

Even in winning at Congressional, Venturi bore no resemblance to the golfer he used to be. Only in flashes. His swing was shorter, inconsistent, the result of back and hand injuries that had almost caused him to quit the game for good.

Even after the first two rounds he didn't look like a threat to the leaders, Tommy Jacobs, who had shot a stunning 64, and Palmer, who had opened with rounds of 68 and 69. Ken was six strokes behind. But then came Saturday morning, when he fired a 66 in the wilting heat despite two closing bogeys, and was attended by a doctor at noon and given salt tablets and cold towels and iced tea to take along in the final round.

After Venturi shot a heroic 70 in the last round for the 278 that became the second-lowest winning total in Open history—second only to Ben Hogan's record 276 at Riviera in '48—his quick wit returned when he faced the press.

He said, "The last time I saw you guys was when you were interviewing me at the Masters and somebody yelled, 'Palmer!,' and all of you ran out of the room and left me with my Coke."

20

BUFFALO, BEAR, ELK, AND PALMER

Billy Casper Beats Palmer at the 1966 U.S. Open at Olympic

NOBODY KNOWS how to cook buffalo, bear, and elk meat, so they probably think Billy Casper eats it raw. What they do know is that he had Arnold Palmer for dessert when he swiped the 1966 U.S. Open from Palmer at the Olympic Club in San Francisco.

What is it about the Olympic Club, anyhow? First, it gave us Jack Fleck instead of Ben Hogan in 1955, and now it gives us Billy Casper instead of Arnold Palmer.

Olympic just has it in for sportswriters, is that it?

"Oh, but look who it gives you for second," said a U.S. Golf Association official in defense of the venue.

Great. The writer could take that to his Olivetti and type happily.

Arnold Palmer was going to win this U.S. Open for three and a half days, or 63 holes, and break Hogan's 72-hole record while doing it, and you couldn't find anyone who would bet against that unless he was one of the Three Stooges.

Palmer confidently went to the last nine holes with a seven-stroke lead over Casper and what seemed like a 4,000-stroke lead over everybody else. Actually, it was nine shots over Jack Nicklaus.

So how could a man lose a major championship after he'd shot rounds of 71, 66, 70, and a spectacular 32 on the front side of the final 18, and needed only to play even par over the last nine to put up a total of 274, which would break Hogan's Open record of 276, which was set 18 years ago at Riviera?

Well, for one thing, Arnold started thinking more about breaking Hogan's record than winning the tournament. Then, as he and Casper were on their way to the 10th tee, it didn't help when he heard Buffalo Billy say, "I'm going to have to play like hell just to finish second."

After that, it came down to incredible golf shots by both men.

If you were Arnold and you duck-hooked into the rough and bogeyed the 10th while Casper parred, you didn't give it much thought. You were still up by six.

They both parred the 11th and both birdied the 12th, and Palmer was still up by six with only six to play. Where was the problem?

Okay, there was a minor one at the 191-yard 13th, where Arnold pulled a 4-iron into the rough to the left of the green and took a bogey, but after both men parred the 14th, Palmer was still ahead by five with only four holes to play.

Then came the short 15th hole, only 150 yards, and Casper was on the green with a breaking 20-footer. That was where Palmer arrogantly went for the flag. His shot bounced into the back rough. He chipped to eight feet but missed as Casper rolled in the birdie. Two-shot swing. Lead down to three.

But, hey, there were only three more to play. Why worry?

This might not have been a problem if the 16th hadn't been 604 yards long and enticed Palmer into thinking he could reach it in two if he swung at the ball as if he were chopping firewood.

While Casper played conservatively by punching a drive into the fairway, and punching a spoon down the fairway, and plopping a pitch onto the green for a 15-foot birdie putt, Palmer was making a mess.

He lunge-pull-yanked his tee shot into the rough. Took two slashes to get out. Pounded a spoon into a bunker. Appeared to be looking at a seven or worse. But he blasted out of the sand and dropped a tough four-foot putt for a bogey six—"the greatest six I ever made," he said.

But Casper sank the birdie, and there was another two-shot swing.

By now Palmer was in something of a stupor, and there seemed to be no question that he would miss a seven-foot par putt on 17 to allow Casper to move into a tie with him. Which he did.

It seemed impossible, but Casper had picked up five shots on Palmer in three holes. Perhaps this was nothing compared to the 50 pounds Casper had lost on his diet of buffalo, bear, and elk meat.

When they both parred the 72nd hole, Casper had registered a 68 to Palmer's 71 and this left them deadlocked at 278. No Hogan record erased, no second U.S. Open victory for Palmer.

In the minds of most observers after Palmer's collapse, it was the closest thing to a foregone conclusion that Casper would win the 18-hole playoff, which he did with a 69 to Arnold's 73.

It's hard to believe, but Palmer has now lost three U.S. Open playoffs in the last five years.

Move over, Sam Snead. You got company.

21

TOUR VET WINS ONE FOR TOUR VETS

Gay Brewer Jr. Takes the 1967 Masters

THE THING about your average touring pro is this: If you give him enough time for his putter to heat up, he can turn a major championship into another Pensacola Open. Gay Brewer Jr., a guy in his mid-thirties with an expanding waistline, a man with a loopy swing who has been strolling along on the PGA Tour for 10 years, achieving no more of an identity than, oh, Mason Finsteraaron, did exactly this in winning the 1967 Masters.

For three of its four days under glorious Dixie skies, the Masters vibrated with excitement. There was something for everybody. Jack Nicklaus, the defending champion, played like Barbara Nicklaus and missed the 36-hole cut. Arnold Palmer made enough meek charges to please his army, or at least hold its attention. For the sentimental, the 54-year-old Ben Hogan came out of nowhere to play a historic nine holes, showing everyone how to hit the golf ball. And during all of this, a pair of youngsters, Bert Yancey and Tony Jacklin—golfers, not songwriters—stormed the landscape with enough frenetic action to give hope that everybody under 30 isn't growing long hair and sitting down in the street.

But then came Brewer with his putter, and the Masters took on its newest look since the Battle of Hastings, or however long ago it was that Palmer and Nicklaus started winning it every year.

Brewer actually won the Masters on the final day over the last six holes when he birdied three holes in a row—13, 14, 15—and parred the others to complete a 67 and leap clear from a jungle of contenders that included Julius Boros, Bobby Nichols, and Bert Yancey.

Brewer's putter seemed to be the only thing keeping him on the scoreboard. He ended the day with 10 one-putt greens, and nine of them were of such length they required pacing, studying, and sweating. There were no gimmes.

A word about the surprisingly poor performance of Jack Nicklaus, who had won the past two Masters tournaments and three of the last four. He hung around the veranda the last two days in the green blazer of a Masters champion, smiling and greeting friends, being the sportsman he is.

"I have no one to blame but myself," he said. "I would make a mistake and press to make up for it and do something worse."

A gloomier explanation for Nicklaus's failure came from Jack Grout, the longtime pro at Scioto Country Club in Columbus, Ohio, who has been working with Jack since he was nine years old. He spoke of it over dinner in the house Jack's dad, Charlie, rents every year in Augusta.

Grout said, "Jack is not the player he was in 1961, '62. In those days, no one could swing a club with such great balance. But he lost it playing against two guys who have no balance at all—Arnold Palmer and Gary Player. Jack used to be able to get back on his right foot and move perfectly onto his left every time. Now he doesn't shift on the downswing. He tries to adjust in the middle of the swing. He needs to spend a month or two working on it and then work some more. But he only half listens now. All he says is, 'I'm laying it off at the top.'"

A word about Ben Hogan's stimulating performance. For some reason, his old brass-head putter made a command performance and over the first three rounds he made 14 birdies—more than anyone in the field—even though he still has trouble pulling the trigger.

Knowing his fans agonized for him as he would continually line up, take a stance, step back, readjust, and freeze, he said after the second round, "I would like to take the putter back quicker, but I can't."

He had no trouble taking the clubs back, then bringing them through with as much perfection as ever. His third-day 66, six under and the low round of the tournament, which included a record-tying 30 on the back nine, will be remembered as one of the epic moments in Masters history.

On the toughest stretch of the course, the 10th through the 12th, his iron shots gave him birdie putts of six feet, one foot, and 12 feet—and he canned all of them.

At the water-guarded par fives, the 13th and 15th, where he had always laid up in two, he took out the 4-wood and gave himself a couple of eagle putts under 20 feet. Both missed, but the birdies were tap-ins.

He parred 16 and 17 and pinpointed a perfect drive on 18 and put a 5-iron shot 15 feet behind the cup. This putt dropped for his 30.

There was something magnificently nostalgic about all of it. At 54, Hogan was still wearing the white cap and the trousers with high pleats and cuffs, and when he came trudging up that last fairway there wasn't a dry eye in the crowd, a throng that even included cynical sportswriters.

You knew it was a last hurrah for Ben Hogan, the greatest shotmaker who ever lived.

Brewer's eyes were a little misty, too, on Sunday. He was the same guy who came to the last hole a year ago with a one-stroke lead but three-putted for a bogey and wound up in a playoff that he and Tommy Jacobs lost to Nicklaus.

This time Brewer drove safely off the 18th tee with a 3-wood and put a 6-iron on the front edge of the green, where he would have an uphill putt of some 16 feet. He rolled it up for a laugher.

"I don't know if I looked nervous out there," he said later. "But I was. Man, I don't know if I was holdin' the putter or it was holdin' me."

22.

SUPER MEX

Lee Trevino Wins the 1968 U.S. Open at Oak Hill

SUPER MEX is what he called himself. Super Mexkin. And there he was in the middle of all that U.S. Open dignity with his spread-out caddie-hustler stance and his short, choppy public-course swing, a stumpy little guy, tan as the inside of a tamale, pretty lippy for a nobody, and wearing those red socks. And here were all of these yells coming from the trees and knolls of Oak Hill Country Club in Rochester, coming from all of the Lee Trevinos of the world. "Whip the gringo," hollered Lee's Fleas, a pack of instant Mexicans enthusiastic enough to rival anybody's army, some of them $30-a-week guys like Trevino himself was a little more than a year ago.

Trevino whipped all of the gringos in the 1968 Open, mainly a gringo named Bert Yancey, the championship leader for three days, in a one-on-one thing, the kind of match a hustler likes. In so doing, he knocked off everything else in Rochester, including Jack Nicklaus and a couple of Open records, the biggest being the one that made him the first guy to shoot four rounds in the 60s when he rang Oak Hill's bell for rounds of 69, 68, 69, 69, for a 72-hole total of 275 that equaled the best ever shot.

But what his four-stroke margin over Nicklaus and six over Yancey did was pump more life into golf than anyone since Arnold Palmer came along. Trevino's wisecracking, hotdogging style is a welcome contrast to a PGA Tour where most of the visor-gripping competitors seem to have graduated from the yep-and-nope school of public relations.

Trevino is a guy who says:

"I used to be a Mexkin, but I'm makin' money now so I'm gonna be a Spaniard."

"Yeah, I been married before, but I get rid of 'em when they turn 21."

"I grew up in Dallas, but I live in El Paso now, so I like to go to the dog track over in Juarez. I been feedin' them dogs for years, but they don't get no faster."

"No, I haven't called my wife yet, but if I don't have the $30,000 check there by Wednesday, she'll call me."

Nobody knew what to predict when Trevino and Yancey went out paired together in the last round, Bert one shot ahead. Who was likely to shoot the 69 and who was likely to shoot the 76?

It was Dave Marr, the 1965 PGA champion, who tried to assess everything at dinner Saturday night. He said, "You know Yancey can play. The man's put up 67, 68, and 70, and he's got the smoothest swing out here ... and you know how badly Bert wants to win a major. You just don't know anything about the jumping bean."

You do now, of course. All the gringos do.

23

THE JUNKMAN COOLS IT

Julius Boros Wins the 1968 PGA at Pecan Valley

A FEW MILES southeast of the Alamo, in a sunken oven of pecan trees and baked Bermuda grass, on land so unpicturesque it makes you wonder why Mexico wanted to keep it in the first place, or why Texans wanted it for themselves—even for shopping centers—a middle-aged man struck a blow for tired, portly, beer-drinking, slow-moving fathers of seven. Julius Boros, who is all of the above, and who says he doesn't so much play spectacular golf as "throw a lot of junk up in the air," won the 1968 PGA Championship, which at one time or another had everybody in contention except Davy Crockett, Jim Bowie, Col. William Travis, and Jack Nicklaus.

With nine holes left to play in the final round, and the sun over San Antonio's Pecan Valley Country Club turning the course into the world's largest hot tub, Boros was one of 10 players all jammed up and sweating and within a single stroke of one another.

Some of the others were Lee Trevino, Arnold Palmer, Doug Sanders, Frank Beard, Marty Fleckman, Bob Charles, and Miller Barber. But not

Nicklaus. Jack despised the course so much, he took the precaution of missing the cut.

Julius then calmly emerged from the pack with a 69 for a four-round total of 281, one over par for the trip, to become, at the age of 48, the oldest man ever to win a major championship. It was his third, and 16 years after his first. He clinched the title by rescuing a par four on the last hole—a brutal, narrow, long, uphill thing that nobody—soaking pro or melting fan—wanted to take home with them. You couldn't have given away a chunk of Pecan Valley to anybody.

It was new and there was an overlarge supermarket-type sign out on the street and it had a small, one-story clubhouse and a row of condominiums straying off in two directions, and it looked pretty much like a place where you pull in, drop off your cleaning, and pick up cheeseburgers for the kids. The fact that the course provided a rousing tournament was, well, astonishing.

Nice finish, too. Only moments before Boros came along to claim the trophy, none other than Arnold Palmer, playing beautifully, hitting some of his finest shots in years, came to the 72nd hole looking like the miracle maker of yore.

He had driven into the rough but smashed a heroic, 230-yard spoon out of the thick Bermuda grass, up the hill and onto the rolling green to within eight feet of the flag, sending his multitudes into a yowling fit. Arnie would make this birdie putt and win it. Just like old times, right?

Wrong. He played a hair too much right break, the ball greased the cup but didn't drop, and for the ninth time in his brilliant career Palmer was a runner-up in a major.

Then Boros came along. Julius never looks like he's playing for anything but self-punishment. He wastes no time. He strolls up and slaps the ball, and good or bad, he walks away expressionless. He smokes and stands under an umbrella, shielding himself from the heat, and yearns for a cold beer.

Boros had a long wait on the last hole while the Palmer melodrama unfolded. His tee shot was in the fairway, but he hit an incredibly poor second shot, a funky 3-wood that never got up and plunked miserably into the upslope, leaving him some 30 yards short of the green and roughly 45 yards from the pin, which was on the back, behind a hump.

"I just threw a junk wedge up there and hoped to get close" was the way he described his third shot with the pitching wedge, a low punch that caught the hump perfectly and skidded down to within three feet of the cup.

As Boros took his stance over the putt that would win him the PGA, a less-than-golfwise Texan in the gallery giggled and said loudly, "You worried about makin' this un, June-is?"

At once, hordes of volunteers in their red hats hollered, "Quiet!"

Of course, "June-is" was very upset and worried. He must have taken at least two seconds before he stroked it in.

24

SORRY, BILLY

1969 Masters at Augusta

OR THREE days the 1969 Masters enjoyed a great inner peace. Billy Casper and his good friend, the Lord, strolled hand in hand through the valleys and pines of Augusta, stamping out petroleum-based pesticides, gas heating, foam-rubber pillows, and assorted sausages that offend his allergies. They also played safe on the par fives while half of Georgia made birdies and eagles. But it was tranquil. Billy had the Masters pressed between his numbed fingers as a result of this careful, calculating golf, while all of his major adversaries, the Jack Nicklauses and Arnold Palmers, were lost in the azalea bushes, perhaps looking for a religion of their own. Billy would go out on Sunday and wander over the course, smiling and shrugging, hit a good chip when he needed it, sink a putt when it was necessary, hum a few of his favorite hymns by the Mormon Tabernacle Choir, and in a matter of a few hours the Masters would be in heaven. There was only one thing wrong with all this. By the time Casper got around to playing decent golf, the Lord was something like six down and five to go—and suddenly Augusta, for the third straight year, had another of those mystery men from the PGA Tour as its champion.

In the proud tradition of Gay Brewer Jr. and Bob Goalby, who preceded him in 1967 and 1968, George Archer, white man, 29, Gilroy, California, was the winner. It was his first major, just as it had been for Brewer and Goalby, and George won it by battling down the stretch with a ragtag group of escapees from some distant Citrus Open.

Toward late afternoon on Sunday, here came this astonishing lineup of contenders. Besides the gangly, 6-6 Archer, who must be the tallest winner of a major since Abraham Lincoln, there were George Knudson, hiding behind his shades, the bewildered Charles Coody, and powerful Tom Weiskopf, a cluster of relatively young guys who had never been this close to a major before and didn't quite know how to handle it.

They all fell apart at the end, which allowed Archer to play one over par on the last five holes and still win with a closing 72 for 281.

Coody was a bigger loser than Casper, as it turned out. Although there were people in the gallery who asked, "Is a Charles Coody anything like a Spiro Agnew?," the Texan was eight under and leading through 15 holes.

"I really don't think I choked," Coody said later. "I just remember holding a 5-iron in my hand on the 16th tee and wishing I could make myself hit a six."

Only the Lord knew what Casper was up to all week. His opening 66 on Thursday was a thing of perfection. He simply played the way a man ought to play if he's won more tournaments than anyone except Sam Snead, Ben Hogan, and Arnold Palmer. He took no chances and explained, "Golf is a game of decisions. I try to keep my mind fresh for the decisions and play my own game."

He kept playing cautiously but steadily for a pair of 71s, and then came Sunday. He started the day off by going to early church and then looked confident in the locker room and on the veranda while the younger contenders looked quiet and nervous.

But out on the course the two-time U.S. Open winner looked like anything but Billy Casper. He bunkered and sliced his way to five over par through the first 10 holes, working on a 77, and the tournament he'd dominated was now devastatingly out of reach. He got home with a 74, but that didn't make any difference.

"I learned a lot of humility on those first 10 holes," he said. "I just got into a series of bad swings and couldn't get out in time. I'm happy I was able to play three under from the 11th in and finish second. It's a great honor to finish second here."

Archer had quite an experience on Sunday, too. He let Casper know right away that he was still in the tournament with a birdie at the second and a tie for the lead. From that point on, his round was a series of good shots and rescue shots.

Archer looks a little like Gomer Pyle, and some of his pals on the tour call him that. He comes from public courses around San Francisco, not from the college ranks. He used to caddie for Harvie Ward when Harvie was the best amateur in the country.

The green jacket they gave him is a 42 extra long, and he said his golf shoes are made by Chris-Craft. That was a joke. That was George Archer's best joke. Say hello, George.

25

THE CROSS-HANDER

Orville Moody Wins U.S. Open in 1969 at Champions in Houston

ALL RIGHT, you wise guys with your tricky sports questions. So you know who was on deck when Bobby Thomson hit the home run, how old George Gipp was when he asked Rock to do him that favor, and who shot Eddie Waitkus. Here's one for you: What was the name of the guy from Killeen, Texas, or Chickasha, Oklahoma, who spent 14 years in the Army and eventually became a civilian and putted cross-handed and won the 1969 U.S. Open that time in Houston?

No, the answer is not Sergeant York. Or Gary Cooper. It's Orville Moody. The very first cross-handed putter to win a major. The former Staff Sergeant E-6 who discovered the U.S. Open paid better than winning the Korean Open three times or the Fort Hood post-tournament.

It was fortunate for Old Sarge, as he calls himself, that the golfers he had to beat over the long, rugged terrain of Champions Golf Club's Cypress Creek course were not Jack Nicklaus, Arnold Palmer, Lee Trevino, Billy Casper, or Gary Player. People of that ilk.

They were people of the ilk of Miller Barber, Mister X, who doesn't putt cross-handed but wears dark glasses and has a baffling swing that only a circus clown can imitate, and 42-year-old Bob Rosburg, now a country-club pro who had won at least 37 cents all year and uses a baseball grip, and Al Geiberger, who lives in a peanut butter jar, and the short-hitting Deane Beman, who wore out his fairway woods before the tournament ended.

It was an unusual Open from the start. To begin with, there was no big creaking clubhouse to wander around in. The one at Champions is small, rustic-modern, and looks more like a ski lodge. That's the way the owners, Jimmy Demaret and Jackie Burke Jr., wanted it. Across the way are cottages and houses woven in and around the quiet streets and swimming pools. Many of the players were staying in the compound for the sake of convenience, and there was backyard cooking going on, and chatting and relaxing after the day's play.

In the mornings, it was eerie to look out of your own cottage and see Julius Boros strolling down the lane on his way to work. In the evenings, it was like being in any other suburban neighborhood where the fellow out in the yard across the street was fooling around with his kids while another man in a car drove up and honked. This definitely wasn't the usual Open surroundings for a Jack Nicklaus or a Gary Player, who happened to be the man in the yard and the man in the car.

Continuing the strangeness of it all, the mysterious Mister X—Miller Barber—held a three-stroke lead going into the final 18 after rounds of 67, 71, and 68. But Miller slowly disintegrated, going four over on the front nine, and this opened the door for everybody. There was a moment on the last nine when there were eight players within two shots of one another.

One by one, all but two of them drifted away, and finally it was down to two men, Moody and Rosburg, the old cross-hander and the old baseball-gripper. They were tied for the lead with Rosburg on the 16th tee and Moody a hole behind him.

Pausing to chat with a friend on the tee, Rossy said, "A birdie and two pars would be 280. That might get it."

"Three pars might get it," he was told.

He grinned and said, "Yeah, and I'd win my bet on no 280."

Rosburg survived the 16th by sinking a tricky three-foot putt. Then he survived the 17th by exploding from a bunker and holing a 10-foot putt. He surely looked like the choice of fate at this point. One more par and Old Sarge might have to reenlist again.

But Rossy didn't have one more in him. His tee shot on 18 caught a limb and left him with a 4-wood out of the thick Bermuda rough. It was a good try, but the ball spurted to the right and caught another bunker. He exploded out marvelously to four feet, but his putt hung on the edge.

Now came Moody. Knowing he had a par four to win the U.S. Open, he hit a cannon down the 18th fairway and crisped a 5-iron into the green like it was the Fort Hood post-tournament. He cross-handed the first putt up to within 14 inches of the cup and let the Open daze stroke it in. For a closing 72 and a total of 281.

To celebrate, he turned his cap sideways for a second and looked dumbstruck. Then he wept, along with a lot of other Moodys, his wife Doris, and his two children. They'd been out at some Holiday Inn, whereas Old Sarge had been driving in hellacious Houston traffic well over an hour every day just to get to the golf course.

Probably more of a reason to weep.

PART THREE

The Seventies

●

"I've never missed a putt in my mind."

—JACK NICKLAUS

26.

A MERRY YOUNG ENGLISHMAN

Tony Jacklin at the 1970 U.S. Open at Hazeltine

LL WEEK long the one-liners dropped like bogeys out there in Minnesota farm country, so it was welcome to the 1970 Henny Youngman U.S. Open. Take this course, please. Let's rent an electric reaper and play 18. Even the locker room has a dogleg. Stir in a lot of talk about cows and corn at the Hazeltine National Golf Club because the pros had stumbled onto a layout that made them look like they ought to be taking lessons from golf writers or their wives. All except one. Tony Jacklin, the young Englishman. He whipped it into the shape of a mealy pudding and made Dave Hill, the mad dog, and all the others look like they were putting up jams and jellies on Route 101 near Shakopee.

Sometimes if a golfer feels at home on a golf course, there can be no surprise if he plays it decently. So it was with Jacklin. The Hazeltine layout tossed and turned on mildly hilly terrain while presenting a few enormous bald spots, and with the way the wind lashed it and the skies chilled it a couple of times, Jacklin had reason to feel at home, as if he were back in England. He said he felt at home, and he certainly played as if he were—at home, all by himself.

Everybody was laid to rest at Hazeltine by Jacklin, who shot four consecutive sub-par rounds on a course the American pros said was unplayable, unprintable, and would better serve mankind as the site of a Marlboro commercial.

What Tony did was shoot 71 on a day when the wind blew 40 mph, then shoot three 70s, including the close-out on a glorious Sunday.

This added up to 281, seven under par, and seven shots ahead of Dave Hill, who was more vocal than anyone on the subject of Hazeltine—and occasionally on Minneapolis, which was supposed to be close to the course but, for all practical purposes, wasn't.

One of the holes that made everyone the angriest was No. 1, a long par four bent around a bunker. The landing area for the drive disappeared from view below a weathered barn perched atop a cornfield.

Led by runner-up Hill, the pros said almost every hole was like teeing up and hitting at International Falls. On the other hand, defenders of Robert Trent Jones's design said the Open had come to the Midwest, so what better way to introduce everyone to the Midwest than to have a layout featuring cornfields and barns?

But Hill was relentless. He was constantly saying such diplomatic things in his press conferences as, "You have to be able to moo like a cow to play golf on this stupid course."

Hazeltine's casualty list was dotted with pre-Open favorites. Arnold Palmer finished 17 over, Jack Nicklaus 16 over, Tom Weiskopf 11 over, defending champion Orville Moody missed the cut, and Lee Trevino, who said at the start, "If anybody shoots 281 here, the Pope is a possum," ended up six over.

Among the rewarding things about Jacklin winning is he now has achieved, at the tender age of 25, the status of a true star. He has added the U.S. Open to the British Open he won last summer at Royal Lytham & St. Anne's. That means Jacklin has two majors, and there aren't many active players today who have accomplished as much. Only Palmer, Nicklaus, Gary Player, Billy Casper, and Julius Boros. All the rest are Lionel Hebert or somebody.

The enormity of Jacklin becoming the first Englishman to win the U.S. Open in 50 years—it hadn't happened since Ted Ray won at Inverness in 1920 by one stroke over Harry Vardon and three other chaps—wasn't lost on Leonard Crawley of the *Daily Telegraph* in London, the only British newspaper that wasn't on strike during the Hazeltine affair.

Crawley, mustache, tweed jacket, and heft, was the only British writer on the scene at Hazeltine. As he dictated his story into the phone on Sunday evening, he paused to make a remark to two acquaintances, Bob Green of the AP and your typist.

He said, "I have, you know, the whole of England at my feet."

So does Tony Jacklin now.

27

VIRTUE IN THE VALLEY OF SIN

Jack Nicklaus Wins 1970 British Open at St. Andrews

MID THE intoxicating old ruins of the town of St. Andrews, and on the golf course that held the first cleat, history and tradition were flogged and caned all week in a musty thing called the British Open by a cast of modern hustlers and legends. It was as if the Wimpy and the Whippy had come to the Royal and Ancient along with black-eyed peas and corn bread; as if, for a while, the Old Course was only a stroll through Carnaby Street. While Tony Jacklin shot the heather off the land for a while, and Lee Trevino verbally shot down a prime minister, Jack Nicklaus played himself into the immortality of the record books, and the lord of nightlife, Sir Douglas Sanders, played himself into the hearts of all those who savor the three-piece, phone-booth golf swing.

It was one of the most thrilling majors in years, one that suffocated in atmosphere. There were overtones of America against the world, elements of the best and worst shotmaking, ghastly pressure, enormous crowds, a buffet of seaside weather, the suspense of overtime—all of those things—until it was concluded by Jack Nicklaus's rendezvous with history.

The fact that the 1970 British Open was being held at St. Andrews was responsible for luring the strongest field of Americans ever. Arnold Palmer had been coming since '60, and Jack since '62, but it was new to most of the Yanks, contestants and fans alike, and they were enthralled all week by the Scots' sophistication in golf.

The first day, when Tony Jacklin completed the grandest 10 holes in the history of major championships—he was eight under through 10—a couple of weathery Scots, a man and a woman sitting in the stands behind the 11th green, were not so dazzled by Tony's tee shot.

Jacklin's iron to the par-three green ate up the flag but went 30 feet beyond to the back side.

"A bit long," said the lady.

"Right on line, though," the man said.

"Well," said the lady, "that's *half* the game, isn't it?"

In terms of sophistication, it was curious the way the British Open began at St. Andrews, in contrast to the U.S. Open, which has at least a touch of ceremony to it. Flags are raised, speeches are made, and someone eventually says, "Gentlemen, play away."

At the Old Course, everybody who got up early enough to be there stood around and watched an elderly gentleman move the No. 1 tee markers back about three feet. Then an aging steward emptied out the trash from the tee box. Somebody coughed. Finally, the starter looked at the Nigerian, who was paired with the Belgian, and said, "Your honor, I believe." That was it.

The first round belonged to Jacklin—and the weather. Tony caught the course in a calm to fire all those birdies, but a rainstorm caught him at the 14th hole, where his ball had found a bush. Actual rivers washed across greens, and ultimately play was suspended for another day.

Jacklin came back out at 7:15 the next morning, promptly took an unplayable lie, lost a total of three strokes to par before he reached the clubhouse, and turned a 64 into a 67.

The next two rounds belonged to Trevino. The second day found Lee moving into the lead with his second 68, which put him a stroke ahead of Nicklaus and Jacklin.

The crowd warmed to Trevino. He loved it, made the most of it.

On the first tee before the third round began, Lee was introduced to Prime Minister Edward Heath.

"You ever shake hands with a Mexican?" Trevino said with a grin.

The R & A building, along with the prime minister, gently swayed with laughter.

Trevino started losing his lead—and the championship—at the fifth hole of the third round. That's where he laced an iron shot at the wrong flag on the huge double green. It left him about 100 feet from the correct flag.

The moment Lee hit the shot, he slapped himself in the forehead and yelled out, "I done hit to the wrong stick! And I'm dumb enough to have done it!"

From then on, the championship alternately belonged to Nicklaus or Sanders. Nicklaus playing beautifully, Sanders scrambling beautifully.

It was after a long day of lead changes in the final round that Sanders faced a two-and-a-half-foot putt on the 72nd green to win the whole thing.

But just before Sanders putted the ball, Barbara Nicklaus, who was standing in the gallery with friends, heard a word from an R & A member with an upper-crust accent. He was Gerald H. Micklem, good friend of golf.

"Congratulations," Gerald said to Barbara. "Your husband has tied for the Open championship."

"What do you mean?" Barbara said.

"Doug's putt looks like it breaks left, you see," Micklem said. "But of course it goes right."

Sanders then missed the putt.

Nicklaus quickly took control of their 18-hole playoff on a chilled, windy day. On his way to an even-par 72, he led by five strokes with four holes to play, but Sanders miraculously made up four of them and Jack held only a one-shot lead when they reached the 18th tee.

Now came a moment of high drama when Nicklaus removed one of his two sweaters, took the driver out of the bag, and went for the green. He smashed a monster drive of 370 yards through the Valley of Sin and to the back edge of the green on the par-four hole.

From there, he chipped to eight feet with his wedge, and after displaying the patience and concentration that earmarks him at times, he jammed the putt into the cup for his second British Open and 10th major.

The British were happy in the end, one felt. Considering the exciting prospects going into the fourth round—Nicklaus, Jacklin, Trevino, even Sanders—it was the same Gerald Micklem who had said, "Quite a show coming up, it appears. But whatever happens, we want a proper champion, don't we?"

Would Jack Nicklaus do?

28

ANOTHER ONE GETS AWAY

Arnold Palmer Loses to Dave Stockton at the 1970 PGA
at Southern Hills

T WAS another chapter in the continuing saga of Arnold Palmer's efforts to find happiness in middle age and save pro golf from the Dave
Stockton people. An episode with the same old ending. You know the
story. Arnold hangs in, makes a move, the leader weakens. Arnold moves
close, closer, and the thundering herds go mad. Then Arnold stands still
and somebody else wins. Tune in next year.

So it went on the lovely and classy but rugged Southern Hills layout
in normally peaceful Tulsa, Oklahoma. The crowds rooted and tromped
and prayed and yearned and leaned in Palmer's behalf as the 40-year-old
hero tried once again to win another major, in particular the 1970 PGA
Championship on this occasion, the one big title that's escaped him.

But this major didn't happen—just as it didn't happen at St. Andrews,
where Kel Nagle happened, or Augusta, where Gary Player happened, or
Oakmont, where Jack Nicklaus happened, or The Country Club, where
Julius Boros happened, or Columbus, where Bobby Nichols happened,
or Augusta, where Nicklaus happened again, or Olympic, where Billy

Casper happened, or Baltusrol, where Nicklaus happened yet again, or Pecan Valley, where Boros happened again.

Boy, Arnold has these silver medals stacking up on him, doesn't he?

Well, he's got those eight majors for consolation, of course.

Palmer bore down and went after it at Southern Hills in the sort of "mood to win" that people have seen him in before. He even had a club he seldom uses, a 4-wood to help him dig out of the thick Bermuda rough. He even had a "cheat sheet," a yardage and diagram chart of the course. He even had lighter woods for swinging easier. "I'm trying everything," he said.

What he didn't have was the hot putter he needed, or even a lukewarm putter. Without that, he wasn't about to overtake a young man as revved up and possessed as Dave Stockton.

From tee to green, Stockton played golf that wouldn't win him much money in a municipal gangsome, but he had the overheated putter going, and he had the right attitude.

"Nobody can putt and chip better than I can," he said after Saturday's 66, which put him five ahead of Palmer. "I just feel like I'm going to win. I'm putting great, and the bad holes aren't bothering me. I've been in the woods and in the bunkers. I've even shanked a shot. But I just keep going. I bounce back."

So he did. Stockton would listen to the plaintive cries for Arnie and only try harder himself. He'd flog one into the trees or the sand, but he would squirt it out one way or another and ram home a putt, and Palmer would get nothing.

He played a fascinating four-hole stretch on the front nine Sunday when he was holding off Arnold with a 73 and his winning 279. With Arnold always rapping birdie putts that refused to fall, Stockton rolled in a 30-footer for a birdie at the sixth, holed out a 120-yard wedge shot for an eagle deuce at the seventh, followed *this* up with a horrible double-bogey five at the eighth, but followed *that* up by coming out of a fairway bunker for a birdie at the ninth.

The one moment of minidrama came at the 13th, an enormous par four of 470 yards with water in front of the green. Palmer played it beautifully, leaving himself a 20-foot birdie putt. Stockton played it like Stockton. He hooked his second shot into the water.

But he stiffed a miraculous pitch shot to within two feet of the cup to salvage a bogey, and when Palmer missed yet another birdie putt, the one stroke Arnold gained was of little consequence. There could just as easily have been a three-shot swing on the hole, but it didn't happen.

At the finish, the soap-opera stuff wasn't for Arnold. It was for Dave Stockton, the fighting 28-year-old Californian. There on the scenic 18th green, as Dave knelt down and looked at a short putt for a par that he knew he could three-putt and still win his first major, he thought: *I'm the PGA champion. I've done it.* Then he looked across the green at his wife, Cathy, and cried.

So did Arnie's Army. But they're used to it.

29

A QUIET MAN AT AUGUSTA

Charles Coody Beats Jack Nicklaus to Win the 1971 Masters

FOR A while in Sunday's final round it looked like Jack Nicklaus had left the 1971 Masters at one of those beach-party movies, the kind where all the chicks clamor after the good-looking blond guy in the tight clothes. That was when young Johnny Miller in the golden hair and Masters-green ensemble was turning the Augusta National inside out, ripping up the flagsticks and holing out a bunker shot, and in general encouraging all the hot-panted things in the gallery to squeal with an affection they usually reserve for rock stars.

The Masters as well as the game of pro golf sure could have used another matinee idol, a Johnny Miller, but that didn't turn out to be where Nicklaus would leave it. Jack left it to a tall Texan named Charles Coody, who even walks with a drawl. A guy who has two different swings in one motion but makes it work, a guy who had lost the Masters two years ago and now deserved it, a guy who admits he's probably lacking in color when he says, "I just play along in living black and white."

Coody was at his best when it came down to the pressure of Sunday afternoon. Maybe it helped that he had been there before. In 1969, he had a one-shot lead with three holes to play, just like Johnny Miller did this time. Except Miller became the old Coody who blew it, and Coody became the quiet man who knocked off the big guys again just as George Archer and Bob Goalby and Gay Brewer Jr.—other living black and whites—had done it in the recent past.

It helped Coody no end that while he played the two par-fives on the back side one under, Nicklaus played them one over even though he had a 4-iron second shot to each while Coody was hitting spoons.

"I never play the par fives well here," Jack said later.

It also helped Coody that Miller butchered three of the last four holes, even though his 68 was the low round of the day. Coody closed with a 70.

"That's quite a walk up the last fairway," said Charles Coody, a native of Abilene, Texas, who was a star golfer for TCU in Ben Hogan's hometown of Fort Worth.

Charles continued, "It's especially a good walk when you're on the green in two and leading by two. I guess I could have gestured a little more for the crowd, but if I ever get in the habit of trying to be somebody I'm not, I may forget how to play golf."

Nicklaus did an entertaining summing up of his losing performance. He said, "I knew all week I was going to win. I was in the right frame of mind, really psyched, and I felt I could bring off whatever it took. But my game was erratic all the way. I'd miss a putt I knew I was going to make. I'd hit in the water when I knew I wouldn't, or couldn't. I three-putted four times today. But until Charles holed his last putt I still thought I was going to win. Big surprise, huh?"

30

REMEMBER THE BATTLE OF MERION

1971 U.S. Open in Philadelphia

F OR THREE days the 1971 U.S. Open at marvelous old Merion, the course on Philadelphia's Main Line that had been enshrined by Bobby Jones when he completed his Grand Slam there, and enshrined again by Ben Hogan when he came back from the car wreck there, belonged to all of the unusual characters who always clutter up an Open. There was the dogged tour veteran, Labron Harris Jr., the obscure transient, Bob Erickson, the man with a bandaged putter, Jim Colbert, and the young amateur, Jim Simons, who had the pouting look of a kid who didn't like his date for the prom. But finally the famous course, short by modern standards but with deceitful targets and speedy greens that are known as "Merion lightning," rose to the occasion and demanded an 18-hole playoff for the championship between the two finest players in the game today—Jack Nicklaus, the country club guy from Ohio, our best shotmaker, against Lee Trevino, the Super Mex from Texas, our best hustler.

The start of the historic playoff blended melodrama with humor. Under the stately elms of Merion's first tee, where the ghosts of Jones and

Hogan still hover about, Nicklaus came out first and took a seat under a tree, his head down, the tension building. Then came Trevino, smacking gum, rubbing his hands together, pacing, waving at the crowd.

Trevino then went over to his golf bag, unzipped a compartment, and pulled out a three-foot-long toy snake and held it up. The crowd shrieked as Trevino laughed and tossed it at Nicklaus. Jack went scrambling in a panic, but when he realized it was a toy, he broke up in laughter. So did the fans. So did the world.

"I need all the help I can get," Trevino shouted.

The only thing more frightening after that moment was Nicklaus's sand wedge. It left him in bunkers at the second and third holes for a bogey and a double bogey and gave Trevino a two-stroke lead.

Nicklaus pulled himself together and made a war out of it, but Lee played steady, solid, two-under-par golf for his 68 to Jack's 71 and his second Open title. Trevino topped Jack at almost every turn in his classic hustler's way.

When Jack birdied the fifth, Trevino birdied the eighth. When Jack birdied the 11th—the legendary "Baffling Brook," where Jones closed out the Slam—Trevino birdied the 12th. When Jack stiffed a shot at 15 for what looked like a birdie that would gain him a stroke, Trevino rolled in a birdie putt ahead of him.

"I'm a lucky dog," Trevino said afterward. "You got to be lucky to beat Jack Nicklaus. He's the greatest player who ever held a club."

The combination of Trevino's smooth, trouble-free closing 69 and Jack's hard-earned 71 was what put them in the tie at even-par 280 and was a compliment to Merion that it had survived a rash of low scores earlier.

Trevino had said at the start, "There are 16 birdie holes on this course, but there are 18 bogey holes, too, and I'll eat all the cactus in El Paso if anybody breaks 280."

Lee was lucky there, too, cuisine-wise.

31

A YANK AT BIRKDALE

1971 British Open

N THE dining room of the massive old Prince of Wales Hotel in South-port, England, on the morning of the last round of the 1971 British Open at Royal Birkdale, the incomparable Lee Trevino started win-ning the championship shortly before eating his poached eggs.

He burst upon a breakfast table occupied by his wife, Claudia, and a few friends, two of them sportswriters, a table that was also surrounded by an assortment of English hotel guests. Lee turned his black baseball cap around backward like a helmet and started babbling, "Where's Tony Jacklin? Tony! Where you at? Man, you're gonna think the German army's after you today."

It was the same display of overwhelming confidence that Trevino had shown a month before in the moments before he went about the business of defeating Jack Nicklaus in their playoff for the U.S. Open at elegant Merion in Philadelphia.

"I believe the Mex will get big Jack today," he had said in the locker room before the playoff. Before he sauntered out to the tree-shaded first tee, where Bobby Jones had stood before completing the Grand Slam, and reached in his golf bag and tossed a toy snake at Nicklaus, causing Jack to set a Merion first-tee high-jump record before he bent over in laughter.

Now Lee was in England after three sparkling rounds holding a one-stroke lead over Jacklin and a little man named Lu Liang-Huan from Taiwan, and hoping to join an exclusive club. On this day, Trevino could become only the fourth man in history—Bobby Jones, Gene Sarazen, and Ben Hogan were the others—to win both the U.S. and British Opens in the same year.

The 35-year-old Lu, who came to be known as Mister Lu by everyone who read the London dailies, was still a complete unknown to all the people around Birkdale—except Trevino.

"I used to play with him in '59 when I was a Marine on Okinawa," Lee said. "He never misses a fairway. I played him in Taiwan one day and he brought me in 8 and 7. Something like that."

Even so, Trevino kissed off Mister Lu, too.

"I'm gonna send him back to the laundry," Trevino said as he went after the poached eggs. "And the German army's gonna get Jacklin."

Trevino's first six holes on Sunday won the championship for him. They gave him the edge he needed to survive a near-calamity later at 17. In those first six holes, he made four birdies to speed away from Jacklin and Mister Lu, and the British Open was over, barring a train wreck.

The clincher came at the sixth hole, toughest on the course, a weird par four requiring a long iron off the tee to avoid a bunker crossing the fairway, then a long fairway wood second, a blind shot to an uphill green. The golfer had to aim at a church steeple far, far away.

Trevino played it with a 1-iron off the tee and a stupendous 5-wood to the green. He clubfaced it. It felt so good to him that when the ball was in flight, he yelled, "Oh, my God—it's perfect!"

And it was, too, unless two feet shy of the flag is two feet shy of perfection.

Trevino was paired with Mister Lu and was working on a 68 and holding a three-shot lead over the slender little man when they reached No. 17. He was also telling too many jokes. But the jokes stopped when he buried his tee shot on this par five in a sandhill left of the fairway.

Lee was forced to hack at the ball twice to get out of trouble, but he still suffered a double-bogey seven, and it could have been disastrous if Mister Lu had managed a birdie on the hole, but he didn't.

Fortunately, the 18th at Birkdale is a phony par-five that Trevino could birdie with a drive and 6-iron and two easy putts, and that Mister Lu could also birdie even though his second shot hit a lady spectator in the head and bounded back into the fairway.

Happily, the lady escaped real harm, but it was a sloppy ending on a rather undistinguished golf course for the historic occasion.

Trevino said, "Hey, I'll take it. I've done won myself the U.S. Open, the British Open, and the Canadian Open. Is there a Mexican Open this year? If there is, I'll be there."

He grinned and gestured a thumbs-up at the two sportswriters who'd walked with him the full 18, then looked around for another friend, Jimmy Dean, the former entertainer who was now in the food business.

Spotting Dean, Trevino trotted toward him across the green, yelling, "Gimme some of that Jimmy Dean sausage, baby!"

32

WEED KILLER

Nicklaus Wins 1972 Masters

POA ANNUA and poa Jack. It was that kind of week down in Augusta, Georgia, at the 1972 Masters. Poa annua, honey, get off them greens you done made so scratchy. Get back in the kitchen and fix up those biscuits, and you stop botherin' Jack Nicklaus, you hear? And Jack, you come in this house. Land sakes, if you ain't actin' like you never been here before. You out there playin' against yourself and the record book and Bobby Jones and all that nonsense instead of settlin' down and winnin' this thing by the 25 or 30 shots you suppose to win by.

That's how it was all week. Poa annua and poa Jack Nicklaus. Poa annua is that weed grass that comes around every four or five years to infect the Augusta National and turn the Masters greens blotchy, fast, uneven, unreadable, and unpredictable, and it's known to send scores scurrying like, you know, upward.

Jack proved once again that he's the finest golfer of our time. He not only beat everybody in this Masters, he showed us that he can even beat himself. He must be the toughest opponent he's ever faced.

Nicklaus won this Masters by three strokes in a manner that would do honor to all the crippled and wounded of highway intersections everywhere. But the thing is, he was *supposed* to win this Masters more than he was ever supposed to win it before, and believe it or not, that can make things more difficult.

Jack Nicklaus was a golfer playing against the record book, his own aspirations, immortality, eternity, the Grand Slam, his private ambitions, and even his own embarrassments. All that adds up to a pretty strong list of opponents, and it was what made the Masters as close as it was.

It was what made Nicklaus come limping down the stretch over the last few holes, trying to play it safe, trying not to let it slip away to some guy who didn't want the burden of winning in the first place.

Jack went to the 11th hole on Sunday with a five-stroke lead on the pack, which included somebody named Jim Jamieson, and *he* was supposed to get you excited? You had to be as drunk as an ad salesman at a table under an umbrella on the veranda.

Nicklaus mainly had to worry about fate. A fate that would prevent him from winning his fourth Masters, his 12th major, which would move him up to one behind Bobby Jones, with plenty of time on his side.

Fate tried hard. It grabbed hold of Jack and made him three-putt the 11th for a bogey, three-putt the reachable 13th for a par, three-putt the 14th for a bogey, and play the 15th like a guy trying to move his hot dog to the hand with the binoculars in it. He bogeyed it by hitting a second shot that looked as if he were trying to land it in a shopping center across the street from the main entrance to the club.

Everyone agreed that the Augusta National with its contaminated greens and gusty winds played about as difficult as it ever had. Only two 72-hole scores had ever been higher than Nicklaus's winning total of 286, although he led all the way after his opening-round 68.

Only three other players broke 290, and one of them was Jamieson, whose main claim to fame is that he comes from Illinois, in a town across the river from Jack Fleck.

Nicklaus succeeded because enough of his game held together to conquer his mind. His driving was good, but his iron play was unsettling and his recovery shots were embarrassing. What kept him going was his attitude, his ability to smile at his mistakes, and his refusal to become demoralized by the weed grass that caused him to miss so many short putts.

"Trying to play safe is the worst thing in the world," he said. "I don't think I would have looked so bad there at the end if I'd been forced to throw the ball at the hole."

Jack has now established himself as a man who has taken the Masters in every conceivable way. He won it the first time by coming down the stretch against Tony Lema nine years ago and winning by a stroke. He won it by nine shots with his record 271 in 1965. He won in a playoff in 1966. And now he's won it clumsily, with rounds of 68-71-73-74, dealing only with destiny and that wicked "Poa annua."

33

THE GLORIOUS QUEST

Nicklaus at the 1972 U.S. Open at Pebble Beach

THE 1972 U.S. Open, the first ever held at Pebble Beach, almost went swimming with the abalone in Carmel Bay before the fierce winds turned loose of it long enough for Jack Nicklaus to get hold of it.

It was certainly the prettiest Open, and in some ways the most important since . . . oh, since Bobby Jones was working on the Grand Slam at Interlachen in 1930. Pebble Beach did its part, providing beautiful backdrops and by being the toughest Open course in modern history.

In this sense, it was only proper that Nicklaus was on call to keep a personal rendezvous. He won when he simply had to win, beating a dazzling array of challengers—Lee Trevino and Arnold Palmer were among them, to drop a couple of names—and by winning he added this Open to his Masters victory in April and put the words "Grand Slam" back into everybody's casual chitchat.

Pebble Beach almost played too great a role. For a while, it looked like the course would be the only winner. Good old Double-Bogey-by-the-Sea, it was absolutely torturous all four days. The scores that it wrought more closely resembled those of the 1900s, when men wore wool suits and swung hickory shafts.

Was that Miller Barber shooting 80? Was that Tony Jacklin shooting 83? Was that Bruce Devlin or Horace Rawlins shooting 85? Was that Mason Rudolph or Willie Park shooting 86? Was that George Archer or Old Tom Morris shooting 87? Who were those guys? Where were we?

In Sunday's last round, when the ripping wind produced the ultimate horrors, only Nicklaus could summon the patience to cope with the place. He had saved his best golf for the last. While his closing 74 and his funny old total of 290 will not look so wonderful in the record books someday, it shall be stated here and now that under the circumstances it was as brilliant a round as he ever shot.

Par is what the course and weather dictate, to borrow from our Scottish ancestors, and par at Pebble on Open Sunday was 76.6. That was the average score of the 20 lowest finishers. And of the nine players Nicklaus had to beat—those that were within five strokes of him after 54 holes—Jack's 74 was the best round.

For a while on Sunday it seemed possible that Arnold Palmer might make it a fight with his old rival. Palmer reached the 14th as Jack was in trouble at the 12th. Arnold faced a makable birdie putt while Jack faced an eight-footer for bogey. A Palmer make and a Nicklaus miss would constitute a two-shot swing. In fact, it would, at this point, give Arnold a one-shot lead.

Didn't happen. Arnold missed, Jack made.

"That putt certainly would have given me more of a personal interest in the Open," Arnold said later.

If that pressure putt didn't wrap up the championship for Nicklaus, then his memorable 1-iron to the 17th green certainly did. Here is one of the killer par threes in the world, 218 yards of wind-aided misery.

Jack stood on the tee, trying to stare down the wind, Bobby Jones, the Open, the Slam, and even Bruce Crampton, who was still in the hunt. That's when Jack hit a shot that made him look like a fighter who didn't want to win on points—he wanted a knockout. His 1-iron knifed into the gale, cleared the ghastly bunker fronting the green, crashed down right at the flagstick, and sat there, two inches from the cup.

It was the damnedest 1-iron in golf history.

Earlier in the round, Nicklaus had enjoyed commenting on the harshness of the course in a brief moment with P. J. Boatwright, the USGA's executive director.

"What did you do with all the grass?" Jack asked him.

Historically, the win made Jack only the fourth player to win the Masters and Open in the same year. Craig Wood did it first in 1941. Ben Hogan did it twice, in 1951 and 1953. Arnold Palmer did it in 1960.

Now the burden grows for Nicklaus. He goes to Scotland with even more pressure on him, facing more talk of the Slam. When it was all over at Pebble Sunday night, it was left to Palmer, the noble ex-king, to say what may be ahead for Nicklaus.

"From now on," said Arnold, "he's going to have trouble even breathing."

34

SLAM SPOILER

Trevino over Nicklaus at the 1972 British Open

HE STOOD against the sandhill, one foot halfway up the rise, a gloved hand braced on his knee, his head hung down in monumental despair. He lingered in this pose with what seemed like all of Scotland surrounding him, with the North Sea gleaming in the background, and with the quiet broken only by the awkward, silly, faraway sound of bagpipes rehearsing for the victory ceremony. This was Jack Nicklaus on the next-to-last hole of the 1972 British Open after another putt had refused to fall. It was Nicklaus in the moment when he knew, after a furious comeback, that he had lost this championship and that his march toward a Grand Slam was over.

If one more putt had dropped for him on any of the last seven holes, Nicklaus, who had already won the Masters and U.S. Open, would have completed what could seriously have been termed the most brilliant rally the game had ever known.

Jack had started the last round six strokes back but had miraculously caught up through 10 holes and had even seized the lead after 11. But one more putt did not drop, and on the same 17th hole minutes later one more chip shot *did* curl implausibly into the cup for the implausible Lee Trevino. So finally, after all the shattering heroics at Muirfield, home of the Honorable Company of Edinburgh Golfers, the whole world had a right to feel overgolfed and oversuspensed.

The honest fact is, there are two incredible players in the game today, Nicklaus and Trevino, and they have been producing so many memorable major championships lately that it's getting hard to keep them straight. The last two U.S. Opens have pretty much been Nicklaus-Trevino sagas, and so have the last three British Opens.

While Nicklaus played too conservatively through the first three rounds, trying to play "Hogan golf" on the same Muirfield where he'd won the championship in 1966, the result was that he trailed the leaders, Trevino and Tony Jacklin, by so much it looked impossible for him to catch up.

But Jack took out the driver in the final round and attacked the place, and it paid off when he blazed to seven under through 11 holes—and a piece of the lead.

Two holes back, where Trevino and Jacklin had more or less been playing each other—they were paired together—the roars for Nicklaus had finally gotten to Trevino.

As they were playing the par-five ninth hole, Trevino said to Tony, "Look at this. Nicklaus has gone crazy. We're out here beating each other up and Jack's done caught us and passed us."

Then they both eagled the hole.

This was when Trevino said to Jacklin, "He might beat one of us, but I don't think he can beat both of us."

The case can be made that this was a lucky win for Trevino, unlike his victories in his three previous majors, when impressive golf won the day. This time he holed out from off the green four times—*four*—over the 72 holes for his 278 that shaved Nicklaus by a shot.

The second day, he chipped in for a birdie three from 40 feet at the second hole. He holed his two absurd shots in the third round, when his

66 allowed him to run off from everybody but Jacklin. The first was from a horrible lie up against the bank in a bunker at the 16th. He slammed his wedge into the sand. Out spurted the ball in a line drive. It took one harsh bounce and dived into the cup. Then at 18 he chipped out of the weeds from some 30 feet and that thing went in for another birdie.

But for all of this, it was one last chip shot that found its way into the hole that, near the finish, won it for Trevino. He was holding the lead as he went to the par-five 17th, knowing Nicklaus's rally had stalled.

Frankly, he played the hole like a man choking on the trophy or a sausage roll. He drove into a bunker, poked it out, poked it again, and ran a short pitch over the green. But he chipped in yet again for his scene-stealing par. Even Lee was forced to break up laughing.

In defeat, Nicklaus was gracious as always.

"I didn't waste a lot of good golf here this week," he said. "I didn't play very well, but what could I have done anyhow about a guy who holes it out of bunkers and across greens?"

As for Trevino, he made no apologies for his luck.

"I think things like that happen sometimes to a man when he's trying," he said. "I was aiming at the cups. I didn't come to Scotland to help Nicklaus win the Grand Slam. If I played golf with my wife, I'd try to beat the daylights out of her too."

35

CASE OF DISRESPECT

Johnny Miller Wins 1973 U.S. Open at Oakmont

T HERE'S NO better way to become an overnight, instant, presto matinee idol in golf than to put yourself somewhere back in the Allegheny hills—about 12 coal mines and six roadhouses behind everybody trying to win the 1973 U.S. Open, including a modest cast of Jack Nicklaus, Lee Trevino, Arnold Palmer, Gary Player, Julius Boros, and Tom Weiskopf—and come cruising along with your blond mane flapping in the breeze, young, handsome, trim, and knock them all sideways with a sizzling round of golf that you've somehow pulled out of nowhere.

Meet Johnny Miller, the proud owner of a record 63 at Oakmont, the young man who demolished the notorious golf course and the elite group of people who contended in Sunday's final round.

What most guys do when they realize they are six strokes and 12 players behind with only 18 holes to play, especially when those 12 players are mostly household names, is go out and shoot a 74 or something, grab a check, and head for the airport.

But what Miller did was go out roughly an hour ahead of the leaders and birdie half the golf course—exactly half the golf course, nine holes—and turn in that 63, the lowest single round in the 73-year history of our national championship.

Okay, it was a perfectly swell round, but now to throw an asterisk into the story. It wasn't the Oakmont of yesteryear, or even a week ago. The rain of Tuesday so drenched the rolling bent greens that they never dried out and became the marble tops for which Oakmont is famed.

And there was another thing. For the first three Opens at Oakmont—those of '27, '35, and '53—every bunker was furrowed, which made them evil, treacherous, and near impossible to play from. But in '62, only the fairway bunkers were furrowed. For this week there were no furrows at all.

Oakmont and the U.S. Golf Association, it seemed, had been found guilty of catering to the complaints of the touring pros. There could be no other explanation.

What did this mean? It meant that in '53 there were only two rounds in the 60s, one by Ben Hogan, the winner, and one by Sam Snead, the runner-up. In '62, Nicklaus's year, there were nine. This time: 23. And they included not only Miller's 63 but a couple of 65s, a 66, three 67s, and more 68s and 69s than you could shake a blue coat and armband at.

Still, an eight-under 63 is an eight-under 63, and it's a pleasure to say that Miller, one of the true stylists in the game, did it with dandy golf shots. Nothing bouncing off hot-dog sheds or tree trunks or sailing out of bunkers and into the cups.

Here's how the 26-year-old with a fine big swing and easy tempo embarrassed historic Oakmont with his disrespectful round:

Three-iron and five-foot birdie putt at No. 1. Nine-iron and one-foot birdie putt at No. 2. Five-iron and 25-foot birdie putt at No. 3. Sand shot and six-inch birdie tap-in at No. 4. Six-iron and two putts for par at No. 6. Nine-iron and two putts for par at No. 7. Three-putt bogey at No. 8. Two-iron and two putts for birdie at No. 9. Five-iron and two putts for par at No. 10. Wedge and 14-foot birdie putt at No. 11. Four-iron and 15-foot birdie putt at No. 12. Four-iron and five-foot birdie putt at No. 13. Wedge and two putts for par at No. 14. Four-iron and 10-foot birdie putt at No. 15. Two-iron and two putts for par at No. 16. Wedge and two putts for par at No. 17. Five-iron and two putts for par at No. 18.

The familiar guys who had started out the day thinking they would settle it among themselves—Palmer, Weiskopf, that crowd—couldn't believe what they were seeing on the scoreboards stationed around the unfurrowed layout.

Palmer thought he was leading with only six holes to go until he glanced at the scoreboard near No. 12.

"What the hell is Miller doing?" he said to John Schlee, his playing partner, who was also a contender.

Schlee, a curious man whose name had never been mentioned any-where near a major, was, in fact, an astrology buff who claimed he was playing well because "Mars is in conjunction with my natal moon."

Schlee would finish second, one shot back, and Weiskopf would fin-ish third, two shots back.

"Johnny Miller?" Weiskopf said, laughing. "I didn't even know Miller made the cut."

36.

TRAINS, PLANES, AND RAINS

Tom Weiskopf Wins 1973 British Open at Troon

T HE REAL Troon never stood up, but Tom Terrific finally did. That's the story of the 1973 British Open, a championship that was played among the trains, planes, and rains of Scotland's west coast.

It's a matter of record that Tom Weiskopf started winning his first major on opening day, and kept right on winning it with the kind of golf he has always been capable of, which is to say a game that combines furious power with artful finesse, a game that looks better in human form than it does in those instruction books and magazine articles with the arrows and dotted lines and shaded areas.

Swing like this. Yeah. Swing like Tom Weiskopf. Or like Tom Terrific, as the British press labeled him. That's what you do.

When the British Open was played at Troon 11 years ago, and Arnold Palmer won it with the best golf of his life, everybody departed saying that Palmer was a god and Troon was a beast. Arnold had shot an Open-record 276, beating runner-up Kel Nagle by six shots and everyone else by 13.

This time it was assumed that the wind would howl again and the heather would leap up and scatter the field and the winner would be the guy who remained on his feet.

But no such thing occurred. The wind never blew; in fact, it stopped. And there was no true rough, the kind you have to slash a wedge out of or turn yourself in to the medics. And because it rained, heavy and light, and the place stayed damp, the greens held everything thrown at them, including Weiskopf's gorgeous irons that sometimes whistled and sometimes punched a hole in the mist.

What remained was not for Weiskopf to prove he could tie Palmer's record with rounds of 68-67-71-70—276, but rather that he could not beat himself, as he had at times in other majors.

Making it even tougher was the fact that Weiskopf was destined to lead all the way and was paired in the last two rounds with Johnny Miller, the main guy Tom had to beat, the guy who had won the U.S. Open a month earlier at Oakmont.

Topping it off, Tom didn't like Troon or the British Open—"It's like camping out over here," he said—and couldn't figure out what he ought to do about it.

"That's okay," a writer informed him. "Ben Hogan never liked a golf course. He wanted to kill every course he played. He thought golf courses were put on earth to keep him from making a living."

"That's what I'll do," Weiskopf said, the lightbulb beaming over his head. "I'll go kill this place."

The biggest obstacles at Troon turned out to be the problems of keeping dry and ignoring the noises. The sound of the trains churning along the railway bordering the course on one side, and the sound of the big commercial jets taking off and landing directly over the course from Prestwick International Airport.

Weiskopf's duel with Miller over the last two rounds was a thriller. Both men played well, but each time Johnny would put a shot close to the flag, Weiskopf would put one inside of it.

This suggested that Weiskopf was going against everything Jack Nicklaus had advised him to do.

Nicklaus had said at dinner one evening, "Tom, whatever you do, don't play Miller. Play the golf course. That's what I do. Concentrate on the golf course."

Weiskopf has a reputation for too often saying what he thinks, and he did it again in victory after winning by three strokes.

"For me to finally win a major, well, you can't imagine what this means," he said. "I'm a sentimental guy, whether anybody knows it or not. But I still don't like the damn golf course."

37

GOING ONE UP ON A LEGEND

Nicklaus Wins 1973 PGA

HERE ARE the words Jack Nicklaus left to history: "Book the hunt." Put them in there with all the giant steps for mankind, praise the Lord and pass the song charts, and we the people in order to form a more perfect par four. Jack finally got No. 14 at Canterbury in Cleveland, topping Bobby Jones and becoming the greatest golfer who ever lived or died.

It was the night before the final round of the 1973 PGA, last of the year's Big Four, and Nicklaus hadn't won any of the others. They'd been grabbed by guys winning their first majors—Tommy Aaron, Johnny Miller, Tom Weiskopf.

Sitting around the dinner table in the house in Shaker Heights that Jack had rented for the week were a group of pals and business associates. Jack was holding a one-shot lead on the PGA through 54 holes, although historic Canterbury wasn't a course to his liking. Too many hills and blind shots, and it was as tight in spots as a pair of jeans on a honey.

Talk got around to an elk hunt Jack was thinking of arranging in New Mexico in November. It's what Jack wanted to do with his fall schedule. But wouldn't it be better to put off the decision and see what happened tomorrow? So said a business partner.

"If you don't win," the business partner said, "you may feel like you need to play more tournaments this fall."

Nicklaus thought it over. Maybe so. Then he thought about how well he was hitting the ball, how strongly he was concentrating on the PGA, how much he wanted to get that 14th title behind him.

"Book the hunt," Jack said.

When Canterbury staged a couple of U.S. Opens back in its past, the Lawson Little Open of 1940 and the Lloyd Mangrum Open of 1946, the last three holes produced playoffs and controversies. Not this time.

The PGA was over by the time Nicklaus reached them. He could even afford the luxury of a closing bogey for his 69 and what would be a four-stroke victory over Bruce Crampton, who was runner-up to Jack for the third time in a major.

After winning, Jack Nicklaus said, "Looking back on it, I have to say I think I was trying too hard—at Muirfield last year, and then at Augusta and Oakmont and Troon. There's no doubt I was hung up on getting the 14th. And the press never stopped talking about it."

But he smiled as he added, "But it's just a number, isn't it? Jones won his 13 in a shorter length of time, and he had fewer tournaments to try for. We need an asterisk, I guess."

38

HOORAY FOR HOLLYWOOD

Nicklaus Wins 1975 Masters

YEAH, BUT Manny, we want Redford for all three leading men. Okay, maybe somebody else for Weiskopf, but Redford's got to play the two blond guys, Nicklaus and Miller. We call it "The Greatest Golf Tournament Ever Played." So people argue. Who'll know? One blond guy makes a putt from here to Encino, and the other two guys miss putts on the 18th from so close the cup looks bigger than Coldwater Canyon. Now, the blond guy who wins, Nicklaus, who is already the best there ever was, he marries his 1-iron and takes his putter for a mistress. Cut and print. *Ciao*, baby.

There was something about the 1975 Masters that was cinematic from the beginning. Honestly, if someone had said to one of those bankable screenwriters, do me a script where the year's first major comes along in Augusta, Georgia, and Jack Nicklaus, Johnny Miller, and Tom Weiskopf—three of the four best players in the world today, with only Lee Trevino missing—go out in the final hours and undergo the most unbearable pressure and provide the most excruciating excitement, hole after hole, until the whole business is decided at the very end, what might have been written was precisely what happened.

You could take all of your double eagles and playoffs and Arnold Palmers and Sam Sneads and Ben Hogans and Byron Nelsons and scrape them into one pile, but altogether they might not equal Sunday's events when Nicklaus bagged his fifth Masters and 15th major.

The record will show that Nicklaus outgutted or outmiracled—whatever—a Johnny Miller who stung the Augusta National with closing rounds of 65 and 66 while Tom Weiskopf stung the course with closing rounds of 66 and 70.

The cold print will reveal that Nicklaus managed it by starting out swifter, with opening rounds of 68 and 67, at which point he would hold a six-stroke lead over Weiskopf and an 11-stroke lead over Miller.

But things got confusing, not to mention close, on Saturday when Miller and Weiskopf were creating storms with their 65 and 66 while Jack was storming backward with a 73. This gave Weiskopf a one-shot lead over Nicklaus, with Miller four off the pace.

So now they go out for the last round, with Nicklaus in the next-to-last group paired with young Tom Watson, and with the twosome of Weiskopf and Miller directly behind.

Since you didn't see it on TV, here's how the front nine boiled over:

Nicklaus bogeys the first hole; they par. Nicklaus and Miller birdie the second; Weiskopf pars. Nicklaus and Weiskopf birdie the third; Miller bogeys. Miller birdies the fourth; Nicklaus and Weiskopf par. Nicklaus birdies the fifth with an iron that swallows the flag; they par. Through five holes, Nicklaus and Weiskopf are tied, Miller four back.

But onward. Miller and Weiskopf birdie the sixth; Nicklaus pars. Everybody pars seven. Miller birdies eight; they par. Miller and Nicklaus birdie the ninth; Weiskopf pars. Miller is out in four under, Nicklaus three under, Weiskopf two under. Nicklaus and Weiskopf are tied, Miller is two back. Can anybody really stand the back nine?

Somebody once said that the Masters doesn't start until the back nine on Sunday. I'm quite sure it was me who said it first. Anyhow, it was true once again.

Johnny Miller will see Nicklaus winning this Masters as his own short birdie putt creeps just outside the cup on the 10th green and his measly two-footer for par twists out of the cup at the 11th green.

Tom Weiskopf will see Nicklaus winning as his "fat 5-iron" plunged into the water at the 11th, costing him a bogey, and as his "fat 6-iron" came up short of the 16th green and the lousy chip that followed cost him another bogey.

And they would both see Nicklaus winning when their eight-foot birdie putts at the 72nd hole burned the cup's edges but missed.

Other observers might see it another way.

They would see Nicklaus winning it with his own heroics. With a crushing 1-iron second shot to the par-five 15th hole that gave him a two-putt birdie, and then with the 40-foot birdie putt he curved into the cup on 16 that made Jack and his caddie, Willie Peterson, do an imitation of ballroom dancers.

On Sunday night Nicklaus spoke of what it was like to be out there in the middle of all that drama.

"It's fun," he said. "You're inspired, you're eager, you're excited. You almost want to break into a dead run when you hit a good shot. It's what you've prepared yourself for, what you wait a year for. I'll tell you. To know you can look back someday and know you were a part of something like that, it's just great."

Other than that, there's not much else you can say about Jack W. Nicklaus. He loves his wife and kids. He's loyal to his friends. He's kind to animals. He can recite the Preamble.

Why does that make a good movie?

39

MADNESS AT MEDINAH

Lou Graham Wins 1975 U.S. Open in Chicago

ROM THE beginning, it was a golf tournament that begged to be forgotten, one that was called everything from the Sauna Bath Classic to the Lost Ego Invitational. So it was probably fitting that on an extra day, on still another steamy afternoon in Chicago, a rather invisible journeyman pro named Lou Graham brought the 1975 U.S. Open to a merciful ending.

Being the last human alive out there on the damp-hot, insufferably humid, and thoroughly oppressive premises of Medinah Country Club, Graham became the Open champion by beating young John Mahaffey 71 to 73 in an 18-hole playoff that the public and press would have been happier with if it had been waged by Jack Nicklaus and Ben Crenshaw.

It came close to involving those two glamour guys.

But Jack and Ben were among the four or five players who blew it over the last few holes on Sunday in an hourlong display of some of the worst golf ever played by familiar stars.

There's no doubt that the main reason Graham and Mahaffey got into the playoff in the first place, after tying over the regulation 72 holes with a three-over-par total of 287, is that, if nothing else, they are straight hitters off the tee. Graham has a kind of flippy swing and just kept hitting low shots a safe distance, never far off line, except on those occasions when he happened to remember that he was in a U.S. Open.

Mahaffey, meantime, is a stylish swinger, one of the bright young lads on the tour. He's a University of Houston guy, an NCAA champion, a kid who swept out the shop for Jimmy Demaret and Jackie Burke at Champions, and he's played in skin games with Ben Hogan and a few rich oilmen—and won money.

In the Monday confrontation, Graham and Mahaffey played exactly as they had through the previous four rounds. Steady golf, but unspectacular to the point of boredom. Graham did manage to make some birdie putts, and Mahaffey didn't. With eight holes to go, Graham had a three-stroke lead. He staggered a bit with two bogeys near the end, but he did shoot that even-par 71, which was good enough.

Graham is known as "a good old country boy" from Nashville. At 37, and after 12 years on the tour, he had won only twice, a couple of tournaments that nobody saw. Once in Minnesota and somewhere else, and they have both been canceled.

Mahaffey said, "This course was never as difficult as the scores looked. I agree with everybody who said it was the easiest Open in history to have won. At least 10 guys could have won it by five shots if they'd only played golf."

Well, maybe not that many. But four others for sure—Nicklaus, Crenshaw, Frank Beard, and Bob Murphy.

Beard, the 54-hole leader after a Saturday 67, agreed with Mahaffey, saying, "This course isn't that hard. Being where I am with a 67 is the greatest rip-off since Riggs and King."

When Frank was the last player with a chance to tie or beat Graham and Mahaffey on Sunday, but bogeyed 16 and 17 and shot 78, he explained that there were too many dogleg right holes at Medinah for his game.

"My best fade hooks 20 yards," he said.

Bob Murphy and Hale Irwin were the leaders in the clubhouse for 30 minutes at 288. Despite a bogey at 18, Murphy put up a 69, the low round of the day, and Hale shot a 70, the second best. Theirs was the number to beat.

Nicklaus knew this as he stood on the 16th tee, one behind Murphy and Irwin. Three pars to the house would have given him 286 and victory. Two pars would have put him in the playoff.

But he bogeyed all three holes. Yeah, Jack Nicklaus did this, with soaring hooks and flubbed chips.

"Jack, did you know you were right there?" he was asked in the locker room, not looking all that perturbed.

"Of course I knew it," he said. "But I didn't play well all week. I was going with an artificial swing, and it caught up with me."

Crenshaw led through most of the back nine, and with pars on the last two holes he'd be the winner at 286. This was true even though he had hit an assortment of wild tee shots but kept finding them in Medinah's jungles and saving pars. Ben described those tee balls as "looking for Jane."

His wait on 17 was far too long, and he didn't quite get enough of a 2-iron to clear the water on the club's postcard hole—the long par three where Sam Snead had three-putted to lose the only previous Open at Medinah in 1949, handing it to Cary Middlecoff.

Double bogey for Ben. Tie for third with Beard, Murphy, and Irwin, one shot away from Graham and Mahaffey.

Explanation?

"I think I hit it with my throat instead of the 2-iron," said Ben.

In the end, Graham and Mahaffey wound up tied after Lou bogeyed the last hole and Mahaffey, who'd dropped a 40-foot putt for a birdie at 14, parred the last four holes.

Mahaffey's birdie, incidentally, was the only one anybody made in the last hour of the championship, when Medinah became Collapse City.

It occurred to historians that the 1975 Open ended like so many old-fashioned Opens had in the past. One guy waiting around in the clubhouse to see if anybody could stay alive to tie him. Finally, another guy makes a par or bogey and does it.

Call it the most thrilling U.S. Open finish since Laurie Auchterlonie shot a 77 and won by six at Garden City in 1902.

40

SWEET SIXTEEN

Nicklaus Wins 1975 PGA at Firestone

E'S A known Communist. He kidnapped the Lindbergh baby. He attacked Pearl Harbor. He peddles dope and he—what? Oh, sorry. We were all just sitting around out here in Akron, Ohio, trying to think up something new to say about Jack Nicklaus.

It's getting difficult. Jack did that thing again. He won another major. Which is like saying a Cadillac has more legroom. This time it was the 1975 PGA at Firestone Country Club, which is a fairly familiar place for Nicklaus. Before Sunday, he'd won five times on this same course—the World Series of Golf four times and the American Golf Classic, accomplishments that had made him second in local earnings to Raymond Firestone.

This PGA represents the 16th major championship for Nicklaus. That's twice as many as Arnold Palmer or any two of Jack's other contemporaries.

Since Nicklaus had shot a 67 on Saturday and had taken a four-stroke lead on everybody, the final round on Sunday only had a chance to be suspenseful if he played as poorly as he did in June when he frittered away a U.S. Open he might have won at Medinah in Chicago.

But he didn't. He shot a cozy 71 and had enough of a lead over Bruce Crampton that he could even afford a double bogey on the last hole to win by two strokes.

Crampton said it pretty well. "We all suffer from human deficiencies. Jack just suffers from fewer of them. He wouldn't have made a six at the last hole if he'd needed something better."

Jack was asked if this was true.

"I wouldn't have," he said, winking.

There was no need to ask Nicklaus if he'd like to play Firestone's long 16th hole again the way he did on Saturday. He would have asked if the questioner was daft. Jack absolutely stole a par five there when he could well have made a 20. It was the single hole that won him the championship.

You can drive as far to the right as you want at the 16th and still be safe. So Jack drove left. High and long left, and into a ravine the Firestone members didn't even know existed on the South Course. Penalty. Shooting three and he was still 7,000 yards from the green. So he dropped 50 yards behind the hazard and hit a 6-iron shot that soared high and far to the right, but it came down behind a grove of tall trees, and he still had a 9-iron left, shooting four. Somehow he hit the world's highest and longest 9-iron and did reach the green, but at least 30 feet from the cup, and in a spot where half the population of the United States usually three-putts. Naturally, Jack sank the putt for par.

It behooves a man to say that from where Nicklaus was on Saturday after that tee shot on the 16th hole, no mortal who ever lived could have rescued a par five—and the championship.

But, of course, Jack hasn't been a mortal for several years now.

41.

STRIKING ANOTHER BLOW FOR YOUTH

Jerry Pate Wins 1976 U.S. Open at the Atlanta Athletic Club

T HAS long been established that you're not supposed to win a digni-fied, ivy-covered, crusty old championship like the U.S. Open unless you're well versed in the history of Francis Ouimet's knickers. But here came Jerry Pate, a 22-year-old rookie, another tall blond guy, a lad of the Deep South himself, to play his way through the Georgia pines and do enough remarkable things on a hazardous course to carry off the 1976 Open, and do it by hitting a 5-iron shot out of the rough and over water on the very last hole, a shot so splendid it even made one or two USGA officials swoon.

Jerry Pate? Maybe you remember he was the U.S. Amateur cham-pion two years ago. Maybe you've heard the rumor that he has the best golf swing since Sam Snead as he goes at the ball with beautiful rhythm and a high finish. Maybe you've heard that he has "the quietest grip" in the game, and that he has "oozed success" since he was a kid.

As a native of Georgia—like Bobby Jones, who before his death cam-paigned for the Atlanta Athletic Club to host a U.S. Open—it seemed appropriate that Pate should prevail in a championship that looked for most of the week to be the property of the cherub, John Mahaffey, or, briefly, of Tom Weiskopf, who had been displaying an uncharacteristic patience and composure, or even of Al Geiberger, who kept lurking near the lead and refusing to go away.

As things unraveled in the last round, Weiskopf with a 68 and Geiberger with a 69 reached the clubhouse in a tie at 279, leaving everything up to Pate, the last man on the course with a chance.

Others had faltered ahead of Weiskopf and Geiberger. Poor Mahaffey, who had lost a playoff to Lou Graham at Medinah last year, had held the lead forever but bogeyed the last three holes, and said, "I just give up too much yardage here—I'm exhausted."

Ben Crenshaw was even a contender for a while, as he was at Medinah, but he suffered a similar fate on the water-sprawled layout. He double-bogeyed the 215-yard 15th hole the last three days in a row. This hole had drowned people throughout the tournament, but it was a hole where Pate made the birdie on Sunday that put him in shape to win.

Now came the 72nd hole and it was all up to Pate. After his birdie at 15, he had scratched out pars on 16 and 17 and was clinging to a one-shot lead when he pushed his drive into the rough and faced a 194-yard second shot over the pond.

Fortunately, he caught a good lie in the rough. The ball was sitting up just enough for Pate to get a 5-iron on it. Still, it was a tremendously long shot over water, with the Open riding on it.

The drama ended the instant Pate's shot came off the clubface. The ball wasn't going anywhere but to the flagstick, and it wound up only two feet away.

As Pate took his triumphant stroll to the last green on his way to a 68 and 277, under the care of several USGA gentlemen, he had only a moment of doubt about the outcome.

"Are you sure I've got two putts to win?" he kept asking Harry Easterly, the USGA president.

Yes, the leaderboard was correct, he was told.

To which Pate said, "Well, I can make the putt anyhow."

Confidence is not lacking in Jerome K. Pate as a competitor, even though he's the youngest U.S. Open winner since Jack Nicklaus in 1962.

"I had to go for it," Jerry said later of his shot at the last hole. "Of course, all I did was hit it two feet from the hole and win the Open. How 'bout that, sports fans?"

42

A BRAW BRAWL

Tom Watson Tops Nicklaus at the 1977 British Open

GO AHEAD and mark it as the end of Western civilization and a special era in professional golf—the Jack Nicklaus era—if you're absolutely certain that Jack's been chased into his sunset years by the steel and nerve and ball-striking talent of Tom Watson.

You could argue it in these hours after Watson has become the new king of the sport in a kingly land; when Watson has defeated Nicklaus again this year in a biggie; when he has done it in the most memorable way imaginable to the greatest player who ever wore a slipover shirt.

Actually, you could say it with numbers. In the last two rounds of the 1977 British Open on the photogenic links of Turnberry along the west coast of Scotland, Watson shot 65 and 65 in the last two rounds to beat Nicklaus by one stroke over two breathtaking days because Jack could only manage the paltry, shabby, humiliating scores of 65 and 66.

Oh, and by the way, they were playing together.

It might also be mentioned that Watson's 72-hole total of 268 was a new British Open record by eight shots, which meant that Nicklaus's total of 269 was seven strokes better than anyone had ever shot before.

Maybe Hubert Green, the U.S. Open champion of a month earlier, said it best after finishing third at 279, 11 shots back of Watson.

"I won the tournament," Hubert said. "I don't know what course Tom and Jack were playing."

After they had punched and counterpunched each other for 50 straight holes, a one-on-one, head-to-head, you-and-me type of thing, they went to the 15th hole of the last round with Watson, the Masters winner over Jack back in April, one stroke behind.

That's where Tom stabbed Jack through his yellow sweater with a 60-foot birdie putt from the hardpan off the green. The astonishing shot struck the flagstick and plopped into the cup for the deuce.

Now they went to the 16th tee and stood there, and looked at each other. The blond and the redhead. Yesterday and today. Then and now.

Tom Watson finally smiled at Nicklaus and said, "This is what it's all about, isn't it?"

Jack smiled back and said, "You bet it is."

They parred the 16th without incident, and so it came down to the last two holes. To the 500-yard par-five 17th, a pushover birdie or eagle hole, and the bothersome par-four 18th.

Anything could happen.

It has to be said that this was where Watson won it. Hitting his second shot first, he absolutely stung a perfect 3-iron right over the flag and onto the green, leaving himself a 20-foot putt for an eagle and an easy two-putt birdie.

The shot seemed to unglue Nicklaus, and just enough to make him force a 4-iron shot that not only missed the green but left him with a difficult chip. Fighter that Jack is, he worked the chip up to within five feet of the cup, but missed the putt. When Watson two-putted for the birdie, it was the first time all week Tom had been in the lead.

On to the 18th. Watson drove with a solid 1-iron and stuck a crisp 7-iron into the flag. It was an arrow into the ribs of a bear. It was marvelous showbiz that Nicklaus somehow recovered from an awkward drive and a miracle-working second shot and managed to sink a 40-foot birdie putt, but he knew the claret jug had been lost.

He could only watch as Watson tapped in from two feet.

"I just couldn't shake him," Nicklaus said later to a group of friends.

With that, he looked off in thought with something of the expression of an aging gunfighter. He did not say he had been expecting *someone* to come along one of these years. But the look seemed to indicate he had finally met him.

43.

SUDDEN DEATH COMES TO TOWN

Lanny Wadkins Wins 1977 PGA at Pebble Beach

FOR MOST of the 1977 PGA Championship on the drought-scarred shores of Carmel Bay, the wrapper that Pebble Beach comes in, there was more interest in the madcap foolishness over the grooves on the faces of the golfers' irons than there was in the first sudden-death playoff in the history of majors. History will say that the playoff ended on the third extra hole when 27-year-old Lanny Wadkins defeated 47-year-old Gene Littler with a four-foot putt for par that caused Lanny to do a bird thing.

The playoff wouldn't have been possible if Lanny's final-round 70 hadn't caught Littler, who'd led the championship all the way from his opening-round 67 until he began trying to nurse his lead over the last nine holes and made a horror movie of it.

With no help from the illegal square grooves that were marauding through the neighborhood, here's how Littler frittered away the title with his unsightly 76:

He bunkered his approach to No. 10 and bogeyed. He three-putted 12 for a bogey. He bogeyed 13 with a poor second shot and a sick chip.

He hit into a fairway bunker and bogeyed 14. He bunkered a short iron and bogeyed 15. Littler pulled himself together and parred the last three holes, but the damage had been done.

In the locker room a few moments before the sudden-death playoff, Lanny turned to a friend who had a beer in his hand.

"Gimme some of that," Lanny said. He took a couple of swigs.

"That ought to do it," he said, grinning, going out the door.

Wadkins made a scrambling par on the first hole to keep his chances alive. They both birdied the second. Then they both tried to bogey the third by missing the green, Littler short, Lanny long. But Lanny chipped better. Gene's was fat, leaving him a 20-footer, which of course he missed.

That's when Lanny jammed in the four-footer and went into a series of leaps and spirals. It wasn't the beer, it was the title.

Until then, the square grooves scandal, if you want to dignify it by calling it a scandal, was the topic of the week. The discussion was all about the width of the grooves in the Ping irons, and how if they're too wide, they give the golfer an unfair advantage. Some golfers took it more seriously than others, even though the space being screamed about was roughly the thickness of a dollar bill.

So it happened that wholesale club testing came about at Pebble Beach to see which golfers might be "cheating," either knowingly or un-knowingly.

Some of the results were as follows: Tom Watson's were too wide. Raymond Floyd's were too wide. Hale Irwin lost two irons. Tom Weis-kopf lost a wedge. Jack Nicklaus's clubs were fine. So were Gene Lit-tler's.

This was actually the first club check at a major in 30 years, or since the U.S. Open at Riviera in 1948. Back then, players who weren't play-ing MacGregor clubs complained about them. They mainly complained about them because MacGregor's staff at the time included Ben Hogan, Byron Nelson, and Jimmy Demaret.

Before that Open, all of the MacGregor irons had to be filed down. So with that disadvantage Ben Hogan shot only 276 to break the Open record by five strokes.

But back to Pebble Beach. For my money, the cerebral Ed Sneed, a member of our Ryder Cup team, put the grooves issue in perfect perspective. He said:

"When you consider that the golf ball, which is either solid or wound and has a Balata or Surlyn cover and must not exceed 1.62 ounces or be less than 1.68 inches in diameter, is struck with a club, the shaft of which may be made of aluminum, titanium, graphite, hickory, or moon rock, and is tipped 3/4 of an inch and is 3/8 of an inch longer than standard, especially when manufacturers on the deflection board drop it 4.3613 inches with a one-pound weight placed two inches from the end, and when the grip on the shaft, which is either rubber, cord, or leather, is 1/64 of an inch over standard, or perhaps 1/32 under standard, and such a shot is struck off of fairways mowed at 29/54 onto a green that is cut to 5/32 on Thursday and Friday and then 7/64 on Saturday and Sunday, it's then of course very easy to see how a groove in an iron club that is a thousandth of an inch off can be one hell of an advantage."

We all can see that, right?

44

THE TRUE SPORTSMAN

Gary Player Wins 1978 Masters

MOST OF the week, the 1978 Masters sat quietly and drearily under peculiar clouds of pollen that turned everything from golf shoes to rental cars into the color of oatmeal. But as usual the tournament exploded on the back nine of the Augusta National on Sunday afternoon, and at the finish jaws dropped and eyes widened as Gary Player leaped out of an antique photo album to win.

What Player did was come from South Africa, middle-aged, seven strokes and 10th place behind, to whisk the green jacket away. He did it with a flaming 64, eight under par, which enabled him to get to the house with a total of 277 and a one-stroke victory over defending champion Tom Watson, last year's U.S. Open champion Hubert Green, and Rod Funseth, the tournament's designated lurker.

While there were brilliant shots occasionally struck out there among the pines and ponds, it looked for much of the time like the world's greatest game of miniature golf.

Player came roaring down the stretch holing everything but his ball marker, and then he settled back to watch on TV as Watson, Green, and

Funseth missed putts that were inside the grip of a hairbrush. It was a reminder that there's no such thing as a gimme in competitive golf.

To get history out of the way, it was Player's third Masters and his ninth major—one more than Arnold Palmer, which is hard for the mind to get around—a list that includes three British Opens, two PGAs, and one U.S. Open. Gary had won the Masters in 1961 and 1974, and he won his first Masters the same way he won this time. In '61, he finished early and watched Palmer blow it on the last hole.

Nevertheless, it was a spectacular victory and told us again what an incredible fellow the 41-year-old Player is. He will fall down, come out of his shoes, hit on the run, and turn the golf swing into something that looks more like a tennis forehand or a baseball strikeout. But he works hard, he out-travels Magellan, and there's never been a tougher competitor.

That 30 he threw at everybody on the last nine holes is worth the retelling. He hit a 5-iron into the 10th green and sank a 25-foot birdie. He hit a 7-iron into the dangerous 12th and dropped a 15-footer for birdie. He fell down launching a 4-iron onto the 13th and two-putted for a birdie. He fell down poking a 3-wood onto the 15th and two-putted for a birdie from 80 feet. He dropped a curving 15-foot putt for a birdie at the 16th. Last, he hit a 6-iron to the 18th and eased a downhill, 15-foot putt into the cup for a birdie.

As Player sank that last birdie, he clenched his fist and jabbed old immortality in the ribs, then fell into the arms of his black caddie, Eddie McCoy, and—well, that was a moment for everyone in sports to rejoice over. That was a fighter we'd been watching, that was a true sportsman, and, my word, that was emotional.

45

LAST MAN STANDING

Fuzzy Zoeller Wins 1979 Masters

WHEN THE 1979 Masters finally ended in its first sudden-death playoff down in Amen Corner amid the blazing dogwood and azalea, the winner was just about the last man on anyone's mind and certainly the last man in the field alphabetically—Fuzzy Zoeller. Most people were preoccupied with watching Ed Sneed slit his wrists.

With exquisite rounds of 68, 67, and 69, Sneed had taken command of the proceedings. He had led at 36, had led at 54, and was still leading everyone by three strokes with only three holes to play.

The playoff came about primarily because the stylish-swinging Sneed suffered three agonizing bogeys on those three holes by missing putts in the range of six to eight feet. They all looked like they were going in, but they didn't. Putts do this sometimes.

Sneed's finishing 76 thus allowed two guys playing ahead of him—Fuzzy and Tom Watson—to join him at the 10th tee for the sudden-death drama. Ironically, Fuzzy hadn't even been seen on the CBS telecast.

Watson had missed birdie putts all day for his last-round 71, and on

Fuzzy's behalf it could be said that at least he played the last four holes in two under par for the 70 that got him into the mix. His big shot was a 235-yard 3-wood to 15 that barely cleared the water and gave him a two-putt birdie.

It need hardly be said that the handsome, well-read Ed Sneed was in the worst frame of mind going into the playoff, having just blown the tournament.

Still, he smacked as good a tee shot as the other two, being first off the 10th tee, and hit his approach to the green first, sticking it six feet from the flag. Problem was, Zoeller and Watson did the same thing. When they all missed their putts, they went to the 11th hole, the start of Amen Corner.

Again, good drives for everybody. Sneed's second shot "looked good all the way," he said later, "until the wind knocked it down." The ball bounced into the back bunker, the worst possible place to be. He would have to explode out toward the pin—and Rae's Creek behind it. Fuzzy and Tom put their shots on the green for birdie putts.

Sneed's dangerous explosion out of the sand was probably the best golf shot of the day. He almost holed it out, missing by inches. But the rescued par under the most trying circumstances did him little good when Zoeller sank an eight-foot birdie putt to grab victory in his first Masters.

The likable, good-natured Zoeller is a guy who usually manages a grin even when the shot goes wrong. He enjoys a smoke. He strolls along, plays to the crowd.

"I just like to play golf," he said. "I think finishing fourth is better than fifth, and finishing 15th is better than 16th."

Of the 3-wood that he hit to 15—his best shot of the day—he said, "Now, believe me, I know exactly how far I can hit a 3-wood. I can hit it 235 yards without any wind. I don't know how it got there."

Although he was dying inside, Sneed put on a cheerful face and joked, "What do you mean Fuzzy won? I thought I won the tournament." Unremarkably, majors are won by shots that get there somehow, and majors are lost by putts that don't drop. Fuzzy's 3-wood got there on the 15th, and Sneed's putt didn't drop at the 18th.

What may have been more remarkable than anything is that either of them was in a position for those things to matter in this Masters.

46

DENTAL PROJECT

Hale Irwin Wins 1979 U.S. Open in Toledo

THE U.S. Open can no more dodge making history than it can avoid criticism or mysterious happenings. The 1979 Open at the Inverness Golf Club in Toledo is where no major had been played since the longest-lasting in USGA annals in 1931—the year of the 72-hole playoff between Billy Burke and George Von Elm—but this time it will be remembered for a spruce tree, an imposter, a clown, and the first Open winner with braces on his teeth. On the course where Harry Vardon, the inventor of the overlapping grip, once walked in the 1920 Open, Hale Irwin invented the underlapping overbite.

A truly fine player who deserved to win another Open after overcoming Winged Foot in 1974, Irwin actually won this one in Saturday's third round when he fired a 67 on the antagonistic old-fashioned greens and humping, curving fairways of Inverness.

He may have won it with a single shot that day, a career 2-iron that soared into the flag at the 13th hole and left him with a gimme putt for an eagle three. All he really had to do on Sunday was not lose, and Hale is too reliable and accomplished a player and tenacious a competitor to do that.

Tenacious seems to be the right word to describe Irwin, a guy who decided to straighten his teeth with braces at the age of 34.

Irwin began the last day with a three-stroke lead over Tom Weiskopf and wound up the day with a two-stroke win over Jerry Pate and Gary Player, 284 to 286, thanks to Hale's "choke-dog finish"—his words—of double bogey, bogey for a four-over 75, the highest closing round for a winner since Cary Middlecoff limped home with a 75 at Medinah in 1949.

Hale apologized profusely for his finish. "Closing with a double bogey and bogey is not my idea of championship golf, but when you wind up two shots better than anyone else, that's what counts. It was a fight out there. This is the Open, and I started choking on the first tee. I found myself out there hoping bad things would happen to the rest of the guys because I used up all my adrenaline on Saturday—I didn't sleep all night."

The special moment of the Open came on that same Saturday. Irwin had to stand in the fairway and watch Tom Weiskopf eagle the 523-yard 13th with a high 4-iron shot and an eight-foot putt. It might have unsettled any other player.

But all Hale did was say to his caddie, "Hell, let's make a damn eagle of our own."

That was when he burned his 2-iron toward the flag. The ball sneaked onto the green and started tracking the cup and stopped two and a half feet short of it.

Hale's low screamer was what the pros sometimes call "a movin' momma." It was the shot of the tournament.

Everything else at Inverness was comedy.

The first day, a tour player named Lon Hinkle found a shortcut to the green at the par-five eighth hole—drive down the 17th fairway—and took it to birdie the hole. His 70 tied him for the first-round lead. Word soon filtered back to the field and six other players took the route to a birdie. This infuriated the USGA. The organization quickly ordered a spruce tree and had it planted in the dead of night in the path of the shortcut before another round was played.

The act was unprecedented. No tree had ever been planted after a major championship had begun, and by doing it the striped ties and gold pins opened themselves up to vicious criticism from the competitors and a spray of jokes from the press.

The eighth hole became known as Hinkle Bells. Writers said they couldn't wait to see a play titled "A Hinkle Grows in Brooklyn."

"Only Hinkle can make a tree" became a standard line.

Lon Hinkle wound up blaming the tree for taking him out of contention. He kept trying other shortcuts at No. 8 over the last three rounds but got nothing for his efforts except scores of 77, 76, 81.

"I should have concentrated on playing golf instead of trying to outfox the tree," he said.

Before the affair with the tree, the USGA had suffered another embarrassment. In the last practice round, Wednesday, an imposter named Barry Bremen played nine holes with Wayne Levi, then had his photo taken with Jack Nicklaus on the practice tee.

It turned out that this was the same Barry Bremen who back in February had managed to get himself into a Kansas City Kings warm-up suit and participate in halftime shooting drills during the NBA All-Star Game.

Finally, on Sunday morning, the USGA felt compelled to make a citizen's arrest of Bobby Clampett, a fine amateur, for conduct considered "demeaning" to the Open.

Clampett had missed the cut but was sent out as a "marker," a noncontesting companion for pro David Edwards, who otherwise would have been playing alone. Clampett has a sort of Harpo Marx look to him anyhow, so maybe that explains what he did.

He drove off the first tee on his knees. He drove off the 10th tee on his knees. He frequently putted between his legs, putted with a sand wedge, and did a number of other routines. He was eventually escorted off the course at No. 12 by Jim Hand, chairman of the USGA's championship committee, and P. J. Boatwright, executive director of the USGA.

"I'll have the last laugh," Clampett said. "I'll turn pro."

47

ADIOS, AMIGOS!

Seve Ballesteros Wins 1979 British Open at Royal Lytham
& St. Anne's

E VERY FEW years the British Open is played at Royal Lytham
& St. Anne's on the frigid Lancashire coast—think Blackpool,
vacation spot for the working man—where if your head isn't tied
on, it could be blown out to the Irish Sea. And every few years somebody
wins at Lytham from South Africa, New Zealand, Australia, or England. You may now add Spain.

This is thanks to a dashing, 22-year-old Spaniard named Severiano
Ballesteros. All he did was become the youngest champion in 86 years
at the 1979 British Open. He defeated and confounded the field with
a combination of brute strength, deft putting touch, and incomparable
luck at finding his tee shots after they wound up in trampled-down
broom, scrub willow, bluebells, heather, and car parks.

Once again Lytham became "an American graveyard," as the British press loved to call it.

Since the great Bobby Jones won the first British Open ever held at
Lytham back in 1926, no American has managed to do it, which means

that Lytham has welcomed such champions as South Africa's Bobby Locke in '52, Australia's Peter Thomson in '58, New Zealand's Bob Charles in '63, England's Tony Jacklin in '69, South Africa's Gary Player in '74, and now Spain's Seve Ballesteros.

Ballesteros didn't earn the title of "the car park champion" for nothing. He hit only nine fairways—*nine*—out of 72 holes in shooting his confusing rounds of 73, 65, 75, and 70 for the 283 that gave him his three-shot victory over Ben Crenshaw and Jack Nicklaus.

Incidentally, if you keep stats on such things, it was Jack's seventh time finishing second in the British Open while winning it three times. This topped the six second places of J. H. Taylor, which stretched from 1896 to 1914. That would be your J. H. Taylor of "the Great Triumvirate," the Harry Vardon, James Braid, John Henry Taylor powerhouse of yesteryear.

Perhaps one reason American pros never fare well at Lytham is that it is such a strange layout. The front nine and back nine are as different as loaves of white and rye.

The front goes out downwind along a railway track, surrendering birdies like pork pies, weirdly presenting par-three holes at one and nine, with two par-fives back to back and reachable with a 7-iron.

But the back nine offers a string of par fours you often can't reach with a limousine, and the golfer has every right to think of par at Lytham as 33-38 instead of 35-36. On top of it all, Lytham's narrow fairways and tiny greens make it the most confining of all British Open courses.

The gallery at Lytham also had a distinct personality. The nearby city of Blackpool, famous for its boardwalk, music halls, carnival rides, and shopworn hotels, is a resort catering to lorry drivers and plumbers on vacation, and they were out in force.

There were record crowds despite the wet, cold, windy weather, and they became moblike as the tournament progressed. They stormed over crosswalks, spilled out of grandstands, cheered for foreigners, and jeered Americans they hadn't bet on. A pub behind the ninth green became the rowdiest place of all, where the Yanks often heard cries of "Miss it, bloke . . . miss it!" as they crouched over putts.

Hale Irwin, the 36-hole and 54-hole leader, gave the British blokes his fist in the third round when he was struggling to fight off Ballesteros and the weather at the same time.

Hale's wife, Sally, smoldered all the way around Lytham in anger, saying later to a friend, "Heckling is cheating."

Irwin, Nicklaus, and Crenshaw were the three Americans poised to make life uncomfortable for Ballesteros in the last round. But Hale double-bogeyed the second hole and was on the way to a 78. He just wanted to go home. Nicklaus bogeyed the easy fourth and knew it would be uphill all day to get a 72. Crenshaw was playing superbly and seemed to have the best chance. In fact, Ben was tied with Seve for the lead on the 17th tee.

This brought to mind the words of Crenshaw's fellow countryman, Jerry Pate, of the night before.

Pate had said to Ben, "Gentle, you're my pick tomorrow. I believe you can rope-a-dope that old hook of yours right into victory lane."

It was noted by a listener that Jerry had put three different sports into one sentence, proving he'd gone to the University of Alabama.

Of course, Gentle Ben found a way to make a double bogey at the 17th, and this was while Ballesteros was hitting his second shot out of the car park on 16 and making a birdie, then driving into some unidentifiable flora on 17 and hacking around and eventually saving par with a 12-foot putt. It was over.

Earlier in the week, Ballesteros had said, "We should play British Open without fairways. Then I might win."

After his victory, Seve said, "I don't aim for rough. It just goes there. My caddie tell me close my eyes and hit it. Maybe I go in fairway."

It seems that accuracy used to be a virtue in golf. It still is for Americans, but it wasn't for the Spaniard at Royal Lytham & Car Park.

PART FOUR

The Eighties

●

"I miss . . . I miss . . . I miss . . . I make."

—SEVE BALLESTEROS, EXPLAINING A
FOUR-PUTT GREEN TO THE PRESS

48

THE REIGN OF SPAIN

Seve Ballesteros Wins 1980 Masters

S EVE BALLESTEROS seemed to be playing a different tournament from everyone else in the 1980 Masters, including most of the recognizable American stars, unless of course you happen to be a close follower of those golfing legends Jeff Mitchell, Rex Caldwell, Ed Fiori, and Gibby Gilbert. Those were the people we sent out to chase the Spaniard as he went about winning his second major and suggesting that he may be the next headline player, or perhaps the real Tom Watson. But in the end, after the expectable and predictable traumas on the back nine holes of the Augusta National, all they determined was that Gilbert was low American.

Ballesteros started becoming the youngest winner of the Masters on Thursday when he lit up the place with a six-under 66. That gave him a share of the lead with Australia's David Graham and Jeff Mitchell of the USA. His 69 on Friday moved him four strokes ahead of the field. Among his closest pursuers was Rex Caldwell of the USA. The four-under 68 on Saturday put Seve seven shots clear of the field, and at this point his closest pursuer was Ed Fiori of the USA.

Well, it was easy to understand why Seve's nearest challengers were Mitchell, Caldwell, and Fiori. They were playing in their first Masters, and among them they held two victories on the PGA Tour. And it shouldn't have been surprising that Gilbert would make the boldest run on Sunday. After all, he'd won the Memphis Classic in 1976.

There was an explanation for what happened to all of the American heroes. As a group they thought the rain-drenched course and resultant soft greens and lack of any wind turned the Augusta National into a pushover public course, thereby disarming the best shotmakers and opening the door to the rabble.

Two of America's fondest hopes were Tom Watson and Ben Crenshaw. They came primed and ready and played superbly, but only in spots. Watson soaked his chances at the deadly par-three 12th on Saturday when he "blocked out" a 7-iron, put it in Rae's Creek, and took a triple bogey. Crenshaw shot the last three rounds in nine under, but he made the mistake of opening up with a 76 and could never overcome it.

He blamed it on "nerves." He was too "up" for the year's first major, he explained, having finished second in the last two majors a year ago, the British Open and PGA, which he lost in a playoff to David Graham.

Aside from that, on the surprisingly slow greens Ben Crenshaw, the world's greatest putter, stroked his putts like Bubba Crenshaw, drunkard.

The Masters suffered its biggest yawn in history when Ballesteros went to the last nine with a 10-stroke lead on the field. He did fritter away seven of those strokes down around Amen Corner, but it was hardly enough to cause him serious worry. He still won by four after he pulled himself together, birdied the 15th, and strolled home.

It was such a slow week that Tom Weiskopf provided the most excitement in missing the cut. He did it making a 13 at the 155-yard 12th hole on Thursday and a seven at the same hole on Friday.

Rae's Creek overflowed with Weiskopf's Titleists.

49

RETURN OF THE BIG DOG

Nicklaus Wins 1980 U.S. Open at Baltusrol

THE HUGE old gabled clubhouse rose up out of the New Jersey countryside looking like it belonged on the jacket of a gothic novel, and Jack Nicklaus walked toward it through the great roaring crowds weighted down with so many records he could have used an extra caddie and a couple of bellhops.

It was a wondrous moment in golf. Harry Vardon was inventing the grip again. Arnold Palmer was hitching up his trousers again. Bobby Jones was impregnably quadrilateraling again. Ben Hogan was smoking a cigarette again as he stared at a green. But this was Jack Nicklaus in 1980, age 40, winning his fourth U.S. Open and doing it with such verve that the Baltusrol course lay in utter destruction behind him.

Nicklaus's golf game not only returned to him at Baltusrol after an absence of two years, but the old gestures came back too: Jack joyously raising his putter high in the air as a birdie falls; Jack grinning and waving to the delirious throngs as he marches jubilantly up the last fairway like the king of old.

The big scoreboard on 18 even honored him with a message:

JACK IS BACK.

It was Jack's Open all the way, and there were Nicklaus records set in every round, but he wouldn't have this 18th major—five more than anyone else—until the final hole had been played and he had nursed a two-stroke lead through the oaks, elms, and spruce of Baltusrol and outlasted an uncanny little man named Isao Aoki of Japan. It seemed unbelievable that although Nicklaus's earlier rounds of 63, 71, and 70 had left the record book looking like kitty litter, he was unable to shake Aoki, a guy who putted with the toe of his putter sticking up and the ball back on the heel of the club.

Aoki would have looked like the best clown act in town, except the ball kept going in the hole.

Not until Nicklaus birdied the last two holes for a 68 and shattered yet another record would he dispose of Aoki. Maybe that's what made it so sweet for Jack in the end. That he had to work for it instead of taking a convivial walk to the clubhouse.

Jack's first-round 63, which was matched by Tom Weiskopf, equaled the lowest Open round ever—the 63 that Johnny Miller shot at Oakmont in '73. Jack's halfway score of 134 was the lowest ever, his 54-hole score of 204 was the lowest, and his winning 272 was the lowest 72-hole score ever.

If all this wasn't amazing enough, it should be mentioned that Aoki's runner-up score of 274 also broke the existing record. Aoki may be a familiar golfing figure worldwide, but he was completely unknown around Baltusrol and the rest of the United States.

Baltusrol, only an hour or so from Broadway, is a fine place to hold U.S. Opens, and it has held its share. It can accommodate crowds and parked cars, and the venerable clubhouse has an "Open look," which is what U.S. Open clubhouses are supposed to look like for us historians—like, for instance, survivors of a more opulent age.

But the playing quality of Baltusrol's Lower Course—there's another 18 called Upper, where Tony Manero won in '36—wasn't up to Open standards due to early-in-the-week rains and a surprising leniency on the part of the U.S. Golf Association. The fairways were wider than usual, the rough shorter, and the greens were hardly what one would call fast.

But as they say, everybody played the same golf course. Everybody had the same chance to do what Nicklaus did.

The words of Tom Watson put it in perspective.

He said, "I just shot 276, the fourth-lowest score in the history of the U.S. Open, and lost by four shots."

Of his comeback, Nicklaus said, "All week long, I had sort of been wondering when the wheels were going to come off. That's what had been happening to me for two years. I was still thinking about it when my driver left me for three holes on the front nine today. But I realized I was getting my head forward on my swing and corrected it. The back nine is about as good as I can play, and it made me think that this old body has a few more wins in it."

Nobody doubts this. Least of all, Lee Trevino, a man who has kept Jack from winning at least four other majors. Trevino handled the commentary in the Baltusrol locker room, where a few other players and a writer joined him to watch TV as Nicklaus birdied the last two holes in his march to victory.

"Get away and let the big dog eat!" Trevino shouted.

When the laughter subsided, Lee grinned at the TV screen and said, "In my dreams, you *always* win, Jack."

50.

SEEING DOUBLE

Nicklaus Wins 1980 PGA at Oak Hill

BECAUSE OF that flying right elbow on his backswing and those small hands that force him to use the interlocking grip and the color blindness and all the time he takes standing over his putts, it's perfectly obvious that Jack Nicklaus will never win 30 major championships. All of it has to catch up with him sooner or later. Anybody can see that.

But of course Jack won his 19th major—now six more than Bobby Jones or anybody else—when he turned the 1980 PGA Championship at Oak Hill in Rochester, New York, into a hunting expedition in which you were supposed to find the rest of the field.

Nevertheless, you could plainly see that because of Jack's age, which is 40, his desire and nerves and the mechanics of his game are rapidly deteriorating. He made a bogey on the next-to-last hole and won his fifth PGA by only seven strokes.

Nicklaus became only the third player in history to capture both the U.S. Open and PGA in the same year. First there was Baltusrol in June, you recall, and now there's Oak Hill in August.

Gene Sarazen did the double first in 1922, when he won the Open at Skokie in Chicago and the PGA on Oakmont in Pittsburgh. Then Ben Hogan did it in 1948, when he won the Open at Riviera in Los Angeles and the PGA at Norwood Hills in St. Louis. The only difference is that Sarazen and Hogan won their PGAs at match play.

This PGA wasn't close after the first two rounds, when Nicklaus's 70-69 found him trailing nobodies by three and then by one. He dropped a four-under 66 on the field in the third round, and everybody else was pretty much done for. His last-round 69 was a ceremonial saunter, more or less, with Andy Bean somewhere back there in second place.

Interestingly enough, Jack was about the only player in the field who liked the course, meaning the changes that had been made by designers George Fazio and his nephew Tom. Everyone else needed a rabies shot.

They didn't like four holes being toughened up. And they didn't like the reshaped greens that were designed to keep the shots as far away from the flags as possible. What made their complaining louder was that Oak Hill was originally a Donald Ross design.

Either Ross or Michelangelo—it's hard to keep them straight.

Tom Weiskopf, a legendary complainer anyhow, appointed himself the spokesman for all and said, "I'm going to start an organization called the Classic Golf Course Preservation Society. Members get to carry loaded guns in case they see anybody touching a Donald Ross golf course."

Tom Watson joined in, saying, "I don't think it's asking too much for a green to have a landing area where a good shot can get closer than 30 feet to the flag."

So how was it that Nicklaus virtually took the place apart when nobody else could break 280?

"I played really well," Jack said. "It's a marvelous layout, but you have to stay after it. I stayed ahead of it. You can't judge it by what I did. Just look at what the rest of the field did."

51

A DRIVE DOWN EASY STREET

Larry Nelson Wins 1981 PGA in Atlanta

THIS BEING a year for unexpected people to win majors—I give you David Graham at Merion and Bill Rogers at Sandwich—most of the suspense at the 1981 PGA in Atlanta centered around the possibility of the quiet Larry Nelson, a Vietnam veteran, one of the rank and file on the tour, tipping his cap as he collected the title. Alas, he did. Right there on the 18th green of Atlanta Athletic Club. Larry's emotional display lasted at least a split second after he wrapped up the last of the year's big ones by four strokes over Fuzzy Zoeller. Nelson had driven into nearly all of the fairways for four rounds, staying as far away from trouble as Acworth, Georgia, where he lives. A commuter won this major. In the final analysis, the winner's biggest problem was traffic.

Nelson won with rounds of 70, 66, 66, and 71 for 273 on the same course where Jerry Pate had captured the U.S. Open five years ago. Fuzzy had stayed the nearest to Larry, four back with 18 to play, but he couldn't manage anything better than the same 71 Larry posted on Sunday.

This was despite all the loosening up in the locker room before the final round began.

When Nelson entered the locker room, Fuzzy and Pate were in the middle of a discussion about hairstyling.

Jerry commented on Fuzzy's current look, a combination of shaggy-hippie with Afro-bouffant.

"I've seen almost that much hair on the back of a dog," Pate said.

"Oh, yeah," said Fuzzy. "How about you? Have you ever seen a bald-headed dog?"

Zoeller then noticed Larry Nelson lugging his own golf bag through the room, having driven the hour and a half from Acworth.

"Hey, Nelly," Fuzzy hollered. "If you're gonna tote that thing yourself, I may have a shot at you today."

Nelson only grinned and kept walking.

It was a weird tournament in which most of the marquee names took a hike. Jack Nicklaus did finish in a tie for fourth—a distant fourth. Tom Watson missed his first cut since '79. Three other noteworthy fellows, Arnold Palmer, Gary Player, and British Open champion Bill Rogers, didn't make the cut until Saturday morning, when, in the rain-delayed finish of the second round, Lou Graham triple-bogeyed the last hole and Brad Bryant double-bogeyed it. That let them back in.

Lee Trevino missed the whole tournament after a first-round 74. That happened because he failed to sign his scorecard. There was much confusion in the scoring tent after Trevino, Tom Weiskopf, and Lanny Wadkins completed their round. Cards were passed back and forth. Trevino thought he'd signed the card but didn't, and later in the day he was DQed.

"I don't have anybody to blame but myself," Lee said.

"Yes, you do," Weiskopf said. "You can blame me."

Trevino said, "Aw, hell, Tom, you get blamed for too many things as it is."

After that, it was Larry Nelson's week. As he stood out there Sunday afternoon in the last fairway facing a 3-iron shot over the water with all those Georgians rooting for him, he knew there was only one way he could lose—by hitting a couple of balls in the lake.

"If I'd had a one-shot lead, that's probably what I'd have done," he said. "I'm a choker. But the big lead allowed me to tell myself I was man enough to hit that 3-iron over the water."

The 34-year-old Nelson was man enough, no question. After all, he'd served in Vietnam as an infantryman when he was 21. He'd seen worse things than a golf shot.

52

THE 1,000-TO-1 SHOT

Tom Watson over Nicklaus at 1982 U.S. Open at Pebble Beach

FROM WHERE Tom Watson stood on the 71st hole of the 1982 U.S. Open at Pebble Beach—in the clawing rough, on a downslope, looking at a glassy green—you don't simply chip the ball into the cup for a birdie deuce to beat Jack Nicklaus, who is already in with a good enough score to win. First, you throw up.

Well, that's wrong. By now, if you're Tom Watson, you're accustomed to beating Jack Nicklaus in major championships. You've done it before at the Masters and the British Open. So you lay open the blade of a sand wedge and plop the lob-chip softly onto the putting surface and then watch the flagstick get in the way of the ball to keep it from running all the way to the Pebble Beach Lodge.

Watson said, "I told Bruce [Edwards, his caddie] I wasn't going to get it close, like he said. I was going to chip it in. I've practiced that shot for hours, days, months, years. It's a shot you need if you're going to do well in the Open, where there's high grass around the greens."

It still qualified as a miracle.

Bill Rogers, who was paired with Watson, said, "You could hit that chip a hundred times and you couldn't get it close to the pin, much less in the hole."

"A thousand times," Nicklaus said later.

This was after Jack said something else. Something that might rank as the Golf Quote of the Year.

Nicklaus had watched Watson play the 17th on a TV monitor behind the 18th green. Jack had shot a 69 and put up a 284 that normally would have been good enough to win. It was even six strokes better than the 290 he shot when he won the first U.S. Open at Pebble Beach in 1972.

When he watched Watson's 3-iron shot to the 17th find the rough and snuggle up in it, he thought: *Bogey, I win.*

Didn't happen that way, and Watson went ahead and made another birdie at the 72nd, a needless birdie, really, to win by two strokes.

That's when Jack smiled as he shook Tom's hand and said:

"You little son of a bitch, you're something else."

So ended one of the more fantastic majors. In reality, it was another Watson-Nicklaus saga. *Watson-Nicklaus III*—check your local neighborhood theater. The first one came at Augusta in 1977 when Tom outbattled Jack in the stretch to win his first Masters. *Watson-Nicklaus II* came later that summer at Turnberry, when in the last two rounds he hung a 65-65 on Jack's 65-66 in a historic British Open.

Watson's chip goes in the memory book with a couple of others in terms of historic stunners. There was Arnold Palmer's chip in the '62 Masters from beside the 16th green for the deuce that enabled him to tie Gary Player and Dow Finsterwald and squeeze into the playoff that he won. And there was Lee Trevino's at the 71st hole of the '72 British Open at Muirfield that ended Nicklaus's gutsy try for a Grand Slam.

"Yes, it's happened to me before," Nicklaus said in a postgame moment. "But I didn't think it would happen again. I suppose I've done it to other people, too, but I don't recall doing it by chipping in. It's especially tough to take when you think you've won. This might be the best golf, tee to green, I've ever played in the U.S. Open."

A case could be made that Watson won this Open with miracles of one kind or another every day.

In Thursday's opening round, he arrived at the 15th tee three over par, staring at a 75 or worse. But he birdied three holes in a row and got to the house with an even-par 72.

He may have won the championship on Friday, when he scattered his tee shots all over 17-Mile Drive but holed two putts of more than 20 feet for bogeys. *Bogeys.* He also got up and down out of a difficult bunker for another bogey, and it all added up to another 72.

He may have won it on Saturday, a calm day when 22 players broke par, and when he carved out a 68 to keep pace with Bill Rogers and stay three ahead of Nicklaus.

Then he did win it on Sunday with two other knockout blows besides the chip-in for his 70 and 282. Tom dropped a 25-foot putt to save par at the 10th hole, and a 35-foot putt for a birdie at the 14th.

Rogers, the '81 British Open champion, said of Watson's birdie at the 14th, "Most humans three-putt from where he was."

Thinking back on it, nobody could have summed up this Open finish better than Frank (Sandy) Tatum, ex-president of the USGA. The evening before *Watson-Nicklaus III* began, Tatum studied the scoreboard and said, "Look at that board. Tomorrow . . . wow."

Wow it was.

53.

BREAKTHROUGH FOR THE HEARTBREAK KID

Ben Crenshaw Wins 1984 Masters

ALL THE years, all the torment, and all the disappointments faded into the blossoms at the 1984 Masters as Ben Crenshaw, the most popular golfer since Arnold Palmer, finally won a major championship. It will be remembered that Crenshaw won it over a scoreboard full of deadly assassins and won it on the back nine of the Augusta National, where so many souls have been lost or misplaced, and that he won it when it was only his to lose. As the 32-year-old Texan walked up the last fairway on Sunday, you could have watered all the botanical wonders on the course with the tears of joy that were creeping down the cheeks of the thousands whose hopes he had crushed so often. In a way, this one was for them.

Here was pro golf's onetime glamour boy finally living up to the reputation he had been dragging through the bunkers and trees for more than a decade, firing a last-round 68 and erasing the sorrow in a dashing two hours with a combination of splendid golf shots and his reliable putter, "Little Ben," the nickname his father had given the club many years before.

We all remember the early Crenshaw. He was "the cute Jack Nicklaus." Just what the sport needed. He seemed to have been born on a magazine cover. He had ravaged amateur golf, and he owned college golf by winning three NCAA titles while playing for the University of Texas, and "Ben's Wrens" had become a popular souvenir button worn by the shapely adorables who followed golf.

There was one problem. Crenshaw's long, loose swing. It was unpredictable, and on the PGA Tour the competition was a little tougher than the amateur circuit. The swing became less and less trustworthy, but Ben could always count on his putting stroke. For example, Tom Kite, his old Austin High School adversary and college teammate, once said, "I don't remember Ben ever missing a putt from the time he was 12 until he was 20."

Crenshaw had been in serious contention for a major many times—at the Masters, U.S. Opens, British Opens, PGAs—but each time unforeseen calamities struck. Five times he had been a runner-up in majors, as recent as last year's Masters, when Seve Ballesteros outdistanced him.

"I've been trying to believe in myself for a year and a half," Ben said after slipping into the green jacket. "I went back to my old swing and concentrated on aiming the ball, and my timing. I spent 10 years working on my swing, and it didn't get me anything but a lot of disappointment. My dad was the one who said I had to go back to my old swing and live with it. There are a lot of funny swings in golf. Who wants to swing like Miller Barber? Nobody. But I've seen him hit as many solid shots as anyone."

On the back nine holes on Masters Sunday there was always the possibility that Crenshaw and his swarms of admirers, including many of us in the press shack, would suffer another heartbreak.

But on the long, picturesque 10th hole, something occurred that gave a hint that this might be Crenshaw's week at last. There, he rapped in his only monster putt of the tournament, a 60-footer for birdie.

Then, two holes later, at the dangerous 12th, he put a 6-iron 12 feet from the pin and rolled that birdie in.

These two putts must have sent shock waves through his challengers, because in what seemed like a jiffy both Tom Kite and Larry Nelson splashed irons into Rae's Creek at the same hole, resulting in a triple bogey for Kite and a double bogey for Nelson.

Of "Little Ben," Crenshaw's putter, a rear-shaft relic that looks like an old Armour, the human Ben would later say, "I've only been without it a few times since I was 15—usually when it ran up a tree."

He said in victory, "I love golf and golf history, and I've dreamed of winning a major. There's no question I've put too much pressure on myself. I'm fortunate to have so many friends, and if there was one thing going through my mind out there on the last nine, it was how I didn't want to let everybody down again."

This time Crenshaw didn't. His victory was by two strokes over Tom Watson, and now the dogwoods and azaleas will be partly his forever. Mainly because he stayed out of them for a change.

54

MAN UNFAZED BY SHARK ATTACK

Fuzzy Zoeller Beats Norman at 1984 U.S. Open at Winged Foot

MAYBE EVERYBODY should play golf the way Fuzzy Zoeller does. Hit it, go find it, hit it again. Grin. Have a smoke. Take a sip. Make a joke. Every so often, win a major championship. That's how Fuzzy went about things in the 1984 U.S. Open on the testing layout of Winged Foot's West Course up in the Manhattan suburb of Mamaroneck, New York, which is not all that far from Three-Acre Zoning, Connecticut.

Most often, Zoeller laughed his way out of trouble, and when he wasn't doing that, he putted his way out. "It's only my career, folks," Fuzzy would say to the gallery on finding himself in the trees or the rough or a bunker or on the opposite side of a green from the cup.

The truth is, it was Hale Irwin's championship for three rounds. He had shot 68, 68, 69, butchering the course he had won the Open on in 1974. But Hale did a curious thing on Sunday. He shot a dreadful 79, thoroughly unexplainable, other than the fact that his putter decided to revolt and turn Hale into a basket case.

It was fortunate for Zoeller and Greg Norman, the Great White

Shark, that they stayed close to Irwin through those three rounds, for they were on hand to inherit the battle when Hale disappeared.

Fuzzy shot a shaky 70 and Greg an iffy 69 to wind up in a tie at 276 over a Winged Foot course that was set up much easier than it was back in '74 when Irwin's strenuous 287 took the championship.

A certain amount of comedy was involved in the conclusion of regulation play. After Fuzzy squandered a three-stroke lead over the first six holes of the last nine, he was forced to watch Norman up ahead of him par the last three long, tough par-four holes by way of Australia.

At the 16th, Greg hit a looping hook with a 4-iron that put him in deep, ragged rough next to a bunker by the green. You don't get up and down in two from there. You make a double bogey. But Norman made a four when he sank a seven-foot putt after digging himself out of the rough.

On the 17th, Norman practically shanked his drive. The ball came to rest almost against a tree. It was between roots and buried in high grass. All he could do was pitch out into the fairway. He was still 165 yards from the green, but he hit a 6-iron to 10 feet of the cup and sank that one for his four.

Greg's drive did find the fairway on 18, but there he hit a half-shank with the same 6-iron into the big grandstand—yes, the grandstand—to the right of the green. "I actually envisioned the shot going about four feet from the flag, but when I started the club back, my adrenaline rushed," Norman explained.

Oh, okay. Makes sense to us medical students.

Greg got a free drop from the grandstand, but his pitch scooted across the green and into the fringe, a hopeless 40 feet from the cup, and downhill. So he made that one, too, incredibly.

Back down the fairway, Zoeller was watching, and when the ball went in, he waved a white towel—a white flag. He was surrendering. It was thought at first that Fuzzy assumed Greg had made a birdie, but he knew it was a par, and he steadily made his own par to tie with a good drive, a good approach, and two putts from 20 feet.

It was the first U.S. Open playoff in nine years, but it didn't last long. It was actually over at the second hole. That's where Fuzzy holed a rambling 68-foot birdie putt while the Shark was three-putting for a bogey from just 25 feet. Zoeller was on his way to a 67, and Norman to his 75.

The tour can use more characters like Fuzzy, the '79 Masters winner who is now the '84 United States Open champion—a guy with two majors. As a personality, he has taken the torch from Lee Trevino, who took it from Jimmy Demaret, who took it from Walter Hagen. Men of levity.

What other player today would pause in the early going of a U.S. Open playoff to walk across a green to playfully shake hands with a sportswriter—yours truly—and kiss a lady fan in the gallery, and try to have a chat with a drunk?

Only Frank Urban Zoeller.

55

GOTT IN HIMMEL!

Bernhard Langer Wins 1985 Masters

H OW MANY times do you have to be reminded that the Masters doesn't start until the back nine Sunday? Arnie's charge was born back there. Sarazen double-eagled back there. Byron caught Guldahl back there. Nicklaus beat Miller and Weiskopf back there. Roberto failed arithmetic back there. And this time, in the spring of 1985, Curtis Strange went back there with a four-stroke lead and before he could get back up the hill to the umbrellas on the Augusta National veranda he was nursing a two-stroke loss to—*Gott in Himmel!*—Bernhard Langer, the son of a Bavarian laborer.

Here was a guy, Langer, who had only won tournaments in places like Germany, France, Italy, Holland, Spain, and Japan. In other words, countries where wars are older and more popular than golf.

Essentially, what Strange did was lose the Masters by going for the par-five 13th and 15th holes on his second shots, once with a 4-wood and once with a 4-iron, and hit them both in the water.

Up ahead, Langer, with nothing to lose, had birdied both holes, not to mention the 12th, and with the boost from Curtis's blunders, he went ahead to win with a closing 68. The fact that this was a major is what probably did it to Strange, who had yet to win one. Make it San Diego, Curtis wins by six.

It might be said in defense of Curtis that he went for both par fives because he was playing superbly. No doubt he felt he could do no wrong, but evidently he'd never read where Ben Hogan said, "You never go for 13 and 15 when you're in the lead."

It's possible that laying up would have been a greater risk for Strange, but in any case he guessed wrong.

It took those two mistakes to allow a fellow who had never won on American soil, who putts cross-handed, for God's sake, to walk away with a championship as immense as the Masters.

Please note that Langer is the first player to win a major putting cross-handed since Orville Moody at Houston's Champions in the 1969 U.S. Open. They are the only two in history, unless there's something we've never been told about one of those Willie Parks or Fred Herds.

This Masters result was okay in a way, if you stop to think about it. The Germans have suffered from really bad press for the past—what—75 years or so?

Let's give them this one.

56

NORTH BY TAIWAN

Chen Folds to Andy North in 1985 U.S. Open at Oakland Hills

THE EVENTS at Oakland Hills Country Club in a genteel suburb of Detroit brought to mind a mystery novel: *The Man Who Can Only Win Opens*, by Elmore Dashiell Chandler Andrew North.

True enough, but the 1985 U.S. Open continually belonged to a little man named Tze-Chung Chen the whole week, and the only reason the championship isn't his today is that he played a single hole in the last round as if he were made in Taiwan, which he was. Does anything made in Taiwan last more than three days?

Sam Snead once lost an Open by making an eight on the last hole. That was at Spring Mill in Philadelphia back in '39. Snead's eight lives on. So will Mr. T. C. Chen's at the fifth hole at Oakland Hills in the last round, and if anything, Chen's was more bizarre.

Mr. Chen carried three wedges in his bag at Oakland Hills: one for sand, one for pitch shots, and now we know what the third one was for—hitting a golf ball twice in one swing.

Confucius say, "Bad head give Andy North Open."

Or maybe it was Mr. Chen who said it.

Through his first three rounds of 65, 69, 69, and through Sunday's first four holes, Mr. Chen was four strokes ahead of the field. He was indeed a unique story. It looked absolutely certain that he would become the first Asian to win a major. For one thing, all of the game's biggest names had either missed the cut and left town or were woefully out of contention.

Twice before, there were Asian gentlemen who made good runs at a major. Mr. Lu Liang-Huan came close at Royal Birkdale in the '71 British Open, and Mr. Isao Aoki had come close at Baltusrol in the '80 U.S. Open. Mr. Lu and Mr. Aoki had failed because of the heroics of a Lee Trevino (Birkdale) and a Jack Nicklaus (Baltusrol).

But this time Mr. Chen failed because of a calamitous quadruple-bogey eight he suddenly suffered at the 450-yard, par-four fifth hole, and just when he was threatening to turn Oakland Hills into so much Moo Goo Gai Pan. It was painful to watch. Mr. Tze-Chung Chen had won the hearts of the press and fans and been responsible for the entire week's wit and wisdom.

He was the Orient Express. He had taken this Open to the cleaners. He was the Bridges of Toko Chen. He was Fu's Rush In. Until finally he became No Tickee, No Trophy.

There was a moment after Saturday's third round, and after being hounded by the press again, when he said, "I no practice now. Press make too tired for golf."

Possibly it's easier to make an eight if you wear a cap that says "Three Bond," advertising an automotive glue. In any case, here's how Mr. Chen went about doing it:

To start with, after a drive in the fairway you aim your 4-iron second shot at the flag but come off of it and find the rough, almost stymied behind some trees. You gouge the ball out but leave it short of the green and stuck in the gnarly rough again. Now comes the soy sauce.

You hit down with the wedge, barely getting the ball in the air, and on your follow-through you hit the ball again, knocking it a few feet dead left of yourself. Most red-blooded American men in that moment would have slammed that wedge against a tree trunk. Mr. Chen, however, didn't look all that outwardly perturbed, being inscrutable. He just hit another poor chip and took two putts, and this added up to a big fat eight.

In one hole, remarkably, he had lost his four-stroke lead. Now in a funk, he quite naturally added three more bogeys to the tragedy and wound up with a horrible 77, leaving the Open for others to settle.

Mr. Chen's collapse catapulted him into a three-way tie for second after a Sunday exhibition of the worst golf ever displayed by athletes in serious contention for a big title. He goes into the runner-up list with Denis Watson, whoever that is, and David Barr, whoever that is.

Watson, who hails from Zimbabwe or Rhodesia, depending on the age of your map, could blame his loss on a two-stroke penalty he endured in the first round for "delay of play"—he waited 35 seconds for a ball to drop when it was hanging on the lip of a cup.

To put himself at ease, Barr, who hails from British Columbia, had kept saying the U.S. Open was "just another golf tournament." Guess not. Once tied for the lead, he found a way to bogey the last two holes.

It should be noted that Andy North, who had won his first Open at Cherry Hills in 1978, did hit one good shot down the stretch. Coming out of his eighth bunker of the day at the 17th hole on the way to a 74, he nearly holed the shot to rescue a par three.

The fumbling and stumbling of others allowed North the luxury of being able to finish with a bogey on the last hole to win. Quick. Name a player who won two U.S. Opens by bogeying the last hole. Answer: Andy North.

It says a lot about him that he kept himself in contention during Saturday's miserable afternoon, when it was cold and rainy. He did it by holing every six-foot putt he looked at, turning an 80 into a 70. Soaking wet throughout the round, and hatless in the rain, he looked like a man whose mobile home had been blown away by a tornado. But he stayed close enough to Mr. Chen that he was there to take the title when nobody else seemed to want it.

A note concerning geography. The Oakland Hills Country Club in Birmingham, Michigan, is only a par five away from the Red Fox restaurant, the last place Jimmy Hoffa was seen. Now there are a lot more suspects who could have done it. The gang that kidnapped the '85 Open.

57

TURNING BACK THE CLOCK

Nicklaus Wins 20th Major at 1986 Masters

F YOU want to get golf on the front pages again and you don't have a Francis Ouimet, a Bobby Jones, or a Ben Hogan handy, you send an aging Jack Nicklaus out in the last round of the 1986 Masters and tell him to kill more foreigners than a general named Eisenhower.

That'll do it.

On the final afternoon of this Masters, the 46-year-old Nicklaus's deeds were so unexpectedly colossal, dramatic, and historic, the taking of his sixth green jacket must certainly rank with the biggest golf stories ever. Up there with Ouimet beating Harry Vardon and Ted Ray in 1913. Up there with Jones completing the Grand Slam in 1930. Up there with Hogan winning the Triple Crown in 1953.

What could be said? That this was a story for the ages? That it may have been Jack's finest hour, this 20th major? As much was said back in 1980 when he surprisingly won both the U.S. Open and the PGA. But here he was again, six years later, hopelessly trailing an imposing group of foreigners by six strokes. There were Spain's Seve Ballesteros, Australia's Greg Norman, Germany's Bernhard Langer, South Africa's Nick

Price, and Scotland's Sandy Lyle, and Jack was so far behind, it looked as if he would need a visa to get on the scoreboard and would have to beat the League of Nations to win.

But he suddenly caught fire, shot a seven-under 65—despite two bogeys—and knocked all of the invaders into a killer funk and took that lovely stroll up the pine-shadowed corridor of the Augusta National's last fairway amid the greatest, weepingest, most joyous roars he or any of us would ever hear.

In the case of Nicklaus, it wasn't so much that he did it but *how* he did it. Six off the pace of Ballesteros, with Greg Norman and Tom Kite moving into contention, Jack did this:

He birdied the ninth, 10th, and 11th, momentarily bungled the 12th with a bogey, but birdied the 13th, parred the 14th, eagled the 15th— yeah, eagled it—birdied the 16th, birdied the 17th, and parred the 18th.

That was a mere 30 on the back nine.

The biggest lick of all might have been the 5-iron with which Nicklaus nearly made a hole in one at the par-three 16th. Frankly, it scored a TKO over Ballesteros.

There stood Seve in the 15th fairway with a one-shot lead on the field. Here was a man who had already made two eagles in the round, at the eighth with a 50-foot chip and at the 13th with a six-foot putt. He had looked indestructible. But the roar greeting Jack's shot at 16 must have got to the Spaniard. Seve jerked the worst-looking 4-iron imaginable at the 15th and put the ball into the front pond with a one-handed finish. He suffered the disastrous bogey that destroyed his confidence beyond repair. Make no mistake. Jack Nicklaus knocked that club out of Seve's hand.

Nicklaus had never won a major watching TV—until this one. In the Jones cottage near the clubhouse, Jack watched the failures of Norman and Kite, the last two players who could beat him. Kite played well, but his 68 and 280 turned out to be one shot too many.

Greg did it a little differently. He stood in the 18th fairway with a 4-iron in his hands needing a par to get into a playoff with Jack. Whereupon he hit a half-shank, push-fade, semi-slice that guaranteed Jack's win.

Later, Nicklaus sat in front of 300 writers and tried to talk about what this meant to him, the roars he'd heard.

"There were only three other times," he said. "The 1972 British Open at Muirfield when I caught Trevino and Jacklin in the last round, even though I wound up losing. The 1978 British Open at St. Andrews when I came from behind to win, and the 1980 U.S. Open at Baltusrol. Those are the other three times I had tears in my eyes."

He said, "I'm certainly not as good as I was 10 or 15 years ago. I don't play as much competitive golf, but there are still some weeks when I'm pretty good."

There were 21 players only five strokes apart when Sunday's final round began. The situation was ripe for someone to go out early and maybe steal the thing. But you had to say that Jack Nicklaus, a 46-year-old golf course designer, was the last one you thought about.

58

TEMPO RAYMONDO

Ray Floyd Wins 1986 U.S. Open at Shinnecock Hills

THE 1986 United States Open came down to a couple of guys who can "make their irons talk," as the pros say, and nothing was more appropriate on a treasured relic of a course like Shinnecock Hills than to have a shotmaker, Raymond Floyd—old Tempo Raymondo— beat another shotmaker, Lanny Wadkins, to win our national championship.

Yeah, there was another runner-up in there. Chip Beck, was it? Beck as in Fleck? Never mind. He spoils the theme. In the end, it was all about Raymond and Lanny, who preserve the sanity of golf by doing things other than driving the ball three million yards, hitting a wedge two million yards, and going on to the next stop on the PGA Tour.

It was earlier in the week that Lanny said to a listener of journalistic bent, "This course ought to reward golf shots . . . and guys like myself and Raymond are among the few people out here who can make our 4-irons talk."

The reference was to a growing list of pros who only know how to hit no-fault irons and a hot ball into watered-down greens.

Everybody was excited about the U.S. Open coming to Shinnecock Hills out in Southampton, Long Island. It hadn't been there in 90 years, or since July 18, 1896, the second Open played, when a man named James Foulis won with scores of 78-74, all in one day.

Only the clubhouse—oldest in America—remained the same, sitting there on a hilltop overlooking the pinched fairways, the old-fashioned greens, the scrub, the windmill from the National Golf Links off in the distance, and the stately crane of ABC-TV.

This was not the course Willie Dunn designed in 1891. It was the Shinnecock Hills redesigned by Bill Flynn in 1931. The pros on hand may have paid the renowned Flynn his finest compliment. More than one of them said it was great to play a golf course without railroad ties or an island green.

The thing that Shinnecock Hills and this Open might best be remembered for is mathematics. At one point during Sunday's last two hours, 10 players either held or shared the lead. Just as dizzy, nine of them were tied for the lead *together* while half of them were finishing the front nine and the other half were going onto the back side.

For posterity, the 10 players were Floyd, Wadkins, Beck, Greg Norman—the 36-hole and 54-hole leader—Ben Crenshaw, Lee Trevino, Hal Sutton, Payne Stewart, Bob Tway, and Mark McCumber.

Granted, it might have been more fun if Jack Nicklaus had been among them, but he had lost this Open back on rainy, chilly, muddy Thursday when he made three back-nine double bogeys and shot a 77, something his last two rounds of 67 and 68 couldn't overcome.

It was the same for Crenshaw. With his three straight 69s, he couldn't overcome his triple bogey on Thursday that led him to a 76. But he did have the most amusing explanation for his triple bogey.

"I drove it in the fairway," he said.

Raymond Floyd, who is known as Tempo Raymondo to many of his contemporaries, basically won the championship on the back nine with his iron play after Lanny's 65 for 281 gave him the number he had to beat.

"There's no question Lanny showed me what I had to do," Floyd confirmed later.

Raymond started shooting his final-round 66 for his two-stroke victory with a 7-iron to the 11th, 6-iron to the 13th, and 8-iron to the 16th, three shots that covered the flags.

After Raymond was cruising along with the lead over Wadkins and Beck, who were now finished, it looked like the last guy who might have a chance was Payne Stewart.

But Payne, who was paired with Floyd, was wearing knickers and a pair of snakeskin shoes that could have come out of Liberace's closet.

So if an old campaigner like Floyd, the winner of three previous majors—two PGAs and a Masters—a guy who incidentally knows how to play for his own money, couldn't handle a guy in knickers and those shoes, he wasn't Tempo Raymondo.

59

MATILDA WALTZES

Greg Norman Wins 1986 British Open at Turnberry

HAPPINESS IN golf is knowing that to win your first major championship, you only have to go out in the last round and beat a midget from Wales, an Oriental in thick eyeglasses, and an obscure man from Yorkshire who used to play cornet in the band of a sauce and pickle factory.

Such was the bliss that fell upon Greg Norman in the 1986 British Open on the cold, murky Ayrshire coast of Scotland. Sometimes it happens like this when you grab your first major. They give it to you. The larger names got lost at sea, or somewhere in the gloom, and Greg waltzed with Matilda to the title, only casually glancing over his shoulder to see what had happened lately to Ian Woosnam, Tommy Nakajima, or Gordon J. Brand, the ex–music maker.

Greg is a player who had been coming close to majors, but three times his suitcase had flown open on Sundays, twice in the U.S. Open and once in the Masters. He can let it soar in a peculiar direction now and then. Greg's feet seem to move on most swings with any club in his hands. He addresses his putts on the toe of the clubhead. He sprays his irons both right and left when he goes bad. He often makes you wonder about his judgment.

Despite those things, his power can be awesome and his touch at times is enviable. At Turnberry he managed to keep all of it together for a spell, and there were moments when it looked like everybody else in the game could forget golf and go play polo with Prince Charles.

It didn't hurt that those strange challengers never put any heat on the transplanted Australian, who breezed home in the final round with a 69 and a five-stroke victory at 280.

The little Welshman, Woosie, 5-foot-4, battled gamely but managed only a 72. Brand, the Yorkshireman with a two-minute pause at the top of his backswing, held on better than most thought but made up no ground with his 71. And Nakajima, who trailed Norman by a stroke through 54 holes, threw away his chances on the very first hole when he three-putted from five feet. It sent him on his way to a 77, and he could be seen nervously scanning the galleries for a death squad of Ninjas.

Under the conditions, nobody else had a chance, certainly nobody from the USA. It was like this: The weather turned every established competitor into a raving, debilitated loon. The wind howled, the rain came down horizontally, and the chill climbed up a man's rain pants. It looked like all any Yank wanted to do was get his butt back to America.

The conditions made it tougher to find a guy from the USA on the scoreboard than a Scot who doesn't like bagpipes. Gary Koch wound up low American in a tie for sixth place.

Congrats to Greg and all that, but Turnberry wasn't really a true test. Only the weather kept it from getting beat up again, as it had in 1977 when Tom Watson and Jack Nicklaus destroyed it.

Consider Norman's record 63 in the second round, when the weather was somewhat polite. It was a 63 with *three* bogeys, including *two* three-putt greens. On a major championship course? In decent weather? Hey, come on. Give Turnberry back to the Coastal Command of World War II, which means digging up the fairways, er, runways. Hell, Greg Norman could have shot a 60. He *should* have shot a 61!

Turnberry *is* scenic, and closer to the tides than any of the other British Open courses. But take away the views of the sea and the lighthouse and Ailsa Craig sitting out there in the distance and nobody would even think of holding a major on the property.

60

OLYMPIC STRIKES AGAIN

Simpson over Watson at 1987 U.S. Open at Olympic

O F ALL the traditions in golf, the one at the Olympic Club in San Francisco is the most annoying. Hold a U.S. Open at Olympic and the wrong guy will win it every time. Olympic is now three for three. Fleck over Hogan. Casper over Palmer. Simpson over Watson. Evidently God likes to punish the press.

Which Simpson is it, you ask? Scott Simpson, that's who. The guy who took Nob Hill, as in the 1987 U.S. Open, and turned it into an urban-renewal project. But why should we be surprised? In 1955, Olympic let Ben Hogan win the Open but gave it to Jack Fleck. In 1966, Olympic let Arnold Palmer win the Open but gave it to Billy Casper. It figured that Tom Watson would win this Open but have Olympic take it away and give it to a journeyman named Scott Simpson.

All week long at Olympic, the big names flickered and sparkled and kept the city and the pressroom buzzing with excitement. This was a major championship that would surely be won by a Tom Watson or a Ben Crenshaw or a Seve Ballesteros. Some guy you'd want to be seen at dinner with. But no. This is what Olympic does.

The big question is why? The answer may lie somewhere in the sameness of the holes. No place on Olympic requires a gamble. Good drives and bad drives can each wind up in the rough. The greens disarm the best putters. A lot of holes seem to be the same par four. There's no Amen Corner, no stretch of dramatic holes. There's only one fairway bunker, and the nearest water hazard is a helicopter ride to the Pacific Ocean. It's a dark course, a stroll through tunnels of trees, a course that rewards patience over risk-taking and shotmaking.

Deep down some of us knew to expect Simpson. He was the most serious lurker all week. Two strokes back at 36, one stroke back at 54. In the middle of that five-way tie on the back nine Sunday.

Which was why all afternoon the writers kept nudging one another and saying, "It's spelled S-c-o-t-t . . . S-i-m-p-s-o-n."

Then Simpson went ahead and rewarded them by closing with a two-under 68 and a 277 total to edge Watson by a stroke.

Simpson's victory more closely resembled Fleck's of 30 years earlier in that he birdied the 14th, 15th, and 16th holes on Sunday just as Fleck had tied Hogan by making birdies on the 15th and 18th. Watson, like Hogan, frittered away nothing. Tom played three under par over the last 11 holes. Good enough to win, normally.

With five holes to go, Simpson was trailing Watson by a shot. But here's how he caught and passed a Tom Watson who had been either first (eight times) or second (seven times) in major championships over the past 12 years.

Simpson hit a nice drive on 14 and stuck a 7-iron in there about eight feet from the cup and rapped in a birdie. At 15 he put a wedge shot 149 yards to 20 feet at this short par-three, and made it for a birdie. At the long 16th, at 609 yards one of the least-birdied par fives on the face of the earth, he drove in the rough but found a good lie in the grass, and quickly pipelined a 2-iron up the fairway, placed a 9-iron 15 feet away, and made that one for birdie.

Watson, playing behind Simpson, watched all of this. But the most depressing thing he saw Simpson do was save a par at the rugged par-four 17th. Scott put his second shot in a bunker at least 70 yards from the flag. Most pros agree that the long bunker shot is the toughest in golf. Certain bogey? Nope. Simpson hit a beautiful bunker shot and sank his putt for the par.

When you totaled it up, Simpson one-putted four of the last five greens of the Open, and none of them were gimmes. When a man does this, it makes it kind of tough to be caught—even by a Tom Watson.

With the trophy in his arms, the winner may have offered the world the best explanation for his victory.

Scott Simpson said, "Jack Nicklaus predicted a plodder would win this Open. He was right."

61

STRANGE INTERLUDE

Curtis over Faldo at 1988 U.S. Open at The Country Club

T HOSE WHO think an 18-hole playoff to decide the U.S. Open is anticlimactic have fallen prey to television. But what else is new? For too many people these days, TV is the only reality. Fortunately, the USGA has another view. It believes that its trophy is steeped in so much prestige, it would be a shame to have it settled at one hole of sudden death, purely for the sake of a network. May it ever be so.

Moreover, anyone who disagrees with this doesn't have much knowledge of U.S. Open history. Playoffs for the Open title may not always be thrilling, but they're at least historic. Some of them in the old days went 36 holes, and one even lasted 72 holes.

A good example was the battle in which Curtis Strange defeated Nick Faldo for the 1988 title at The Country Club in Brookline, Massachusetts, which is part of Boston for most people's money. Curtis finally bruised his way into golf's elite by winning a major when he shot a 71 to Faldo's 75, but it wasn't easy. It wasn't a browse through a boutique.

"Damn, it was hard out there," Curtis said.

Strange and Faldo had tied at 278 when Curtis made a clutch up-and-down for par out of a bunker on the 72nd hole.

"This is for my dad," Curtis said in a tearful victory statement. "He died when I was 14, but from the age of nine everything he taught me about the golf swing is still with me."

A key hole in the playoff was The Country Club's 13th, the Primrose, a tight, 433-yard par four. When they got there, Strange was holding a threadbare one-stroke lead. But Nick three-putted for a bogey and Curtis ran home a 25-footer for birdie, and for all practical purposes the championship was his. He was three ahead with five to go, and he didn't squander it.

Some facts: It was the 28th playoff in Open history, seven of which have occurred around Boston—three of them at Brookline. Others have taken place at Worcester, Brae Burn, and Myopia Hunt.

Faldo should feel no shame in joining a list of Open playoff losers that includes Arnold Palmer (three times), Bobby Jones (twice), Ben Hogan, Byron Nelson, Sam Snead, Gene Sarazen, and Jack Nicklaus.

Opens are always more romantic when the club and the course have an "Open look." The Country Club still has it. The old yellow-framed clubhouse, looking like the color of Harry Vardon's breath, and the knobby, rocky, tree-infested, curving layout with its USGA touches of Open shag contributed to the atmosphere all week.

History hung heavily over the place. People wondering what it must have been like 75 years ago when Francis Ouimet did that thing to Vardon and Ted Ray, and wondering what it must have been like 25 years ago when Julius Boros did that thing to Arnold Palmer and Jacky Cupit.

After presenting two world-class, well-dressed players in a playoff, history will be kind to Brookline again, even though Peter Jacobsen said, "The Country Club? Couldn't anybody think of a name for this place?"

62

KING CURTIS

Strange Again at 1989 U.S. Open at Oak Hill

LL U.S. Opens are a little goofy in a way, some more so than others, but the 1989 edition at Oak Hill Country Club in soggy old Rochester, New York, would surely be remembered as a Strange one, and not just because Curtis won it. Don't you hate that kind of humor?

Among other things, it was a championship in which holes in one for a while were cheaper than junk food, a championship in which casual water at times was deeper than Lake Ontario, and a championship in which Tom Kite demonstrated the proper way to take the wheels off of a car and drive it into a ditch.

Finally, it was a championship that ushered Curtis Strange into the select company of Willie Anderson, John J. McDermott, Bobby Jones, Ralph Guldahl, and Ben Hogan. They now happen to be the only six men in history who have won U.S. Opens back-to-back.

"It's not who's done it," Curtis said after doing it. "It's who hasn't." He had won last year at The Country Club in Brookline in a playoff with Nick Faldo, 71 to 75.

The last time back-to-backs happened was Hogan in 1950 at Merion and 1951 at Oakland Hills. Before that it was Guldahl in 1937 at Oakland Hills and 1938 at Cherry Hills. Before that it was Jones at Winged Foot in 1929 and Interlachen in 1930. Before that it was McDermott at Chicago Golf in 1911 and the Country Club of Buffalo in 1912. And before that it was Willie Anderson at Baltusrol in 1903, Glen View in 1904, and Myopia Hunt Club in 1905.

Anderson remains the only guy to win three in a row, unless you count Hogan in '48-'50-'51—as Hogan fans do. Ben might well have won four in a row if he hadn't been forced to miss '49 because of a prior engagement with a Greyhound bus.

Curtis closed with an even-par 70 at Oak Hill for a winning total of 278. He even enjoyed the luxury of a three-putt bogey on the final green, but make no mistake about the fact that he earned this championship. He was a bulldog coming down the stretch.

It was a day Curtis had been preparing for all season. He said, "I've played a lot of rounds on the weekend this year when I was out of it, but I kept grinding just to make my game better and not get in the habit of giving up. Those rounds won this for me. I didn't let myself give up."

It should be said that his record-tying 64 in Friday's second round helped him not give up. This gave him the cushion to go all the way to the 16th hole on Sunday before making another birdie. There, he dropped a 15-foot putt after a day's string of pars during which he hit 15 greens.

"He is one tough bastard" was Peter Jacobsen's description of Curtis.

There is always at least one big loser in Opens. This time it was Tom Kite, the 54-hole leader, a player who tends to live on leaderboards, bank money, but has yet to win a major.

Kite had shot 67, 69, 69 through three rounds and was one under through the first four holes on Sunday—to say nothing of leading the Open by three strokes. Kite was trying out a cross-handed putting grip and telling himself that it might work for him as it had for Bernhard

Langer at Augusta four years ago, and for Orville Moody at Champions in 1969. Why not him?

But as soon as you started thinking that Tom's time had come, he took a triple bogey at the fifth hole, a double bogey at the 13th, and another double bogey at the 15th.

"What can I say?" Kite said, forcing a weak smile. "My golf stunk. Every time I missed a shot, I got killed."

Not really. What made his nosedive into a 78 astounding is that he received the biggest break of the week on the first hole of the last round. He had hooked his tee shot into the rough, then poked at his second shot and put it deeper into the rough. But enter the casual water rule.

The relief he received from Bill Battle, current president of the USGA, allowed Kite to drop the ball in the fairway, from where he pitched up and sank a 15-foot putt to save par.

If Kite had played on to win the Open, he would have won it with that free drop, and it would have been recalled that Battle, as captain of a ship during World War II, was the man who rescued future President John F. Kennedy from the water after *PT-109* went down.

Kennedy from the water, Kite from the water. But Tom fouled this up by finding *more* water. So much for angles.

If you want the names of the four players who made a hole in one at the 167-yard par-three sixth hole over a period of one hour and 57 minutes on Friday, they were Mark Wiebe, Nick Price, Jerry Pate, and Doug Weaver.

Each man hit a 7-iron. Each shot landed to the right and beyond the flag, then sucked back into the cup.

There were moments when people in the gallery would tell the players how to play the shot.

"Hit it to the right just past the flag," someone would holler.

"The pin might have been too easy on six," a USGA wizard said.

The press naturally took delight in forming a new rock group at Oak Hill. It was called the Four Aces.

Assorted photos were taken of the Four Aces together. Weaver wearing his Spalding visor, Wiebe wearing his Titleist visor, Pate wearing his Wilson cap, and Price bareheaded.

The photo begged a caption saying, "Which one of these golfers doesn't have a hat contract?"

PART FIVE

The Nineties

●

"I want to thank the press from the heart of my bottom."

—NICK FALDO, AFTER WINNING THE BRITISH
OPEN AT MUIRFIELD IN 1992

63

SHOOT A USGA OFFICIAL ON SIGHT

Hale Irwin Wins Sudden Death at 1990 U.S. Open

OMETIMES IN a U.S. Open it matters not who wins or loses but how the course plays, especially when the course invites every garment worker in the neighborhood onto the scoreboard and lets them stay there like a bad rash, curable only if you have any Hale Irwin ointment handy.

Poor old Medinah with its clubhouse that looks like the Babylon Marriott. Its famous No. 3 course caught the fever early in this 1990 championship and never got over it, despite Irwin's victory in the first sudden-death playoff in Open history.

When last seen, many of Medinah's bloodied members were looking for USGA officials—P. J. Boatwright, the executive director of rules and competitions, and all of his helpers—to throw into Lake Kadijah and watch them go down for the third time.

Going into the 1990 Open, Medinah No. 3 was recognized as one of America's sternest tests. In its two previous Opens, those in '49 and '75, its par of 71 amid the tall oaks and swollen willows had stood up to golf's heroes and even slapped them around. Cary Middlecoff's two-over 286 had won in '49, and a three-over 287 had been the winning number in '75 before Lou Graham won in a playoff over John Mahaffey.

But this time the layout had not only been revamped on the back nine holes—in one absurd way by turning the decisive and historic par-three 17th hole into the 13th hole—but by increasing par to 72 and even widening the fairways and thinning the rough.

This invited all the nobodies to the party. There were a record 39 sub-par rounds on Thursday, a record 47 subpar rounds on Friday, a record 24 subpar rounds on Saturday, and 14 more subpar rounds on Sunday, led by Hale Irwin's 67 that got him into the playoff with Mike Donald, a strange presence at best.

Added up, that was 124 subpar rounds on glorious Medinah No. 3 and it devastated the USGA's old record of 64.

More than one Medinah member staggered around in a daze and said, "Jesus, *we* play a tougher course than these guys. The USGA clowns have embarrassed us and turned us into the Quad City Classic."

Who were some of these garment workers that were doing this to glorious Medinah? Aside from the members of the International Ladies' Garment Workers Union who were honking their horns and boycotting the Open on avenues surrounding the place because they didn't think it was fair that LaMode knitwear ought to be manufactured by non-union people?

Well, they were the likes of Tim Simpson, Scott Simpson, and Jeff Sluman on Thursday, Tim Simpson and Mike Hulbert on Friday, and Billy Ray Brown, Mike Donald, Tom Sieckmann, and Mike Reid on Saturday. All of them ripping the course apart.

A couple of known quantities, Nick Faldo and Greg Norman, made gallant moves on Sunday but didn't quite get there. Nick finished one shot out and Greg three, largely because he turned the new par-five, birdie-hole 14th into a bogey at the exact moment when he was lead-ing.

The Great White Einstein killed his chances with an ill-advised club selection when he was five under on the day and seven under for the Open. He smashed a drive down the center of the 14th fairway, but instead of going for the reachable green in two, he made the mistake of trying to "think." He tried to lay up with a 3-iron—*he would try to play Hogan golf?*—but he hit one of his patented right-to-right shots into the woods. That was it.

There was a question whether the 45-year-old Irwin would have enough energy left for a playoff after his jogging, high-fiving war dance around the 72nd green when he holed a 45-foot birdie putt for his 67. That round brought Hale back from a tie for 20th place, four shots behind the leaders. But he did finish two hours ahead of Donald, so that was helpful.

In the windy Monday playoff in regulation, Irwin and Donald both shot 74, but Donald led by two with only five to go. Hale caught him and took him into sudden death in a Hale Irwin kind of way.

First, Hale covered Mike's birdie at the 14th, and next he fired a 2-iron uphill and into the wind from 207 yards away and put it eight feet from the cup for a birdie. After which he steadily parred the 17th and 18th holes and let Mike Donald make the kind of mistake a guy makes when he's never won a major. Donald hit a quick hook off the tee and bogeyed. Then, on the first sudden-death hole, Irwin hit a perfect drive and a perfect wedge and sank a perfect birdie putt from 10 feet to win his third U.S. Open.

This did three things. It made him the oldest Open winner at 45 years. It lifted him onto a level where only four other men had won more—Willie Anderson, Bobby Jones, Ben Hogan, and Jack Nicklaus. And it's worth noting that Hale became the only guy ever to win U.S. Opens wearing glasses ('74), braces on his teeth ('79), and contact lenses ('90).

64

FAIRWAYS AND PUTTS

Ian Baker-Finch Wins 1991 British Open at Royal Birkdale

AN BAKER-FINCH had spent his career being low hyphen in the clubhouse, but as of now the slender Australian dude is the only hyphenated name ever to appear on a major championship trophy, unless, of course, you want to count Ben Immortal-Hogan or Byron Streak-Nelson.

And so what if the 1991 British Open was one of the gloomiest majors since Mungo Park took it all at Musselburgh? And so what if Ian did it with an inconsequential bogey at the last hole? And so what if he did it in the last round when he only had to beat a bunch of slum people since the glamour names were taking the week off from their golf games? And so what if he did it on Royal Birkdale, a course sunken amid jagged sandhills covered in dark green brush, a place with a peculiar white Art Deco–type clubhouse that looks like the airport in Entebbe?

The hyphen fellow with the name of a clothing designer or a community theater director mainly did it with a fiery display of sub-par golf over the last two rounds, closing with 64-66, the latter effort offering a front side of 29, which had more than a little to do with preparing an early burial for the notorious favorite, Seve Ballesteros, who was poised with his friend Destiny to win it again.

A 29 in the last round of a major, when you're already tied for the lead, will tend to eliminate a considerable amount of drama, so the final 18 at Birkdale was over almost as soon as it started.

The 30-year-old Australian who now lives in Florida quickly birdied the second, third, and fourth holes, then birdied the rugged sixth and added a birdie at the seventh and encountered no real problems on his way to a 66, other than risking injury to his back by bending over so often to take his first putt out of the cups.

Baker-Finch didn't even realize that his 64-66—130 tied Tom Watson's 65-65 at Turnberry in 1977 as the lowest final 36 in British Open history. And he didn't realize that his 29 was the lowest final-round nine ever shot in a major.

He carried a four-stroke lead into the back nine and could have finished with a double bogey and still won, inasmuch as the contestants who threw low rounds at him—your Jodie Mudd with a course-record 63, your Fred Couples with a 64, and your Mike Harwood with a 67—were never in serious range of catching him. Harwood, another Australian but certainly more obscure than Baker-Finch, wound up second.

Yeah, it was that kind of week.

Going into the last round, Ballesteros thought he was in perfect position to win his fourth Open. He was only two strokes back.

THEY'RE SCARED OF ME, blared a tabloid headline, supposedly quoting the Spaniard.

On Saturday night he actually said, "I am so confident. The crowds are with me. They give me an extra club in the bag. You must be brave and play solid golf to win the Open. I have done it. They haven't. It is my destiny."

As it happened, Seve's destiny was to slash a one-over 71 out of the sandhills while everyone else was breaking par and finish tied for ninth place, seven back of the winner's total of 272.

Adding to the gloom was the venue. Southport is to Liverpool what Sing Sing is to New York, but with less elegance. It's a seaside town of sleazy arcades and endless redbrick houses and buildings. Southport, as I have known it through three other British Opens—those captured by Americans Lee Trevino, Johnny Miller, and Tom Watson—hasn't changed. It's basically a vacation spot or weekend retreat where the well-to-do of Liverpool go to wrap themselves in freezing wind and terminal dampness as they picnic on a muddy beach and watch the dark sea recede toward Ireland.

Much of the fun of going to British Opens revolves around a game called house-renting, a game that was started back in the 1960s when American pros rejuvenated the championship and hordes of tourists and journalists began attending the tournament.

In Southport, many of those redbrick homes are huge and stately and look promising from the outside, and the ads make them sound truly wonderful. A typical ad reads:

"Woofington House is a magnificent Victorian structure in the lovely coastal town of Southport. Spacious drawing room, dining room, sitting room. Five bedrooms. More than adequate bathing facilities for 10 people, including baths, showers, basins, lavatories. Quality cooking and cleaning services available. Contact Oldwalls, Hardwood & Throwrug. Solicitors & Estate Agents."

Then you arrive and discover that the estate agents left out a few minor details.

It seems that the adaquate bathing facilities consist of one bathroom for 10 people. Thus, you finally learn why Queen Victoria wanted to conquer the world—England needed more tubs and basins.

Next you discover there are only three soggy towels to the household, and they also double as rags with which the cleaning lady wipes off countertops. Then the chef the estate agents have hired for you turns out to be a 15-year-old schoolgirl who knows how to make 7,000 pieces of toast to go with one fried egg, or 7,000 fried eggs to go with one piece of toast.

Meanwhile, throughout the week you are visited upon by the owners, who drop by to water the tomatoes in the backyard, unplug the phone, turn off the hot-water heater, and leave a note saying, "I respectfully ask that you NOT SMOKE in the house, as my wife and I gave it up many years ago."

But it's all part of the charm, and in Southport so is the mammoth old Prince of Wales Hotel in the center of town. This redbrick fortress is always the headquarters for officials of the R&A and the name contestants, and its lobby bar is usually teeming with activity.

The lobby of the Prince of Wales was where you could observe crusty old R&A members, who are easily identified by their gray hair, gin-red faces, navy blazers, and dark blue neckties gaily speckled with oxtail soup. You stand and stare at the gorse and thatch in their noses and hear one say to another, "Yes, quite so. That was the year of Henry Cotton, Lord Derby, and that business with the casual water."

This one, of course, was the year of the hyphen.

65

KILL IT, JOHN

John Daly Takes 1991 PGA at Crooked Stick in Indiana

HASTA LA *vista*, Greg Norman and all you other long hitters. I have seen the future of golf and it comes from Dardanelle, Arkansas, it has a baby face, it wears a blond wig, and it drives the ball so far, it makes everybody else look like an interior decorator.

Meet John Daly, who became the greatest unknown since Jack Fleck to win a major when he trampled everybody in the 1991 PGA Championship and made a joke of feared Crooked Stick Golf Club out in Indiana with his mesmerizing length from the driver down to the sand wedge.

He stood near Indianapolis, took the clubhead back to Rhode Island, swung it around Texas, and finished in Georgia.

"Kill" is all his caddie told him to do each time he addressed the ball.

Small wonder he carries around the nicknames Wild Thing, Macho Man, Killer John, Long John, and Dude the Terminator. John Daly is alien golf. He's golf in the cosmos.

Finesse? Knockdown shots? Course management? Who needs it when you can reduce a 525-yard par five to a driver and a 6-iron? Who needs it when you can reduce a 449-yard par four to a driver and a sand wedge?

His tempo is to swing as hard as he can. What does he use for a swing key? "Look, a golf ball!"

Daly was a guy who got into the PGA as an alternate because Nick Price's wife was having a baby. He drove all night from Memphis and didn't have time to play a practice round at Crooked Stick, a pure Pete Dye course with bulkheads and sandy islands and water and twisting fairways designed out of a cornfield. But, of course, you don't need a practice round if you can drive over all of Pete Dye's trouble.

At 25, John was a graduate of the South African tour, the Hogan tour, and the Q-school, as if anybody cared before he shot four sub-par rounds of 69-67-69-71 for the 276 that dusted Bruce Lietzke by three strokes.

In triumph, Daly said, "I'm not gonna become a jerk. If I become a jerk, I'll quit golf."

When you think about it, there wasn't a more suitable golfer to lose this major than Bruce Lietzke, the proud runner-up. Lietzke is a journeyman pro who makes a point of not playing in the U.S. Open and the British Open. He hadn't played in the British Open since 1981 and he hadn't played in the U.S. Open since 1985. He doesn't like the U.S. Open because of what the USGA does to the courses, and he doesn't like the British Open because he doesn't like England or Scotland, except on TV. Why root for a guy to win majors when he won't even play in them? On top of everything else, Lietzke was using one of those unsightly long putters at Crooked Stick. A long putter should never win a major.

It's a pleasure to report that Daly would have won this PGA even if he'd gotten the two-stroke penalty that briefly haunted him after the third round.

The world of golf is populated with rules junkies, as we know, and there is nothing wrong with this unless one of them watches golf on TV and has a telephone.

Three rules junkies phoned Crooked Stick on Saturday and somehow got through to inform PGA officials that Daly had violated Rule 8-2b on the eleventh green. They saw it on TV with their own eyes.

Rule 8-2b, as literature, rates up there with Chaucer, as far as I'm concerned. I quote: "When the player's ball is on the putting green, the player, his partner or either of their caddies may before, but not during, the stroke point out a line for putting, but in so doing the putting green shall not be touched. No mark shall be placed anywhere to indicate a line for putting."

PGA officials went into a dither or funk, whichever was closer, and rewound the tape to study the incident. What they saw was Daly and his caddie, Squeaky Medlin, on the 11th green. The caddie was holding the flagstick and waving his arm, as if to say the eagle putt breaks left to right. Squeaky put the flagstick down and moved away. Daly missed the putt, leaving it outside the cup on the left.

It took only one glance of the rerun to see that the flagstick Squeaky placed on the green was on the opposite side of the cup from where the putt broke. There was no violation.

People, hear me. Nobody gets to call in to a football telecast and penalize a team for holding. Nobody gets to call in to a baseball telecast and strike out a batter. Nobody gets to call in to a tennis telecast and foot-fault a server.

I looked it up. Rule 8-2cbd in golf says you can hang up the phone on a rules junkie.

66

JUST FRED

Couples Wins 1992 Masters

WALLOW AROUND all you want in pro shop merchandising and it's doubtful you can find a golf ball capable of stopping short of the water when it's rolling straight downhill. But Fred Couples had one. He used it to win the 1992 Masters. Maybe you'll be seeing it in the ads soon. Play the Maxfli HT, the ball that's afraid of water.

This was the ball Couples hit short of the 12th green in the final round of the Masters. The shot had doom written all over it. Amen Corner and Rae's Creek were up to their old tricks again, giving us a whole new golf tournament on the last nine holes.

Cinch catastrophe if Fred's ball trickles down into the creek after it hits the steep bank. It would have been, as more than one British TV announcer has said, "consigned to a watery grave." No ball hitting that bank had ever stopped before. Not on Sunday. Not in all the Masters tournaments in all the towns in all the world.

If Fred's ball had gone into the creek, it would have been anybody's

Masters. Probably Raymond Floyd's or Corey Pavin's. They were the closest. Or perhaps Mark O'Meara's. Or Jeff Sluman's.

But the ball didn't go in the water, even though it was heading down a slope as steep as the side of the Augusta National clubhouse. Couples then pitched up nicely and tapped in for his divine par—and that was basically the Masters.

Couples constantly came to his own rescue throughout his round on Sunday and what became a two-stroke win over the 49-year-old Ray Floyd. Fred went out in the last pairing with Craig Parry, the young Australian who was in the lead after 54 holes, and the results their games achieved were as different as kangaroos and jackrabbits.

Parry played far better than Fred from tee to green, but he missed 10 putts inside 10 feet on his way to an incorrigible 78 and a tie for 13th place, while Couples never missed anything from 15 feet or less for his 70.

Some of the stunts Couples pulled were these:

His putter saved par at the first. His drive deep into the woods at the second could have cost him a triple, but he escaped with a bogey. His second at the eighth put him in jail, but a no-brain putt got him a birdie. He made a miracle sidewinder at the ninth. He came out of a bunker at the 10th for a par. Wild tee shots cost him birdie chances at the 13th and 15th. He tried to three-putt the 17th, but his putter wouldn't let him. He hit a picked-clean approach out of a fairway bunker at the 18th but somehow found the green.

But Fred would best be remembered for the unbelievable break he got at the 12th hole. Sometimes you get a big break when you're winning a major. Bobby Jones once had a wood shot skip across a lake to help him win a U.S. Open. Gary Player won the Masters one year after a fan leaped up to bat Gary's ball back onto the 15th green when it was bounding toward the water behind the green.

A hero-starved media welcomed Couples to its bosom after his Masters victory. They ordained him a superstar, and they like him because, as one of them said, "He's just Fred."

Fred does bring a new kind of nonchalance to playing golf. He's the most effortless golfer out there. He's the first to win the Masters without wearing a glove since Ben Hogan. He sort of plays the game like a man who's not really keeping score.

He said he never answers the phone at home because "there might be someone on the other end of the line."

"I just play golf," he said.

Asked what he does when he goes home, he said, "I don't play golf."

It might have taken Couples 12 years on the tour to win his first major, and it may be the only one he ever wins, but he's a new hero, and hey, in the sportswriting dodge we make do, okay?

67

THE CONSUMMATE GRINDER

Tom Kite Wins 1992 U.S. Open at Pebble Beach

TOM KITE walks around today as living proof that if you work hard enough at golf, even though you may have limited ability, a day will come when the cups on the greens of a major championship will expand and consistently inhale your golf ball at a precise moment in history, and suddenly all past disappointments will become a quaint memory.

When Kite withstood the wind and rough and pressure of the final round to capture the 1992 U.S. Open at Pebble Beach, and did it on a day that turned hordes of talented players into comic figures, it called to mind the words of Cary Middlecoff from years ago: "Nobody wins the Open, it wins you."

That wasn't necessarily the case with Ben Hogan or Jack Nicklaus or Bobby Jones, but it's certainly been the case with numerous others, and it was probably the case with Kite. Fate wouldn't allow Tom to lose this Open. It was payoff time for the Texan who'd been out there grinding for 20 years and who didn't seem to know how to do anything but win money and tournaments of little consequence, other than the Players Championship in Ponte Vedra Beach, Florida, in 1989.

Kite joins Nicklaus (1972) and Tom Watson (1982) as the winner of a U.S. Open at Pebble Beach, and he shares with them a remarkable shot in the last round. Whereas Nicklaus and Watson did it on Pebble's long par-three 17th hole, Kite did it on the short par-three seventh, where he turned a certain bogey into a birdie by pitching in from 30 yards away.

File this with Nicklaus's great 1-iron that was nearly an ace in '72, and Watson's chip-in from the deep rough left of the green in '82.

To give you an idea of how the wind can change in the vicinity of Carmel Bay, Kite hit a sand wedge to the 107-yard seventh on Saturday, but Sunday he needed a 6-iron. His shot wound up in the rough behind the green. That's when his wedge shot barely cleared a bunker and darted across the green and hit the flagstick and dived into the cup.

That shot was the biggest in his round of even-par 72 that included other key shots. Kite could look back on several occasions where the cup grew to bathtub size. An 18-foot birdie putt at the first. A 12-foot par putt at the fifth. A 20-foot birdie putt at the sixth. A six-foot par putt at the ninth. A 35-foot birdie putt at the 12th. All this plus the pitch-in.

It's impossible to recall another American who waited longer to grab a major. Kite is 42. You have to think of a struggling actor who toils at his craft for years, then one day you see him accepting an Oscar because he finally got a part where he could chew the furniture. The Open at Pebble Beach was that movie for Tom Kite.

"I don't know why it took me so long," Tom said. "I think my game is right for the Open."

He was proud of the aggressiveness he showed in the last round. He attacked the course. But he was upset with the fact that common sense told him to play safe coming home.

"I hate myself for going into the prevent defense," he said—meaning he cautiously played for bogeys at 16 and 17—"but that's what I had to do."

It's a reflection on the gritty, grinding, gutsy round that Kite played when you look at the Sunday scores of some of the dignitaries. Gil

Morgan, the 54-hole leader, 81; Raymond Floyd, 81; Davis Love III, 83; Payne Stewart, 83; Craig Stadler, 81; Scott Simpson, 88; Paul Azinger, 80; Peter Jacobsen, 80; Mark Calcavecchia, 80.

Kite started the day one stroke behind Gil Morgan and tied with Ian Woosnam and Mark Brooks. When Morgan, Woosie, and Brooks all took a powder, Tom was asked to hold off the late runs of Jeff Sluman and Colin Montgomerie to win by two shots with a nostalgic total of 285. All except Kite, Sluman, and Montgomerie looked like they'd never seen rough or wind before.

The frustrated Gil Morgan would take no pride in joining the list of third-round leaders to suffer an Open collapse. In relatively recent times, the ones that come to mind are Tommy Jacobs (76) at Congressional in '64, Marty Fleckman (80) at Baltusrol in '67, Miller Barber (78) at Champions in '69, Frank Beard (78) at Medinah in '75, T. C. Chen (77) at Oakland Hills in '85, and Kite himself (78) at Oak Hill in '89.

In Kite's case at Pebble Beach, it's nice to be able to say that nobody waited longer for a major championship, and no hardworking fellow ever deserved it more.

68

REVENGE OF THE SHARK

Greg Norman Wins 1993 British Open at Sandwich

WELCOME TO *Masterpiece Links Theatre* on BBC, starring— in order of their appearance—Greg Norman, his golden tresses, and his occasional talent of striking the golf ball on the clubface.

In this episode at Sandwich along a gray, damp, mushy, blustery coast of Kent in the game's oldest professional championship, Norman played a round of golf in the 1993 British Open that has long been expected of him. Under gripping conditions against the best players in the world, he fired a 64 that is certain to be headed for a place in the Louvre or the British Museum.

Greg's final 18 left Nick Faldo, holder of five majors, scratching his head, wondering how he could shoot so low and still lose. It was the lowest finishing round for a winner in the ancient competition, and Norman did it with authority, hole after hole. But the best thing is, he did it without wearing that silly planter's hat.

Norman's rounds of 66-68-69-64 established a new 72-hole record of 267, erasing the 268 that Tom Watson painted on Turnberry in 1977 when he narrowly defeated Jack Nicklaus in their head-to-head duel, and it clipped Faldo's wondrous 269 by two strokes.

But Greg's golf shots on that 64 will be remembered better than the numbers. He never missed a fairway Sunday. Put a 9-iron to six feet and birdied the first. Rolled in a 25-foot putt for a birdie at the third. Drilled a 12-footer into the cup for a birdie at the sixth. Spun a 9-iron to within one foot of the cup for a birdie at the ninth. Out in 31 and on to the back side with a two-stroke lead.

His first nerve check came at the 11th, where he had to drop a seven-footer for par, and did. Armed with that confidence-builder, he stiffed a sand wedge at the 12th for a four-foot birdie. Then it was at the defining par-five 14th hole, most dangerous hole on a course that goes by the official name of Royal St. George's Golf Club, that Norman looked absolutely sure of himself, as if he knew this was his day, his week, his time.

With the boundary stakes looming on the right, Greg took out the driver when the situation begged for him to use an iron and play for a safe five. A wild drive was the only way he could lose.

But he rifled a beauty down the middle, smashed a 3-wood up short of the green for a pitch, and cut as pretty a wedge as you could diagram up to a foot of the cup for yet another birdie.

For all practical purposes, the championship was history. Norman had conquered Sandwich's mysterious slopes, steep moguls, cavernous bunkers, and blind shots. Visitors could go back to roaming the village's narrow, cobbled streets dating back to medieval times. Or wander on to Dover and gaze at the white cliffs, or mosey over to Broadstairs to see the house where Charles Dickens overlapped his quill.

Heavy rains hours before the championship got under way made for a sloppy week. To accommodate everyone, the R&A ordered metal ramps and wood-shaving pathways placed all through the course and village.

When the paths of wood shavings quickly turned into mush, they became of special interest to one R&A official in particular. Staring down at a bed of the mush outside the press tent, he said to a companion, "Alicia could do with a bit of this for her rhododendrons, I shouldn't wonder."

Having taken his second major against a record of no fewer than five heartbreaking losses in the big ones—three of them in playoffs—Norman took satisfaction in saying, "I never mis-hit a shot all week. I hit every drive perfect. It was a championship you had to win, because nobody was going to give it to you."

Greg's 64 at Sandwich cries out to be ranked with some of the epic closing rounds in history. Which is to say with Ben Hogan's 67 at Oakland Hills in 1951, with Arnold Palmer's 65 at Cherry Hills in 1960, with Jack Nicklaus's 65 at Augusta National in 1986.

It was the night before the final round when Faldo, who was tied for the lead with Corey Pavin, studied the scoreboard and said, "It gives you a great buzz. We're all there . . . Greg . . . Freddy . . . Bernhard . . . Corey. All the right names."

The thought occurred that someone should have said this *for* Nick, and you had a suspicion that the gods might punish him for it. Of course, the punisher turned out to be Greg Norman instead.

69.

HALF A SLAM

Nick Price Wins 1994 PGA at Southern Hills

I**T WAS** the noted historian Ben Crenshaw who tried to pay Nick Price the ultimate compliment at Southern Hills in Tulsa when Nick's rounds of 67 and 65 gave him a five-stroke lead through 36 holes of the 1994 PGA Championship. "He's a man in full flight," Crenshaw said. "He's striking the ball better than anyone since Hogan and Nelson." This indeed set the stage for Price to go out in the third round and strike the ball like Hogan and Nelson—Walter Hogan and Roy Nelson, two carpet salesmen from Duluth.

This was okay, though. Because it was in Saturday's third round that Nick Price actually won the PGA, his second major of '94 and his third in three years. His first came in the PGA at Bellerive in St. Louis in 1992.

The reason: Price's third-round 70 when all of his pursuers were throwing birdies at him could well have been a 76 or worse. It was his only bad ball-striking round of the championship, but he somehow escaped with a score of even par.

It was Nick's sand wedge and his backup mallet putter that helped see him through the day. He mistakenly played "defense" on Saturday. Tried to nurse along his lead. "Wait for something to happen," he said.

The result was a half-dozen tentative approach shots, even with the 9-iron, that left him in bunkers. Six different bunkers. But he got up and down from five of them for four pars and one for a birdie.

"There's no question I won the championship Saturday," Nick said later. "It's difficult to sleep on a lead. I fought to maintain a lead going into Sunday. It almost cost me."

With his play-safe round behind him, Price played nothing but near-perfect golf on Sunday to close with a 67 and a total of 269 that served two purposes: It humiliated Southern Hills members who watched their proud course torn apart, and it gave Nick a whopping six-stroke victory over runner-up Corey Pavin.

Price's win gave him half a slam for the year. He had won the British Open a month earlier at Turnberry, where he had to fend off a curious Swede named Jesper Parnevik, whose cap with the turned-up bill made him look like he, not Price, could become a man in full flight.

Nick also closed the deal on America in '94. We were wiped out in the majors for the first time since 1903, what with José María Olazabal taking the Masters in April, and another South African, Ernie Els, taking the U.S. Open at Oakmont in June.

The year 1903 was the last time America went winless in majors. Willie Anderson, a Scot, won the U.S. Open, England's Harry Vardon won the British Open, and Alex Smith, another Scot, won the Western Open, which was then a major.

If you're wondering about the last time anyone took the British Open and PGA in the same year, that would be Walter Hagen in 1924 at Hoylake and French Lick.

One more thing. Nick Price may have three majors now, but that's not the best thing about him. He's as nice a guy as you'll find in the game.

70

A SENTIMENTAL JOURNEY

Ben Crenshaw Wins 1995 Masters

DID BEN Crenshaw really win the 1995 Masters, or did all of us spend the week watching him star in the remake of two old movies, *Angel on My Shoulder* and *God Is My Co-Putter*?

Uh, Co-*Pilot* . . . sorry.

At their best, Jack Nicklaus and Arnold Palmer never put on a better show than Crenshaw at the Augusta National Golf and Predestination Club.

For a while in the final round, it became a place where some of the flowery names of the holes changed from Carolina Cherry, Golden Bell, Azalea, Redbud, and Nandina to . . . well, Harvey Penick.

These were the specific holes, the ninth, 12th, 13th, 16th, and 17th, where Crenshaw called on the last golf tip from his old friend and teacher to sink the crucial putts that won the tournament for him.

Take two practice strokes on the green before you putt. Don't let the head of the club pass your hands on the stroke.

Harvey's last tip. Told to Crenshaw two weeks before Penick passed away in Austin, Texas, at the age of 90.

You could see Crenshaw applying the advice throughout the Masters, forward pressing an instant before the stroke, nearly to the point of exaggeration. If you believe in such things, you could say it almost looked as if Ben were hearing a whisper.

"I had a 15th club in my bag this week," Ben said Sunday evening after winning his second Masters. "It was Harvey Penick."

The kind, soft-spoken, unselfish Harvey had become a best-selling author, but he had never stopped being a teacher, and Crenshaw and Tom Kite were his favorite pupils. Harvey had taught them as teenagers, as collegians at the University of Texas, and as successful touring pros.

Ben and Tom had never stopped living in Austin and consulting Harvey for advice. To them, Penick was more than a friend and coach—he was family.

There had been something going on for four years with Penick's bestseller, *The Little Red Book*, and the successes Kite and Crenshaw had. Something that can only be understood by people who sit on hilltops.

It was only a month after *The Little Red Book* came out in 1992 that Kite won the U.S. Open. It was quite a moment for the Kites when Tom's wife, Christy, took the trophy to Austin and put it in Harvey's lap. A month after that, Crenshaw won the Western Open, his first victory in two years.

Crenshaw and Kite have continued to win once a year, and now this storybook Masters happened to Ben.

Neither Crenshaw nor Kite looked eager to play in a golf tournament on the Thursday the Masters started. They had returned the night before from Harvey's funeral and were both teary-eyed on the Augusta National veranda that morning as they spoke with friends.

Crenshaw got choked up trying to quote from a eulogy given by Bud Shrake, coauthor of *The Little Red Book*. "Heaven is a better place today," Shrake had said. "Harvey Penick is there. Harvey is not the only golfer in Heaven, but we can be certain the angels will be lining up to see him very shortly to get their grips checked."

Crenshaw was four back after the first round and two back after the second, but he was tied after 54 holes with someone named Brian Henninger, who was destined to go where Brian Henningers usually go in the last round of a major—to a 76.

It came down to Crenshaw holing those birdie putts on the back nine for his closing 68 and the 274 that held off Davis Love III by a stroke.

Ben called his 6-iron to the 16th for a six-foot birdie putt that dropped "the best 6-iron I've ever hit."

Then, after his wedge shot left him with a 12-foot birdie putt at the 17th that he cozied into the cup, he said:

"It was the prettiest putt I've ever hit. It came off the putter at the perfect speed and you could tell it was heading home. It's like someone just put a hand on my shoulder and guided me through."

So true, Ben. Not to bury the lead, but all in all, this Masters was a bad week for atheists.

71

REVERSAL OF FORTUNE

Norman's Epic Collapse in 1996 Masters

O N THE morning of the last round of the 1996 Masters, smart money knew to have several leads handy because we were dealing with a Greg Norman thing. Every possibility from his planter's hat being found floating in Rae's Creek to Greg finally winning and hopping into one of his helicopters and skywriting a message to his favorite group of people: "Put This in Your Pressroom, You Middle-Income Jerks."

Lead one, Norman wins:

AUGUSTA, Ga.—Da-dum, da-dum, da-dum, da-dum ... how do you make "Jaws" music on a laptop?

Lead two, Norman loses:

AUGUSTA, Ga.—Don't jump, Greg, you have too much to live for. Think of your G-4, your yacht, your choppers, your six or seven Ferraris—who's counting?

Lead three, Norman wins:

AUGUSTA, Ga.—Greg Norman brought the palsied putting method to the Masters, adding a dreaded hour of slow play to recreational rounds throughout America, and possibly the Middle East, although things have always been a little shaky over there.

Lead four, Norman loses:

AUGUSTA, Ga.—Greg Norman did his famous imitation of the *Titanic* again on Sunday at the Masters, but this time he didn't go down by the bow, he went down by the throat.

●

AT THE END of the bizarre occurrence in the final round, Nick Faldo, the winner, uttered a true statement. After slipping into his third green jacket, to go with his three British Open claret jugs, he said, "I hope I'm remembered for shooting a 67 today and not for what happened to Greg. But obviously it will be remembered for what happened to Greg."

How could it not? A strange object slowly bled to death before our very eyes. For four hours. Although Norman did it to himself and unleashed every Great White Can of Tuna joke in the book, his undoing also wrought sympathy from his most cynical critics.

On the one hand, you could appreciate why Faldo hugged Greg on the final green. Why wouldn't you hug a guy who's been so nice to you?

Or it could have been a Heimlich maneuver—what do you think?

At least Faldo added another known personality to his victims in the six majors he's captured. Among his runner-up victims are Rodger Davis ('87 British Open), Scott Hoch ('89 Masters), 47-year-old Raymond Floyd ('90 Masters), and Mark McNulty ('90 British Open).

Any golfer could understand what Norman had gone through. Even

Harvey Penick's best-selling instruction books can't tell you how to stop the bleeding. It's the hardest thing in the world to do.

Future historians won't know what really happened when they read Norman's daily scores: 63-69-71 . . . 78! Here's what they may think:

1. Boy, the wind must have howled that day.

2. Boy, I hope I never get food poisoning that bad.

3. Boy, Greg must have gotten some terrible news that morning about one of his nine private jets.

Norman's collapse goes into the history books with some of the other great crumbles in majors. With Macdonald Smith's 82 in the last round of the '25 British Open, Joe Turnesa's 77 in the last round of the '26 U.S. Open, Dick Metz's 79 in the last round of the '38 U.S. Open, Sam Snead's eight on the last hole of the Open in Philadelphia in '39, Ken Venturi's 80 in the last round of the Masters in '56, Arnold Palmer blowing a seven-shot lead on the last nine of the Open at Olympic in '66.

One theory about Norman's collapse is that he'd played so well for three rounds, he went out on Sunday to let divine intervention take care of everything—and when it didn't he came apart.

It started immediately. He hit a bad drive, a rancid second shot, and missed a four-foot putt for a bogey on the first hole. It was the first putt he'd missed all week. Then, oops, he wrong-clubbed at the fourth and sixth and snapped one at the eighth, caught a case of the shorts at nine, trashed up the 10th, three-putted the 11th from close, and did a water thing at No. 12.

All of a sudden, Greg realized he'd lost six strokes to Faldo in five holes. He now trailed Nick by two shots. He hadn't hit a decent shot all day, so to try to correct this, he began swinging longer and faster, hips spinning, feet flying. Bad went to worse. Finally, there was nothing for Greg to do but start thinking about what to say in the pressroom.

This display brought back memories to those of us who had seen him find a way to finish second in seven prior majors, sometimes by his own coming apart and sometimes by bad luck that should never happen even to a Greg Norman.

There was the '84 U.S. Open loss to Fuzzy Zoeller in a playoff, the second-place finish by a stroke to Jack Nicklaus in the '86 Masters, the loss to Bob Tway in the '86 PGA when he'd led by five with nine to go, the Masters playoff in '87 where Larry Mize chipped in on the second sudden-death hole, the loss in the four-hole playoff to Mark Calcavecchia in the '89 British Open, the loss in the sudden-death playoff to Paul Azinger in the '93 PGA, and last year's loss to Corey Pavin in the '95 Open at Shinnecock.

Even before this Masters, Norman was alone in being able to look back on the fact that he had lost a playoff in each of the four majors—he owned a Grand Slam of silver medals.

In Augusta it was good of Greg to remind us in his post-Masters interview that his financial worth is still in the $40 million range, and that he still considers himself a winner, and that he's still a perfectionist. To which he added, "I feel confident in my belief and my approach to whatever I do that I can do it. If I wanted to be a brain surgeon and take the time to study that, I could."

Maybe so, but he wouldn't operate on this cowboy—not on Sundays, anyhow.

72.

THE LATE SHOW, STARRING . . .

Mark Brooks Wins 1996 PGA

T HE 1996 PGA Championship was lost by a fellow named Kenny Perry, a local hero, who started celebrating too soon and then spent too much time auditioning for an announcing job on network TV. Which left it to be won by a cool, tough Texan named Mark Brooks, a guy who looked like he might smile only if he heard the press tent was on fire.

It was an unusual championship, to put it mildly. One that was held in a suburb of Louisville, Kentucky, that didn't exist until the PGA came to town and put the tournament at Valhalla Golf Club, a course that didn't exist until the designer Jack Nicklaus came to town and rounded up all of the limestone, power lines, and bent grass he could find.

In what passed for a conclusion to the week, Brooks couldn't have whipped Perry worse on the 18th hole of the handmade Valhalla if he'd chained him to a wall and given him a taste of the lash.

On the last hole of regulation and in the one-hole playoff, Brooks played the 540-yard par five in birdie-birdie, or four-four, while Perry, discovering all sorts of bluegrass, played it in 6-DNF.

Right. A bogey in regulation while he was waving to the crowd and celebrating a two-stroke lead—and shooting a 68 despite the bogey—and then pocketing the ball in the playoff after five strokes found him still eight feet from the cup.

Perry's bogey and Brooks's up-and-down out of a bunker a little later on for his birdie was what created the playoff. Perry might have fared better in the playoff if he hadn't devoted so much time to enjoying himself up on the CBS TV tower with Jim Nantz and Ken Venturi, oblivious, no doubt, to the possibility that someone might tie his 277 total.

Perry was given the option of leaving the tower, and he took the blame himself for not doing it. He said, "They told me, 'Feel free to do whatever you like,' but I hung around. I was caught up in the moment. All the fans and everything. When Mark made the birdie, I went down and asked the officials if I had time to hit some balls. They said no. You could say I learned a good lesson, I guess."

Aside from the fact that nobody liked Valhalla very much except a few of us, the hottest issue of the week was the all-important dress code for caddies.

Before the rain came and cooled everything off on the weekend, the temperature hovered around 118, and when you factored in the humidity, it wasn't all that different from standing under a perpetually warm shower. So a few caddies came out in short pants.

Two of them were the caddies for Tom Lehman, the newly crowned British Open champion, and Steve Jones, the newly crowned U.S. Open champion. They were apprehended on the second hole Thursday morning by a group of indignant PGA officials.

The players and caddies protested, pointed to the fact that they were already soaking wet and miserable, and pointed to the fact that there were two female caddies, one for Nick Faldo and one for Steve Stricker—his wife—who were permitted to wear shorts.

The rule didn't apply to female caddies, they were told. Furthermore, the male caddies could either put on long pants or be escorted off the course. The caddies began slipping into the trousers that were in the golf bags.

Why was the PGA of America doing this? the players inquired.

"Because" was basically the answer.

Another memory that will linger from Valhalla was the deeply emotional way in which Mark Brooks handled winning his first major.

When he was asked in his press interview what this PGA meant to him, he said, "I don't know yet."

Then he glanced down at a slip of paper.

He answered some other questions with the highly quotable comments of "No," "Yes," and "It's possible."

Eventually, Brooks was challenged by a group of writers about his unhappy appearance, his overall attitude. Wasn't he the winner of a major title that, among other things, gave him a 10-year exemption on the tour?

Brooks threw up his arms and said, "What do you want me to do? I was taught a long time ago that if you drop your guard, the other guy will know what's going on."

Okay, Mark. We get it. Here's an idea. How about we don't bother you anymore—ever?

73

HE'S HERE!

Tiger by 12 at 1997 Masters

XCUSE ME for a moment while I write this TV commercial for Tiger Woods, the 1997 Masters winner. It will be sponsored by his agent, ITG—International Tiger Group—and some of his new companies: Time Woods Warner, Saks Fifth Woods, Merrill Woods Lynch, BloomingWoods, Diet Tiger, and American AirWoods.

Fade in Nick Faldo, bent over and battered:

"I'm not Tiger Woods."

Fade in Fred Couples, thin and wan:

"I'm not Tiger Woods."

Fade in Tom Lehman, haggard and short of breath:

"I'm not Tiger Woods."

Fade in Greg Norman, old and lifeless:

"I'm not Tiger Woods, but I'm putting '97 behind me the way I've put '96 behind me."

As you've probably heard by now, Tiger's overwhelming performance on the Augusta National may have made this Masters the tournament that changed golf forever, changed golf course design forever, and changed society forever.

Such things remain to be seen, but what is easy to see today is that Tiger's rounds of 70-66-65-69 for a stunning total of 270 broke the old 72-hole record that was held by Jack Nicklaus and Raymond Floyd.

In doing this, Tiger won by 12 strokes. Another record in majors, for modern times anyhow. It's topped only by the 13-shot victory of Old Tom Morris in the British Open of 1862, which took place over 36 holes when only four people owned a set of clubs. And that mark has only been equaled by Young Tom Morris in the 1870 British Open, also at Prestwick, when only eight people owned a set of clubs.

Going into the last 18 on Sunday, the nearest thing to Tiger on the scoreboard was Constantino Rocca, which, contrary to reports, was not a forbidden dance. It was a man from Italy nine strokes back.

Next closest was Paul Stankowski, who put aside composing his symphony long enough to be only 10 strokes back.

What? One of those guys was going to throw a little 55 at Tiger?

Tom Kite was actually the guy who inherited second place.

There was no drama to Tiger's last-round 69. Just good golf shots. Down around Amen Corner, where trouble for leaders is often found, Tiger went birdie-par-birdie. In fact, he played the testing Amen Corner seven under for the week.

Kind of hard to beat a guy who doesn't three-putt a single, undulating, highly varnished Augusta National green for four days, and drives it so far off the tee he has a wedge to 11 of Augusta National's 18 holes.

So now at the age of 21, Tiger has added a professional major to go with his three U.S. Amateur titles. Four majors is the way you have to count it. "You envision dueling it out with Faldo or Nicklaus or Watson, someone who's awfully tough to beat down the stretch," he said in the glow of victory. "You dream of doing that or getting into a playoff, weird things like that, but never to do it in the fashion that I did it."

A question remaining is whether anything can be done to stop Tiger, or at least slow him down, before he makes some of us forget that we ever saw Ben Hogan, Byron Nelson, Sam Snead, Arnold Palmer, and Jack Nicklaus swing a club.

It so happens that I have a 10-step plan to suggest:

1. Make him wear Harry Vardon's tweed coat.
2. Make him wear Greg Norman's planter's hat.
3. Make him wear Tom Kite's glasses.
4. Make him use Phil Mickelson's clubs.
5. Make him play the gutty.
6. Make him use a long putter.
7. Make him travel by train.
8. Make him carry his own clubs.
9. Make him stay in press hotels.
10. Make him get married and have to go to Ace Hardware a lot.

74

SOMEWHERE UNDER THE RAINBOW

Davis Love III Wins 1997 PGA at Winged Foot

IRST ROMAN numeral to win a major, Davis Love III. First guy in Softspikes cleats to win a major. First guy to win a major while looking like he's taking a nap. Wake up, Davis, you're the 1997 PGA champion.

He may be in jail by the time this finds print. You can't turn rugged, ornery, intimidating Winged Foot into a par-66 golf course and shoot a 72-hole total of 269. Heavens, that's seven strokes lower than Fuzzy Zoeller shot when he won the U.S. Open in '84, and 18 strokes lower than Hale Irwin shot when he won the U.S. Open in '74.

It's against the law to do this. There are signs everywhere.

Winged Foot is a proud place, tucked away in an enviable part of Westchester County amid lovely mansions, gardens, lawns, forests. Which made it all the more amusing when Paul Azinger, the 1993 PGA champion, and two other guys endured what they considered to be a harrowing experience in the neighborhood.

It was after practice on Wednesday that Azinger, Phil Blackmar, and Mike Standly went to a nearby park to take a fly-casting lesson. There, however, they found themselves threatened by a group of teenagers. The kids hid behind trees and peppered the fly-caster/pros with crab apples and chunks of asphalt.

"It was weird enough that we decided to leave before 15 of them showed up and circled around us," Azinger said. "But when I thought about where I was, I thought this was probably normal."

Sure. Why not? Azinger was trapped in that hotbed of gang terrorism, where the Crips and Guccis strike fear in the hearts of fly-casters. Only 15 minutes from Greenwich, Connecticut, where the Bloods and the Ralph Laurens have been known to shout insults at Hermès handbags.

This is mentioned only because it was part of the fabric of PGA Week. Now back to the Roman numeral.

Davis Love III finally played the kind of golf people had been expecting of him for—what—10 years? He fired three rounds of 66, finished at 11 under par, and won the thing by five shots over his nearest competitor, the newly crowned British Open champion Justin Leonard, and by what seemed like 500 strokes over everybody else.

In truth, it was by 17 over Tiger Woods, who found a way to make four double-bogeys and wound up tied for 29th place. Still, Tiger managed to have the time to pose for photo ops with Evander Holyfield and Miss Universe. Where were Fergie and Costner?

Hey, Tiger. Dump the celebs. Straighten out the tee ball.

That's what Davis Love III started doing a few years ago when he was considered the longest hitter in North America—in any direction. He's still among the top five in distance, but he's hitting more fairways now. What he worked on was to acquire "quiet feet," as the gurus say, and to stay down and be stronger through impact.

Sunday's final round started with Davis and Justin tied for the top spot, but Davis grabbed a four-stroke lead through the first five holes, being well on his way to yet another 66.

The only moment of drama came at the 13th hole, a 212-yard par three. Davis jerked a 4-iron into the rain-matted rough, while Justin put a 3-iron shot to within 15 feet of the cup. But Davis almost holed out his pitch, saved par, and Justin missed the birdie putt.

Leonard demonstrated that he could be as gracious a loser as he was a winner a month earlier at Royal Troon.

"Naturally I'm disappointed," the young Texan said. "But I'm happy for Davis and his family. He never let up and hit the ball solid all the way. I was glad I was with him and was there to watch."

Then there was the rainbow thing at the finish. Love, whose father, Davis Jr., was killed in a plane crash in 1988, admitted he was fighting emotions over the last few holes. Especially when twin rainbows appeared to arrive on cue as he was walking up the 18th fairway.

"I didn't want to look," Davis said. "It was very strange. I guess there was something to it . . . son of a PGA member. Who'd ever have thought?"

With his 11th victory on the tour in 11 years, Davis no longer will be known as The Best Player Never to Have Won a Major.

"It's nice to have been in that category," he said. "It's nice to be out."

75

URGENT CALL FOR A NAME

Mark O'Meara Wins 1998 British Open at Royal Birkdale

THE FIRST battle cry at the 1998 British Open was: Who in the name of Ben Hogan are Brian Watts and Justin Rose? Another was: Why do rules (27-1), (20-3c), and (20-2c) spell Mark O'Meara? Finally, there was: Why shouldn't Mark O'Meara win another major championship since he looks like Billy Casper's long-lost brother?

Not many majors have been contested sillier than the one that unfolded at Royal Birkdale, which lies only two sneezes and three coughing spells from the redbrick seaside town of Southport, England, where people go to enjoy the icy mist and sit on beach chairs in the mud and stare at incoming squalls.

So it was a good thing that O'Meara won it in the end. His name was among the few that made sense. In fact, given Birkdale's history of allowing only the winners of multiple majors to emerge victorious on its zigzagging moonscape of a layout, O'Meara made even more sense.

With the exception of Ian Baker-Finch in 1991, Birkdale had anointed only the likes of Peter Thomson, Arnold Palmer, Lee Trevino, Johnny Miller, and Tom Watson. Men with majors. And O'Meara has now added the British Open to the Masters he won in April and the U.S. Amateur he won in 1979. He's had half a six-pack of majors.

The win puts O'Meara on an elevator we never expected him to ride. Three majors lift him into the elite company of Jimmy Demaret, Cary Middlecoff, Ralph Guldahl, Hale Irwin, Denny Shute . . . uh, Tommy Armour, Julius Boros, Francis Ouimet . . . and, let's see . . . Chick Evans, Henry Cotton, Nick Price, Larry Nelson . . . and, of course, Billy Casper.

That's not too long a list when you consider the game is older than the plumbing in Southport.

Speaking for himself in the afterglow, O'Meara said, "I felt if I went out and played well and kept my composure, I'd have a chance here."

But that's not the best thing he said. The best thing he said was "Just make the call—whatever you say, I'll live with it."

He said that in Saturday's third round when he escaped from the 480-yard sixth hole with a bogey five that could have been a buzzard-albatross-alien-monster-with-wings type of deal.

O'Meara's ball was lost in the gorse after his second shot, and although he didn't find it before the allotted five minutes was up, a spectator did—in his pocket.

After much discussion, the R&A officials allowed O'Meara to "find" the ball (27-1), drop it (20-3c), place it (20-2c), and then make the (5) instead of the (7-8-or-9) that eventually led to his winning (280).

And the incident took only 25 minutes, or 25 hours, depending on how cold you were as you stood there watching.

Otherwise, in the freezing, windblown carnage of Birkdale's meandering layout, there were illustrious victims strewn everywhere, from Tiger Woods's 77, to Fred Couples's 78, to Justin Leonard's 82, to Nick Price's 82, to Phil Mickelson's 85.

Birkdale's routing goes off in all directions. In the wind, therefore, you can be looking at a 130-yard 4-iron on one hole and a 217-yard 7-iron on the next. Puts a strain on the mind, Birkdale does.

It probably took a 41-year-old gentleman to handle it, a man who has joined the short list of players who have won the British Open and Masters in the same year: Hogan, Palmer, Nicklaus, Player, Watson, Faldo.

"The golf ball sitting on the ground doesn't know how old you are," O'Meara said.

A word about the two strangers O'Meara was called upon to beat.

First, there was Brian Watts, the guy O'Meara defeated in the four-hole playoff by two strokes after Mark's closing 68 tied him at 280. Watts had led at 36 and led at 54, and this led to the discovery that he was from Oklahoma and had been winning money on the Japanese tour since 1991.

Watts's big claim to fame two months before Birkdale was to intentionally miss the cut in the Fuji Sankei Classic because he wanted to go home and see his wife and son. He did it by hitting both a driver and 3-wood into the ocean when he had a wedge to the green.

Justin Rose, the other stranger, was a thin 17-year-old English amateur who missed the playoff by only two shots. It was the best finish in the British Open by an amateur since Frank Stranahan tied for second behind Hogan at Carnoustie in '53.

A big moment for Justin Rose came after his 66 on Friday when a proper British radio interviewer said, "All well and good, Justin, but I *regret* to inform you that, *should* you win here, you *shan't* be the youngest winner of the Open championship. I'm afraid that will still be Young Tom Morris, who was 17 years, 5 months, and 8 days in 1868."

Justin could only blink and say, "Really? Huh."

THE PAYNE STOPS HERE

Payne Stewart Wins 1999 U.S. Open at Pinehurst

ONE TRICK in the sandhills of North Carolina at the 1999 U.S. Open was to see if Payne Stewart, the only man in the field dressed like Donald Ross, could win it coming down the stretch against the furious challenges of Tiger Woods, Phil Mickelson, and Vijay Singh. Another trick was to see if a U.S. Open could be held at the Masters.

Both proved to be true, and they combined to make the '99 Open one of the most magnificent championships in history.

Even before Donald Ross, the designer, got rid of the original sand greens at Pinehurst No. 2 and put in grass—ostensibly for the 1936 PGA Championship—the place had things in common with the Augusta National. Old South, old pines, old money.

Long before Stewart outlasted those other three brand names and beat them with a 15-foot putt on the 72nd hole—the last stroke of the tournament—Pinehurst No. 2 had a reputation as the South's first truly great golf course, and the resort had a reputation as the South's first enchanted destination for those of the golf-nut persuasion.

For many years, the old North and South Open on No. 2 was sort of a Masters before there was a Masters. Touring pros and golfing enthusiasts alike remember the North-South and Pinehurst as the tour's annual brush with charm and elegance. Black tie and evening gowns for dinner.

Eventually, it was the favorite tournament of Ben Hogan and Sam Snead, who each won it three times and in fact considered it a major, as did the equipment and apparel companies who gave bonuses to the North-South winner just as they did for winners of the U.S. Open, PGA, and Western Open. Win the North-South and you could endorse cigarettes whether you smoked or not, and soft drinks whether you drank them or not.

For decades there were worshippers who wondered why Donald Ross's jewel, Pinehurst No. 2, couldn't hold a U.S. Open. When it finally installed bent greens, it had a chance. And now it's been the host, complete with old-world charm, slick greens, plenty of length, clear sight lines off the tee, and the rigid requirement of precise iron shots.

At first glance, Pinehurst No. 2 looked more like a Masters than an Open with its tightly shaved undulations and relatively little rough, and it presented every bit as much of a problem getting up and down as the Augusta National does.

Nobody put it better than a pro named Brandel Chamblee when he was on his way to a tie for 46th place: "It's Augusta on steroids."

Helped along by some rain, No. 2 played easier than was expected on Thursday, and a foursome led at three-under 67. Mickelson was one, David Duval was another, but the other two were oddities, Paul Goydos and Billy Mayfair.

As the course hardened, Mickelson and Duval were still in the lead after 36, and Payne had joined them. Then after 54 it was Payne all alone on top, but nipping at his heels were Phil, only one back, Tiger, only two back, and Singh, only three back. Duval and his hook grip had done a disappearing act along with everyone else.

Adding to the drama of it all was Mickelson's announcement that if his wife, Amy, started giving birth to their first child—she was expected to deliver any minute—he'd be out of town, gone, WD'd, on his way home. Even if he was leading.

How would he know? Well, Phil's caddie, Bones McKay, was carrying a beeper, and if the beeper went off with the proper code punched in, that would be the signal—and Mickelson swore he would immediately leave the golf course.

For some curious reason this brought to my mind the lyric of an old country-and-western song: "If the phone don't ring, you'll know it's me."

Of course, pros aren't permitted to have portable phones on the course during a competition—for obvious reasons. They might call up David Leadbetter, Hank Haney, Chuck Cook, or Butch Harmon, and say, "I'm out here on the 10th hole and it looks like I've either got an 8-iron or a 9-iron—what do you think?"

All four guys had a chance to win on a Sunday packed with the suspense of tremendous golf shots, great recovery shots, narrowly missed putts, and critical putts that dropped. The misses were more numerous, however, for those trying to catch Payne.

Mickelson kept it in the fairway all afternoon, surprisingly, but his putts lipped out repeatedly. Singh missed two makable birdies at 13 and 14. Tiger spun out at the 10th, three-putted the 11th from kick-in distance, and blew it from seven feet at 17.

It was left to Payne Stewart to make the three big putts that mattered the most. He holed a 25-footer to save par at the 489-yard 16th, the longest par four in Open history. At the 191-yard 17th, Payne played a gorgeous iron to within four feet of the flag, and made it for the birdie that put him one ahead of Mickelson.

At the 446-yard 18th, Stewart pushed his drive into the rough where he had no chance to reach the green. Mickelson found the fairway and also found the green. Phil had a 25-foot putt for birdie and no doubt an easy par. A playoff looked inevitable.

Payne dug his ball out of the rough but was still 80 yards from the green. He had to get up and down in two to win. On one of Donald Ross's "crown jewels."

Payne Stewart was up to the task. His splendid pitch under pressure got him to within 15 feet of the cup, and his putt for par—for a final round of 70 and 279, for the win, for his third major—had nothing but throat written on it the instant it left the putter's face.

By way of explaining his victory, Payne said, "I got here last weekend when nobody was around. I walked the course two or three times. I took an 8-iron, 9-iron, pitching wedge, and sand wedge and hit a bunch of chip shots and pitch shots to these greens from all sorts of places. I think it might have helped me."

You might say so. You might also say that Pinehurst No. 2 had helped itself to a few more U.S. Opens in the future.

77

THE INSPECTOR CALLS

Jean Van de Velde at the 1999 British Open at Carnoustie

ONG BEFORE Inspector Clouseau asked the sheepherder from Aberdeen if he had a "lee-cense" for his "min-key," and then gave him the 1999 British Open, the testy old links of Carnoustie proved once again how the best golfers in the world will scream, curse, whimper, ask for their mommies, and go home and pull the covers over their heads if they aren't allowed to go out and make birdies, eagles, and golden-cheeked warblers.

The comical Frenchman aside—Jean Van de Velde is the name that will live in infamy—it was also comical to listen to the best golfers in the world talk about how much they were unfairly tortured by the legendary course that borders the Firth of Tay in this gloomy little town.

The course was tough enough, they said, and didn't need the help of the R&A and Carnoustie Course Superintendent John Philip to turn it into a combination of wheat field, wild-game preserve, and duck blinds.

In other words, a course that could only be played by someone like Jean Van de Velde, who had all the traces of a character stepping out of a Pink Panther movie.

The best golfers in the world would no doubt be pointing out for the rest of the year that Van de Velde was the pro from Disneyland Paris, and it would obviously take a Goofy to play a Mickey Mouse track like Carnoustie.

Of course, not even Goofy could have thrown away a major the way Van de Velde did. When a double bogey can win a major on the last hole, you don't turn yourself into a martyr and make a triple. But that's what Jean of Argh did at Carnoustie's 487-yard finishing hole, where the Barry Burn winds around and around, yearning for a mis-hit shot.

You can only wonder why Van de Velde, a smallish, highborn gentleman who winters in Geneva and summers in Biarritz, didn't play the hole with, say, just for example, 4-iron, wedge, wedge, and three putts. That would have been a six, but good enough to make him the first Frenchman—and only the second ever—to win the championship since Arnaud Massy at Hoylake in 1907.

But instead he Clouseau-ed it. He played it driver, 2-iron, grandstand, wall of burn, rough, burn, drop, bunker, blast, and putt. Actually, when you think about it, he made a rather miraculous seven.

As Van de Velde took seven hours to take those seven strokes, it was a scene straight out of Mel Brooks's *Young Frankenstein*, the one where Gene Wilder and Marty Feldman, Dr. Frankenstein and Igor, are digging through the prison cemetery to come up with parts for the monster:

Dr. Frankenstein: "What a filthy job."

Igor: "Could be worse."

Dr. Frankenstein: "How?"

Igor: "Could be raining."

Your normal, everyday golf historian could think of only two tragic examples to compare with Van de Velde at Carnoustie. Sam Snead's eight and Roland Hancock's six-six.

Sam made his triple in the '39 U.S. Open on the last hole of the Spring Mill course at Philadelphia Country Club. Drove in the rough, tried to hit a brassie out, and started counting. A five would have won and a bogey six would have tied. If there is any such thing as an excuse for Sam, he was finishing early and thought he needed a birdie to win.

"Hell, I could have played the hole with three 7-irons if I'd known what I had to do," Snead said.

Roland Hancock, a 21-year-old nobody, was a different story. At Olympia Fields in Chicago in the '28 U.S. Open, he needed only to play the last two relatively easy holes in five-five, or bogey-par, to beat Bobby Jones and Johnny Farrell, who were already tied and in the clubhouse.

"Make way for the new champion!" people hollered as Hancock went to the 17th tee. Whereupon he strayed shots all over the South Side of Chicago and finished six-six.

It was also part of the doings at Carnoustie that a Scottish qualifier named Paul Lawrie shot a final-round 67, and our own Justin Leonard, the '97 champion, shot a 72 to wind up tied at 290.

They watched while Van de Velde, the leader at 36 and 54 holes, did his Clouseau thing, thrusting the three of them into a playoff for the claret jug. Which wasn't much of a playoff. Lawrie hit the only golf shots, beating the other two by three strokes in only four holes.

Van de Velde said of the ill-chosen 2-iron shot that caused him all the trouble in regulation, "It hit the grandstand and bounced backward, but you know, it could have hit someone on the head and bounced forward."

Love that. So you take the young Scot who won the claret jug. I'm keeping the Frenchman who won the story.

78

DON'T LOOK NOW

Tiger Wins 1999 PGA at Medinah

N THE last major of the last decade of the twentieth century—the NASDAQ Nineties—it seemed fitting that the 1999 PGA Championship at Medinah Country Club in a suburb of Chicago would wind up in the hands of the playing pro from Nike, Titleist, American Express, Rolex, Wheaties, All-Star Café, CBS Sportsline, Asahi Beverages, and Electronic Arts.

That would be your Tiger Woods and his current endorsements that guarantee him $30 million a year in the foreseeable future whether or not he makes a single cut.

Of course, the PGA almost wound up in the hands of a bubbling young Spaniard, Sergio Garcia, who ought to think about signing up with a circus troupe in Vegas or Romania so he can take his death-defying tree-trunk shot on the road. What a world.

Although Tiger shot three over par for the last seven holes of the last nine, he did get in with an even-par 72, and it gave him the total of 277 that was good enough to keep the Spaniard in second place in the last major of the rich old twentieth century, which made touring pros almost as wealthy as rock stars and dead portrait painters.

This was appropriate. Harry Vardon, the dominant player of his time, won the last major of the nineteenth century, the 1899 British Open at Sandwich. You might want to argue that Willie Smith did by winning the U.S. Open three months later, but was the U.S. Open a major at the time? It was only four years old. Doubtful. More likely it was considered a weekend off for the hired help.

So Tiger and Vardon. That's one thing.

Another thing is that the century ends with foreign players achieving the prominence they enjoyed back around 1910, in the dwindling days of the Great Triumvirate—Vardon, Taylor, and Braid.

Foreign players won virtually half of the majors in the 1990s. It barely wound up 21–19 for Americans because Tiger held off Sergio.

Maybe you can only appreciate this global emergence if you're reminded of how the USA used to dominate things.

In the 1980s the U.S. had an edge of 29–11. That's when Jack Nicklaus and Tom Watson were carrying the ball, and Seve Ballesteros was becoming a Brit in the minds of English and Scottish journalists.

It was 34–6 in the 1970s, with Nicklaus and Lee Trevino doing the heavy lifting, and the foreign contingent had little going for it but the globe-trotting Gary Player.

The score was 31–9 in favor of the Yanks in the 1960s, with Arnold Palmer in the lineup and Nicklaus helping out. Player got a little help from Roberto De Vicenzo, Bob Charles, Kel Nagle, and Peter Thomson.

The only reason America didn't have a greater edge than 31–9 in the 1950s was that nobody but Ben Hogan took the trouble to go over and win the British Open.

Led by Hogan, Byron Nelson, and Sam Snead, America was 23–3 in the war-torn 1940s. Before that, Gene Sarazen got some assists from

Denny Shute and Horton Smith and others to give America a 31–9 edge
in the 1930s, and before that, we had Bobby Jones and Walter Hagen to
thank for the 27–13 edge in the Roaring Twenties.

Hope the stats haven't spoiled your dinner.

The PGA didn't turn into a drama until Sergio birdied the 13th, which
had something to do with Tiger over-puring his own tee shot moments
later and stumbling to a double-bogey five. Still steaming, Tiger pushed
his drive into deep rough at the reachable par-five 14th and had to settle
for a par. Then came an impulsive second shot at the 16th and another
bogey.

That was followed by a tee shot at 17 that put him in more deep rough,
and another gunch chip left him with a left-to-right eight-foot putt for
par—to hold the lead. He squeezed it in. Big moment.

But the biggest moment of the championship had come ahead of it,
when Sergio hit that open-face, 189-yard circus shot with his 6-iron. The
ball was cradled in roots, almost up against the trunk of the tree. His
view was of trees to the far left of the green.

He hit a 30-yard slice from the root-infested lie and went running
after it while the ball was in the air, jumping up and down for a better
view, and finally saw it reach the green safely.

The mind shudders to think of what might have happened. One. The
ball hits the root and bounds back into Sergio's knee, turning him into a
lifetime sweater salesman. Two. The ball hits the root and bounds back
into Sergio's forehead, turning him into Jean Van de Velde. Three. The
ball hits the root and bounds back into Sergio's heart, turning him into
dead, and Stewart Cink ties Jay Haas for runner-up.

PART SIX

The Two Thousands

•

"It doesn't suck."

—PHIL MICKELSON, UPON HEARING AFTER THE THIRD
ROUND OF THE 2004 MASTERS THAT TIGER WOODS WAS
TOO FAR BACK—NINE STROKES—TO BE A THREAT

79

A LEAGUE OF HIS OWN

Tiger by 15 at 2000 U.S. Open at Pebble Beach

O N BOARD THE U.S.S. *TIGER WOODS* SOMEWHERE IN CARMEL BAY NEAR ABALONE CORNER—The only aircraft carrier in golf, comma.

The story could stop there. After the fog set in on Pebble Beach at the 2000 U.S. Open, it made you wish they'd crowned Tiger the first 36-hole Open champion since Joe Lloyd in 1897, which was the last time they settled things at 36 holes.

They could have. Tiger led by six strokes after two rounds. He led by 10 after 54 holes. Then he did the Secretariat thing in the final round and won by 15. Tiger lifted the fog and himself at the same time.

It was epic, is what it was. Goes in there with some of the other all-time moments. You know them. Jones and the Slam. Hogan and the Triple Crown. Palmer's comeback at Cherry Hills. Nicklaus grabbing his sixth Masters.

Tiger not only won this U.S. Open by 15 shots when he finished with rounds of 65-69-71-67. He shot the low first round, the low second round, the second-best third round, and the low fourth round—for a 272 that tied the Open record. To go on about it, his 12 under was another record, and it would have been 16 under if Pebble Beach had played to its usual par of 72 instead of 71 this time, the USGA having chosen to convert the second hole into a par four.

By contrast, consider what happened to many of the game's other top players. There was an 84 by Jim Furyk, 83s by Hal Sutton and Darren Clarke, an 82 by Greg Norman, 80s by Vijay Singh, Bernhard Langer, and Jesper Parnevik, and 79s by Phil Mickelson, Davis Love III, David Duval, and Colin Montgomerie.

Tiger's competition was so pathetic that somebody named Miguel Ángel Jiménez tied Ernie Els for second at 287.

It took some players all day to shoot an 83. John Daly did it in 15 minutes. He made a 14 at the 18th hole. It made Tiger's triple bogey on Saturday look like Gene Sarazen's double eagle at Augusta.

Only Tiger could have grinned at a triple. It happened at the third hole on Saturday when his drive took a bad hop and wound up in deep rough. His 7-iron carried inches shy of the green and buried itself in deeper rough. Worse. In a spot where he had to chop it out sideways. His first swing hardly moved the ball. His second just dribbled it. He chipped poorly and he two-putted.

But he grinned as he came off the green. What? He grinned at a triple?

"I knew it was the result of two bad breaks, that's all," he said. "It had nothing to do with how good I was playing."

At 24, Tiger has bagged his sixth major, putting him one step ahead of Jack Nicklaus at the same age. Tiger has one U.S. Open, one Masters, one PGA, and three U.S. Amateurs. Nicklaus at this stage had accumulated one Open, one Masters, one PGA, and two U.S. Amateurs.

You count the Amateurs after a guy wins a professional major. Intelligent historians do. Otherwise, Bobby Jones won only seven majors—and why would *that* make sense?

In Jack's defense, it must be said that he had to compete against the likes of Arnold Palmer, Gary Player, Lee Trevino, Tom Watson, Gene Littler, Johnny Miller, and Tom Weiskopf, among others.

Jack had dogfights. Right now, Tiger just has dogs.

80

BROKEN RECORD

Tiger by 8 at 2000 British Open at St. Andrews

TIGER WOODS did it again. This time at St. Andrews when he turned the 2000 British Open into a plate of mince, neeps, and tatties, with bubble and squeak on the side.

Oh, but heck, darn, he only won by eight strokes this time, as opposed to the 15 he won by at Pebble Beach last month. Nevertheless, his 269 total for the 72 holes was 19 under, and that's never been matched by anyone in any major.

One reason is that Tiger dropped only three shots to par all week as he fashioned rounds of 67, 66, 67, and 69, largely by avoiding every one of the Old Course's treacherous pot bunkers, which are everywhere and named after obscure Scots or their body parts.

Another reason is that he pays so much attention to details.

"I'm rolling my putts really well," he said during his dismantling of the oldest course.

Okay, but don't everybody's putts roll?

"Yeah," he said, "but I mean, mine really hug the ground."

Another reason is that he hit a shot in the first round that only he can hit. It came at the 17th hole, the Road Hole, the world's meanest par four.

Tiger pulled his drive into the vegetation left of the fairway. We're talking deep here. Knee-deep brush. What he did was slash an iron that lifted the ball out of the brush and moved it 160 yards to the front of the green. It was a swing so violent, he wound up on one leg and stumbling.

"A shot like that," Tiger explained, "you have to lay the face wide open and hold on tight and get your right hand into it as much as your left. It's not the lie that stops the clubhead, it's grass that stops the shaft."

Yet another reason is the second shot Tiger hit in Saturday's third round to the 581-yard 14th hole. He smacked a 3-wood with full force that he hoped would reach the green. It was only an instant after he swung that you knew he liked it.

You had to imagine that Steve Williams, his caddie, had said something to him on the order of "Show me that 290-yard draw of yours." And that was when Tiger, knowing he'd pured it, with the ball halfway there, knifing through the air, casually said to Steve:

"That the one you're talking about?"

Not cocky, just confident. The most talented and self-assured player in the game. At the tender age of 24, he's now completed the career Grand Slam of winning the British Open, U.S. Open, Masters, and PGA, joining Jack Nicklaus, Ben Hogan, Gary Player, and Gene Sarazen, the only others who had done it.

Furthermore, my wife says he even outdresses everyone.

81

TRIPLE PLAY

Tiger Wins 2000 PGA at Valhalla

THE GOLFER who is going to challenge Tiger Woods and keep him from owning all the oceans, mountains, and air we breathe, to say nothing of our tacos and fruit groves, is a kid only 10 years old that we haven't heard of yet. But he's been playing golf since he was two, he's been on the back tees since he was seven, he's already 6-3 and 195, he lives in Texas, California, or Florida, he hits balls on the range 16 hours a day, and he has bleeding lash marks on his back from his daddy punishing him with a bullwhip every time he shoots worse than 62 in practice.

Otherwise, until Tiger turns 35, or somewhere in there, and perhaps becomes bored with the game, he's basically going to be humming that song, "Show Me the Majors," which was first introduced to the charts by Ben Hogan.

This happens to be true because the lame and halt who are out there trying to compete with Tiger these days are becoming, with each passing day, lamer and more halted.

Most people were aware that when Tiger went to Valhalla in Louisville, Kentucky, in August for the 2000 PGA, the year's last major, he was mainly there to compete with Hogan, the only man ever to win a Triple Crown, or three professional majors in one year.

Hogan's were slightly different—the Masters, U.S. Open, and British Open in 1953—whereas Tiger has now captured the U.S. Open, British Open, and PGA. Back in April, Tiger made the mistake of not winning the Masters, primarily because of a triple bogey and a double bogey along the way, which left him in fifth place, six strokes back of Vijay Singh, who even flaunted a brief smile in victory.

One of the burning questions around Valhalla's media center during the week was, Why didn't Hogan seek the pro Grand Slam in '53 by going for the PGA after he won the other three?

It's a question most often asked by what has become a predominantly youthful membership in the sportswriting lodge—it seems at times as if their knowledge of golf history begins with the Nike swoosh.

I'll say this one more time. After the automobile accident in '49, Ben was never going to enter the PGA again. His legs wouldn't withstand the rigors of so many 36-hole matches. Also, the dates conflicted. The PGA that year at Birmingham Country Club near Detroit started on a Wednesday with the first of two qualifying rounds to decide the 64 contestants who would enter match play. This meant that the PGA final wasn't played until Tuesday the following week, which was the day before the first round of the British Open at Carnoustie.

As it happened, Ben was busy playing two qualifying rounds in Scotland while Walter Burkemo was marching through his match-play opponents at the PGA in Michigan. The Tuesday when Burkemo was winning the PGA final was the same Tuesday that Hogan was playing his second qualifying round at Carnoustie—and even Ben Hogan couldn't be in two different places at once on two sides of the Atlantic Ocean.

Ben wouldn't have and couldn't have. Got it now?

Tiger led for three rounds at Valhalla, but he had the misfortune of having to go out in the final round on a windless and rain-softened course and confront all kinds of lurkers who invited themselves to the party.

Lurkers with names like Greg Chalmers, Scott Dunlap, Stuart Appleby, Thomas Bjorn, Franklin Langham, J. P. Hayes, and Bob May.

When Bob May turned out to be one lurker too many and shot three straight 66s, Tiger was forced to call on all of his resources to prevent May, who resembles so many other nameless PGA champions, from becoming the Jack Fleck in his life.

Woods fell behind by two strokes through the first six holes of Sunday's final round, but then he was seven under over the last 12 holes, dropping pressure putts like no one had since Jack Nicklaus in his prime, just to wiggle into the playoff with the almost comatose Bob May.

Think about it. Tiger broke his third tournament record of the year in a major, but he had to scratch, claw, and dig for a tie at 72 holes to squeeze into the three-hole playoff. He eventually won it with a birdie at 16 and scrambling pars at the 17th and 18th after his tee shots went first to Lexington and then to Paducah.

The astonishing athlete prevailed, however, and now the only question is whether there will ever be a Jack Fleck in Tiger's future.

82

A SLAM BY ANY NAME

Tiger Slam at the 2001 Masters

WHEN LAST seen on Sunday night in the press emporium at the 2001 Masters, sportswriters from around the globe were feverishly hammering on their machines to come up with a suitable name for Tiger Woods's grand achievement of holding all four professional majors at the same time, even if it took another calendar year for him to do it.

Actually, I had been working on this all week, long before Tiger would prove his mastery again, and long before Phil Mickelson and David Duval would do their anticipated pratfalls on the Augusta National course to ensure Woods's victory.

Something that would go down in history with the Impregnable Quadrilateral, which some scribe labeled Bobby Jones's feat in 1930, when men were men and some were amateurs and they all played golf in shirts, neckties, and knickers.

My efforts resulted in:

Phi Granda Slamma.

Thai Slamma Granda.

The Tiger Slam.

Four for the Road.

The Mulligan Slam.

Personally, I leaned toward the Mulligan Slam, inasmuch as it took Tiger two years—last year and this year—to win the Masters and hang the green jacket in there with the U.S. Open, British Open, and PGA that he won in 2000.

But then I strained two muscles in my back and accidentally broke a leg off a chair to come up with the Woods Wins Quartet.

This is not to belittle what Tiger did. It ranks among the greatest accomplishments in golf. Not that it deserves to be put ahead of Jones's same-year Grand Slam, Ben Hogan's Triple Crown—and five out of six wins for the year—Byron Nelson's streak of 11 in a row, or Jack Nicklaus's 20 majors in a career spanning four decades. But it goes in there somewhere.

Tiger trailed by five shots after the opening round, when he shot a 70 while Chris DiMarco's 65 led. Tiger sculpted a 66 in the second round and pulled to within two of DiMarco. Then his 68 on Saturday gave him the lead by one over Mickelson, by two over DiMarco, and by three over Duval and Ernie Els.

Mickelson and Duval were the two who stayed with Tiger down the stretch, but they basically wound up bringing more heat on themselves than on Woods.

When Duval birdied five out of six holes from the fifth through the 10th, it looked as if he were Darth Biker the Tiger Killer, but just as suddenly he turned into David Duval again, flubbing up the 16th hole for a bogey and blowing short birdie putts on 17 and 18.

Mickelson, meanwhile, was still trying to overcome his previous mistakes. Such as the three- and four-footers he'd blown the day before, the 7-iron he'd put into the water at the 12th on Friday, and the flop shot he'd bungled from the front edge of the 14th on Saturday that cost him a double-bogey six, and finally the wild tee shots he fought with all day

Sunday that held him to a 70 instead of the lower round he desperately needed.

The thing about Phil is, even when he hits a good shot, the expression on his face seems to say, *I wonder where this one's going?*

Tiger sealed the deal with four consecutive clutch putts of eight and nine feet at the seventh, eighth, ninth, and 10th greens. And the flop shot *he* hit at the eighth showed Mickelson how it's supposed to be played. Tiger took a full swing at the ball with a lob wedge on a 25-yard shot that the rest of us can hit either three feet or 100 yards, and pulled it off as near to perfection as possible.

He played smart golf through the back nine and his drive on 18, the 72nd hole, said it all. Here was a guy with a one-stroke lead for the Masters, for the Woods Wins Quartet, and what does he do? He goes with the driver, the only club that could cost him dearly—that could send him into the trees on the right.

But he blistered it exactly 327 yards, around the corner of the dogleg and into the heart of the fairway, leaving himself a mere 78-yard pitch shot to the green.

Pure gravy that he holed the birdie putt to win by two over Duval and three over Mickelson. But it was back on the tee with the driver that Tiger let everybody know who was still the boss.

83

MAJOR SURPRISE

Retief Goosen Wins 2001 U.S. Open at Southern Hills

THE BIG news in Tulsa at the 2001 U.S. Open was that Tiger Woods lost a major championship—golf is dead.

This was shocking. But it may have been even more of a surprise that Tiger lost this Open at Southern Hills Country Club in more ways than a person can go to sleep trying to read Proust.

In other news, some guy won the U.S. Open in a playoff after one of the most shamefully grotesque Sunday finishes in history. The winner turned out to be a 27-year-old Retief Goosen of South Africa. He beat a 40-year-old Texan, Mark Brooks, 70 to 72 in the uneventful playoff.

Goosen had either led or been tied for the lead all the way, so the question continually came up: What was a Goosen?

Was it a member of the winged flock that was in the running for Oklahoma's state bird, an honor ultimately bestowed on the swallow-tailed flycatcher that became Southern Hills's logo for the 2001 championship, beating out a buffalo, a cowboy, and an oil derrick?

Was a Goosen one of those TV-advertised power tools that has so many uses? It cuts, it slices, it dislodges, it tightens—the Retief Goosen makes life easier around your home.

Was the Goosen a traditional holiday dinner in Johannesburg?

Actually, this Goosen was an unperturbed, mild-mannered fellow who shot a 66 in the first round and did it the hardest way possible. By shooting three under through seven holes on Thursday before play was halted at 3:15 by rain and lightning, then rising at 5 A.M. on Friday and shooting one more under for the next 11 holes.

Bad weather brought on the lightning incident. Goosen was 17 when he was struck by a bolt on a golf course, knocking him out of his shoes. It charred his clothing, melted his clubs, and left him with the loss of hearing in one ear. After that, maybe this Open didn't seem like much of a chore to him at all.

The comedy of the finish of regulation play started with Mark Brooks, the guy who made a clutch up-and-down birdie out of a bunker at Valhalla in the 1996 PGA to force the playoff he won over Kenny Perry. Brooks birdied the first playoff hole in Kentucky to win, and now he looked like a good bet on the 72nd hole in Oklahoma.

That was until he ran his 50-foot putt eight feet past the hole and the putt coming back hung on the right lip. This was Three-Jack No. 1.

Next came Stewart Cink and Retief Goosen, now the co-leaders after Brooks's bogey. Cink missed the green to the left, into the Bermuda rough. Goosen then looked golden after his 6-iron from 171 yards uphill stopped 10 feet from the flag.

Cink slashed his third shot 15 feet short, and figuring Goosen could do no worse than a two-putt par, he ran his own par putt 18 inches by. Tap it in, get out of Goosen's way. Oops. Cink jabbed his putt to the right and entered double-bogey world. Son of Three-Jack.

Maybe Goosen shouldn't have been watching all this. With two putts from 10 feet to win the U.S. Open, he promptly three-putted. Return of

Three-Jack. But he did make the last one to avoid becoming the first man who ever four-putted the last hole to lose a major.

As for Tiger Woods, the whole world knew he was after his fifth straight major, but apparently the Southern Hills layout knew it, too. It forced him to hit an endless variety of misbehaving wedge shots and short irons to the greens. He was either long, short, or wide right. Southern Hills did let him make numerous 10-footers for pars that kept him awake.

It's interesting about Southern Hills, a course with an assortment of doglegs going left and right. It continues to be a burial ground for the game's dominant player. It pulled Ben Hogan back into a tie for 10th in the '58 Open. It lured Jack Nicklaus back into a tie for 10th in the '77 Open. It wheeled Tom Watson back into a tie for ninth in the '82 PGA. And now it had dragged Tiger Woods back into a tie for 12th place.

The members must be swollen with pride.

84

GOLFING ROYALTY GOES PUBLIC

Tiger Wins 2002 U.S. Open at Bethpage State Park on Long Island

W E ALL know that Tiger Woods's main adversaries are Bobby Jones, Ben Hogan, and Jack Nicklaus, but there's a handful of guys who keep telling themselves they have a chance to duke it out with him, except they keep losing. This time in the 2002 U.S. Open it was wishful thinking again for two of them—for Phil *(I'm proud of myself)* Mickelson, and Spain's Sergio *(Mommie likes Tiger best)* Garcia.

For the first time, the U.S. Golf Association took the Open to a pure public course, to the rigorous layout of Bethpage Black in Bethpage State Park in Farmingdale, New York, one of four courses designed sometime after the fall of the Roman Empire by the celebrated architect A. W. Tillinghast, "Tillie the Terror," who had also given the game, most notably, Winged Foot in Westchester County, Baltusrol and Somerset Hills in New Jersey, San Francisco Golf, and Brook Hollow in Dallas.

Bethpage is in a part of Long Island that no tourist had ever seen. By my count it was at least four traffic jams from Manhattan, five from the Hamptons, and six from a view of the ocean.

The USGA obviously knew that nothing can daunt a New Yorker, that 42,500 paid spectators each day wouldn't mind going to Jones Beach and lining up to board shuttle buses that would slowly take them to Bethpage, where they might get a glimpse of Tiger. It would be easier than what they did in their everyday lives.

It was not only the largest crowd in Open history, it was the loudest, even though beer sales were shut off as the leaders made the turn each day. The fans also came out to sing "Happy Birthday" to Mickelson on Father's Day and to serenade the petulant Sergio after he flipped them off over something he considered an insult on Friday.

Bethpage's added attraction for the USGA is the immense real estate. The other four 18-hole golf courses (three of them Tillinghast's), a polo field and picnic grounds, had been sitting around for years waiting for corporate-hospitality tents. It's a known fact that the USGA loves corporate-hospitality tents as much as it loves the minimum 1.68 inches in diameter of the golf ball. Small wonder there'll be future Opens on Bethpage Black.

It's a strong course—only Tiger's 277 broke 280—but not a great course. It offers no memorable stretch of holes. Many of them look the same: a hole ringed by bunkers with old-timey round greens that look as if a squadron of flying saucers have glided in from another galaxy and gone splat. There's no out of bounds and only one water hazard, the small pond at the par-three eighth that would only terrorize your partner in the Member-Guest.

Bethpage Black did present length and narrow fairways and thick rough, and the Black's rough was rougher than normal. The ball loved to sink deep, out of sight.

Which brings up the shot of the championship—the lob wedge Tiger hit from behind the 17th green on Friday when he was working on a 68 to go with his opening 67.

He hit what he thought was a perfect 4-iron right of the flag, but it carried 210 instead of 207 and buried itself in the deep rough, visible only to an ant. Getting it out would be one thing. Stopping it would be another, for the cup was located close to the fringe and down a vivid slope.

Tiger dug the ball almost straight up with the lob wedge, landed it precisely on the fringe, from where it trickled lazily and amazingly down to the cup for a gimme par.

Now, folks, although Tiger was leading by two at the time, he was in double-bogey territory with that lie, and Ben Hogan at the top of his game would never have attempted that shot. Hogan would have made sure he got on the green, even 30 feet past the pin, and gladly taken his bogey.

But such is the artistry and confidence that Tiger brings to the game. Just another reason why the week was more or less his from start to finish. Phil and Sergio threatened off and on and hung with him for three rounds, as they did when Woods won the Masters with a certain amount of ease back in April, but at the finish it was the same old story.

So there's nothing left to do but let the Slam talk begin again.

85

DR. JEKYLL AND MR. ELS

Ernie Els Wins 2002 British Open at Muirfield

IGER WOODS, like Arnold Palmer and Jack Nicklaus before him, went to the British Open chasing a modern Grand Slam, but he saw it go fluttering away somewhere over Scotland like a wounded seagull. This was just as Arnold did in 1960 and Jack did in 1972. Meanwhile, scads of writers when last seen were pestering Ernie Els to let them coauthor a best-seller for him titled *Watch Out for Your Lap, a British Open Might Fall in It.*

The second bit of news from the 2002 championship at Muirfield, which is not terribly far from Edinburgh, is that the championship produced the first four-way tie—and resulting playoff—in the entire history of majors.

Els won in a battle with a Frenchman named Thomas Levet and two Australians, Steve Elkington and Stuart Appleby. The Aussies were eliminated in the first four holes of playoff regulation, then Els topped Levet on the first hole of sudden death with a remarkable bunker shot from an awkward stance followed by a nerve-testing five-foot putt for par.

Over the years, there'd been playoffs in majors involving three players. Harry Vardon had been in one, Byron Nelson had been in one, Ben Hogan had been in one, Arnold Palmer had been in two.

But never a foursome. They tied because Appleby shot a final-round 65 while Elkington and Levet shot 66s and Els scratched out a 70.

The victory gave Ernie his third major and was a reminder that he was once the top candidate to become what Tiger Woods is.

"It hasn't been easy," said the fellow they call the Big Easy because of his manner and his swing. "I've had a good career, but I've got a little Jekyll and Hyde in me, I guess."

An obvious reference to the times he's disappointed his fans, not to mention himself. Since winning the 1994 U.S. Open at Oakmont, Ernie had been second in four majors and third in two others while soothing his followers by taking his second U.S. Open in '97 at Congressional.

But back to the bigger news.

Woods came to Muirfield with the Masters and U.S. Open in his stash. He cruised past everyone at Augusta by three strokes, and he won by the same margin in our Open on Bethpage Black, an overpraised public course in Farmingdale, New York.

Tiger was riding high. He'd won six of the past nine majors, and the press had already given him the British Open. After his first two rounds of 70 and 68, it appeared that he was right on track to take it. He was only two back of people like Duffy Waldorf, Bob Tway, Padraig Harrington, and Shigeki Maruyama, and only one back of Søren Hansen and Des Smyth, whoever they were. Oh, yeah. Ernie Els was in there, too, but Tiger had handled Ernie every time it mattered.

So what was not to like?

The weather on Saturday, that's what.

What blew in was Agatha Christie weather. Rain, chill, wind, mist, and a gray gloom fell upon Muirfield, and Tiger got caught in the worst of it. The result was his disastrous 10-over 81, no doubt the highest round he'd shot since he was in diapers. What he did was have an I-surrender-get-me-outta-here-and-turn-up-the-thermostat round of golf.

His body language told you everything as he teed off on No. 1 in the whipping wind and freezing rain. It said: "Why are the elements doing this to me? Don't they know I'm Tiger Woods?"

So after starting out only two strokes away from the lead, Tiger wound up 11 strokes and 66 players behind with only 18 to play. It didn't matter that he would close with a superfluous 65 on Ideal Weather Sunday. He still finished six strokes back and tied for 28th place.

This was in contrast to Arnold Palmer's Slam effort at St. Andrews in '60, when he lost by one to Kel Nagle, and to Jack Nicklaus's Slam effort at this same Muirfield in '72, when he lost by one to Lee Trevino.

Tiger topped off his performance by refusing to come to the press center and be interviewed. Bad taste, but probably just as well. He might have been reminded that Ernie Els shot a 72 in the same weather.

86

THAT WONDERFUL YEAR

Ben Curtis Wins 2003 British Open at Sandwich

WELL, WHY shouldn't a man ranked 396th in the world, a complete unknown, a guy playing in his first major championship, on his first links course, fool around and win the 2003 British Open at Sandwich? It's a crazy year, right? Aren't we still wearing our "I Support Hootie" buttons that we bought at the Martha Burk protest in Augusta in April? Aren't we still wearing our "Go, Annika" buttons that we bought at Colonial in Fort Worth in May when she took on the guys?

Incidentally, which Ben Curtis was this? Ben Curtis, the world's fastest hurdler? Ben Curtis, the UCLA wide receiver? Ben Curtis, the wiley old coach at Vanderbilt?

None of the above. It was Ben Curtis, the 26-year-old PGA Tour rookie, a native of Ohio, who made it into the championship only because he'd tied for 13th in the Western Open—his best finish until now.

It was the Ben Curtis who played four over par on the last seven holes and sank an eight-foot putt for par on the 72nd hole that he didn't think mattered because his total of 283 wouldn't be good enough to win on this true links near the white cliffs of Dover where camouflaged Spitfires and steel-gray Messerschmitts once did their air shows in the skies. But it did matter, and in victory Ben Curtis was able to mutter, "Oh, my."

Curtis's score shouldn't have been good enough, but he got a lot of help along the way, especially from such challengers as Tiger Woods and Thomas Bjørn, a fuzzy-minded Dane. Bjørn was leading by three strokes when Curtis finished with his 69 and limped to the clubhouse, more than happy to be earning third- or fourth-place money.

Curtis had started the last round three behind Bjørn, the 54-hole leader, and two behind Davis Love III, who was in second place, and in a tie with Tiger Woods, Sergio Garcia, Vijay Singh, and Kenny Perry.

Of that group, which one would you have bet on to birdie six of the first 11 holes on Sunday? Not Ben Curtis, naturally. It wasn't until his game and reality finally caught up with him that he bogeyed the 12th, 14th, 15th, and 17th holes on the way to the house.

Tiger could say that he gave this British Open to Ben Curtis on the first hole Thursday, where his tee shot found the rough and was lost, costing him a triple bogey.

He must surely have been the first superstar to lose a golf ball in front of 10,000 people, some of whom were standing only a few feet from where the ball landed. A triple seven and yet he finished the championship just two back of Curtis.

But Thomas Bjørn was the solid loser. He left a shot in the bunker at the 17th hole on Thursday, angrily slammed his wedge into the sand, and absorbed a two-stroke penalty for an eight. Then, at the 16th on Sunday, with a two-shot lead, he took three to get out of another bunker—the ball kept hitting a knob on the green and rolling back down to his feet in the sand. A double-bogey five resulted. And he lost to Curtis by one.

It was a tragicomedy, to be sure, but someday Bjørn will be able to tell his grandchildren that he once saw more sand than Lawrence of Arabia.

87

AT LONG LAST

Phil Mickelson Wins 2004 Masters

KINDLY HOLD still for a moment, if you don't mind, while I try to do a Phil Mickelson thing and take six or seven sizes off of this typeface so I can get it down to 14 point and maybe birdie the first page of this piece on the 2004 Masters.

It shouldn't be any more difficult than Mickelson taking six or seven yards off that 146-yard wedge shot that gave him a tap-in birdie at the Augusta National's 14th hole on Masters Sunday—the shot of the day, probably of the tournament, unless you want to count Phil's 18-foot birdie putt that dropped on the 72nd green to beat Ernie Els by one.

Pause now while all of us scream: *A hundred-and-forty-six-yard wedge? Are you kidding?*

Feel better?

Speaking of things that dropped, there was a free drop Els received in Saturday's third round that kept him in the tournament and was, well, basically disgraceful. It saved him from a triple bogey.

He'd hooked his drive off the 11th tee, and it went so deep into the trees, you'd have had a hard time getting a photographer for *National*

Geographic to go in there. It was amazing that Ernie even found the ball. It was tucked in there among roots, twigs, leaves, sticks, rocks, and limbs.

But here came this rules official—and his name shall be withheld out of kindness to his family—to give Ernie a free drop from what he determined to be "ice storm debris." It looked like a lift out of Uganda and onto I-20 near Augusta, and it helped a very fortunate Els get out of the hole with a bogey five.

If Mickelson hadn't played so well on his way to a third straight 69 and his winning 279, it would have been The Drop That Won the Masters.

But Phil finally did it. Got his first professional major. It took him only 10 years, but maybe this made it more special.

All of us had been waiting, waiting—he had come out with so much talent and a huge amateur reputation. We watched him finish third behind Nick Price in the '94 PGA, fourth behind Corey Pavin in the '95 U.S. Open, third behind Nick Faldo in the '96 Masters, second to Payne Stewart in the '99 U.S. Open, third behind Tiger Woods in the '01 Masters, second to David Toms in the '01 PGA, third behind Tiger Woods in the '02 Masters, second to Tiger in the '02 U.S. Open, and third in the Masters last year, which was won by Mike Weir.

One of the nicest things about Mickelson's victory is that he's a guy who's loyal, unlike another star we know. Phil's caddie, Bones McKay, and his business manager, Steve Loy, go back more than a dozen years with him.

Phil is also accessible, unlike another star we know, plus he's talkative, interested in other sports, other aspects of life, and despite his fame and fortune, he's been working hard lately to improve his game, and he arrived a week early at Augusta this time, Hogan-style. It paid off.

Attention, Tiger lovers: In case you missed it, Tiger tied for 22nd, was never a factor, and lost his seventh major in a row. That's close to being called a slump.

88

IT SHOULDN'T HAPPEN TO A SPORTSWRITER

Todd Hamilton Wins 2004 British Open

FOR THREE days the 2004 British Open at Royal Troon on the chilly, windy west coast of Scotland had more strangers in it than a pot of haggis. Intruders like Thomas Levet, Skip Kendall, Barry Lane, and Todd Hamilton. It was almost saved at the end by Ernie Els and Phil Mickelson, but just like last year, when it wound up in the clutches of the indistinct Ben Curtis, the same thing happened again. This Hamilton person won.

The result of Todd Hamilton tying Els at 274 and both of them nudging Mickelson by a stroke, and then Hamilton upsetting Ernie by one shot in a four-hole playoff, was that those of us with a sense of history were given to picking ourselves up off the floor.

We were thrown—mentally, if not bodily—back into the Depression Thirties, when hamburgers were a nickel, movies were a dime, radio was TV without a picture, and another major championship, the U.S. Open, was stolen back-to-back by two woefully unfamiliar names, Sam Parks Jr. and Tony Manero.

Parks stunned the world by winning at Oakmont, and Manero

stunned the world by winning on the Upper Course at Baltusrol—and it's hardly any wonder that this was the only time the Upper Course was ever used.

Parks and Manero then. Curtis and Hamilton now.

You could say it's part of the charm of it all, or you could say it shouldn't happen to a sportswriter who's only trying to feed his family.

The first day was wholly forgettable as majors go. A man looked and searched and scraped around in the heather, peered into ditches, scanned the wind, and after meandering past the Frenchman and the Englishman who tied for the lead, a New Zealander, another Englishman, a Korean, a Swede, an Australian, one more Englishman, a Scot, a Fijian, another Swede, and one more Scot, there were the Americans.

One of the veterans in our lodge, Art Spander of the *Oakland Tribune*, adroitly typed, "First in war, first in peace, and 13th on the British Open scoreboard."

Friday was Skip Kendall Day. A creamy and crunchy guy who seems to have been on our tour for 4,000 years. Skip's big moment came when he was permitted to meet Prince Andrew, a known golf nut.

"I had never met anyone like that before," Kendall said. "He shook my hand and seemed like a good guy. I don't know . . . is he?"

Saturday was when Els and Mickelson plunged into the fray, but Hamilton, playing what he called "ugly golf," and evidently the only player in the field with a hybrid—basically a 1-iron with loft and a clubhead—shot a 67 to seize the lead.

It was basically his 40-foot chip/putt with this weird hybrid that enabled him to get up and down for the par he needed on the last playoff hole to beat Ernie Els, the Big Easy having never been easier.

For those who wish to play "ugly golf," the prediction here is that hybrids will immediately become a trend.

89

LAND RECLAIMED BY DRACULA

Pete Dye and 2004 PGA at Whistling Straits

PETE DYE came from behind to win the 2004 PGA Championship. That's my lead and I'm sticking to it.

Dye won it way up there in Try-to-Find-Me, Wisconsin—it's not even *close* to Milwaukee, folks—when Whistling Straits finally got the strong wind it needed off Lake Michigan on the last day of the championship. This made it possible for the course to do what Dye, the designer, and the Professional Golfers Association of America, and Herb Kohler, the owner, had hoped it would do, which was beat up on the world's best players.

Pete Dye has long been known as the Bela Lugosi of golf course architects, and Whistling Straits might have retired the trophy for him.

The basic fear is that the design will become a trend—like all those TPC courses did. There are rich guys everywhere, other Herb Kohlers, who may decide they want their own "links-style course," their own monument, built out of a forlorn hunk of real estate.

"Hey, Pete, do me one of those Whistling Straits. You know, with the dunes and the caverns and all that stuff, and if you need a lake, just say so, and we'll dig one for you."

But let's get something straight. Whistling Straits is not a links. A links is a course that happens to be located on land reclaimed from the sea. Whistling Straits is on land reclaimed from an antiaircraft range.

Flatland at that. Land on which something like 4,000 bulldozers moved something like 480 million tons of dirt and created Bela Lugosi's theme park of towering dunes, dotting bunkers, cavernous wastelands, and mammoth bent greens.

The result was an incredibly scenic layout that accommodates the following adjectives: magnificent, shocking, terrifying, infuriating, mystifying, stunning, and bewildering.

With no wind off Lake Michigan to protect it, however, it was a pushover on Thursday despite its length of 7,514 yards. It was kicked around by people like Darren Clarke, Luke Donald, Briny Baird, K. J. Choi, and Geoff Ogilvy. But Vijay Singh, Justin Leonard, Chris DiMarco, and Ernie Els were among them—the men who would ultimately decide things.

The course got a little tougher each day, and then on Sunday it got its licks in on everybody and showed the field what things would have been like if the wind had blown for four rounds. It dragged the winning score back to 280, which was the highest PGA total since Shoal Creek in 1990.

Moreover, it came up with Vijay Singh for the real winner, a man who not only failed to make a birdie over the final 18 but whose 76 was noteworthy for two reasons.

One, the 76 with which Singh luckily tied Justin Leonard and Chris DiMarco at 280 to get into the playoff was the highest score by a winner since the PGA switched from match play to stroke play in 1958. Two, it was the highest last round by the winner of any major since—whoa—1938.

It was that long since a chap named Reg Whitcombe shot a 78 as he survived the gales of Sandwich—a storm that blew down the exhibition tent—to win the British Open that year.

That 76 may or may not be an embarrassment for Vijay, who now has a third major to go with his 1998 PGA and 2000 Masters. You never know what Vijay's thinking, and you certainly never know what he's saying, since he never says anything—to the press, anyhow. He didn't even say anything after he won the three-hole playoff over Leonard and DiMarco with a birdie and two pars. So he did finally make a birdie on Whistling Straits.

Thus, at the conclusion Herb Kohler, the commode king, was a happy man. Pete Dye and Kohler's Whistling Straits were the big winners. The PGA Championship will return to this place, and most likely pretty often, even though the easiest way to get there is to be washed up on a remote shore of Lake Michigan.

90

THE PEOPLE'S CHOICE

Phil Mickelson Wins 2005 PGA at Baltusrol

T MUST be the PGA, the year's last major, if it's August and you can sit down and talk to the heat, or reach inside your shirt and grab handfuls of humidity. But what was different this time at familiar old Baltusrol in this summer of 2005 is that Phil Mickelson won the championship. Yeah, Phil. Of all people.

In case you've forgotten, Baltusrol is in Springfield, New Jersey. Baltusrol used to be only 45 minutes from Broadway, but that was back before every family had three cars. It's the place that has this enormous, spooky old clubhouse that would look more natural on the moors of Devon. It's a clubhouse that would make a mystery writer want to prowl around inside and look for a corpse behind every door.

The historic and celebrated Lower and Upper Courses at Baltusrol have a certain tree-lined, botanic charm, but they are arguably the most overrated works of A. W. Tillinghast, the legendary designer.

It's hard for a historian to forget that Baltusrol has given us Tony Manero, Ed Furgol, and Lee Janzen as U.S. Open winners. But at the same time, it's rather revered as the place where Jack Nicklaus won two of his four U.S. Opens, and now it can boast that Mickelson won his third major on the premises to go along with his 1990 U.S. Amateur and last year's Masters. So, okay, we'll let Baltusrol live.

Not only did Phil win, but he did it the hard way, and on Monday, an extra day, due to weather delays, and because he was up against so many strange and surprising contenders.

Making it even harder on Phil was that he did it without anything happening to him or for him—no chip-ins, no pitch-ins, no lucky bounces, no putts that were rapped off-line but veered into the cups. How unlike him. How unlike most winners, really.

Mickelson simply did it by steadily hitting good golf shots, not to overlook his sensational birdie on the last hole.

What an odd collection they were, these contenders who refused to go away until the final moments.

There was Davis Love III, a household name but one who hadn't won a tournament in two years. Davis somehow managed to remain a presence even though he kept hitting his ball off the golf course every chance he got.

There was Thomas Bjørn, the solemn man from Denmark who specializes in meltdowns. This one was more gradual. No resemblance to the three swings he took out of the bunker at Sandwich to hand the British Open to Ben Curtis two years ago. Or the 86 he shot in the European Open earlier this summer when he was the 54-hole leader but managed to make an 11 on the 71st hole.

There was Steve Elkington, the '95 PGA winner, who had pretty much done a vanishing act the past five years, although he did pop up as one of the thousands in the 2002 British Open playoff won by Ernie Els.

One could only assume Elkington had been devoting most of his time to finding the ugliest golf shirts on the planet. His most hideous frock at Baltusrol was the blue-and-white polka-dot job he wore on Sunday that he must have bought on eBay as an investment, believing it had once been worn by Joan Crawford.

Mickelson was either leading or tied for the lead after each round, which led to a few stressful moments and trouble sleeping, and when it came down to crisis time, he had to make a birdie four on the last hole to win.

That's the spot where he produced one of the best drives of his career under the circumstances—it gutted the fairway—and then lofted a 3-wood second shot that looked high and perfect but drifted slightly right and wound up in the rough beside the green.

But the dramatic chip/pitch out of the rough was a shot Phil knew well, and he played it exquisitely—to within two feet of the cup.

His finish with a nerve-biting round of 72 for the 276 that nailed Elkington and Bjørn by one stroke was set up by his opening-round 67 and his spectacular 65 in the second round—low score of the championship. It was those rounds that made it Phil's tournament to win or lose.

So what we now have on our hands is a confirmed superstar of the game, another one the game badly needs—three majors will do it for you—and besides that, the fans and the press both love Phil, even if some of the other players roll their eyes at his aw-shucks public routine.

Fine. Let them win majors too.

91

FULL BODY SLAM

Geoff Ogilvy Accepts 2006 U.S. Open at Winged Foot

BURY MY laptop at Wounded Foot. Sorry. Make that *Winged* Foot and put it next to Phil Mickelson. The 2006 U.S. Open was grim from start to finish, and Mickelson will be saying, "I am such an idiot," for months, if not years, to come, for giving away this Open with the worst driving exhibition since the Greyhound bus ran into Ben Hogan.

Phil had hit just two fairways in the last round at Winged Foot, and yet the Open was still his with three holes to play. He held a two-stroke lead, thanks largely to the unsightly riffraff that was loitering near the lead, a throng that looked as if they'd shopped for their apparel in the women's department at Labels for Less.

Over the last few holes so much dizzy stuff happened you wanted to shout, "Nobody gets this trophy—nobody!"

Jim Furyk, who'd won the 2003 Open at Olympia Fields in Chicago, had a four-foot putt for par on the 72nd green that would have put him into a playoff, but he blew it.

Padraig Harrington, the Irishman with a scary glare, missed by two after bogeying the last three holes—and tripling the 18th the day before.

At one point, the championship even seemed to belong to the much-maligned, long-suffering Colin Montgomerie, who is either Scottish or English, depending on which newspaper you read in Great Britain.

Colin stood in the 72nd fairway with a clear second shot to the green for a par four that, as it turned out, would have wrapped up the title. Yes. Majorless Monty. That guy. He'd kept hanging around and had astoundingly holed a thousand-yard birdie putt at the 71st hole.

So . . . cue the bagpipes for Monty.

Oops. Kill the bagpipes.

Monty's approach shot went wide right into the rough, not far from the Greg Norman Pavilion, where the Shark put a shot in the '84 Open. It buried in the high grass and the double bogey left Montgomerie one shot short of glory.

"You wonder sometimes why you put yourself through this," Colin said after his fifth runner-up finish in the majors—three of them in Opens.

In the meantime, this thin Geoff Ogilvy person holed out a chip on the 71st for a par. So Ogilvy, 29, with only two PGA Tour wins to recommend him, was only one back of Phil.

Ogilvy then made an All-Australian up-and-down from 20 yards short of the 72nd green to reach the clubhouse with a 72 and what appeared to be good enough for second place, a five-over 285, on tough old Winged Foot.

Now back to Phil. After a bogey at the 70th and an All-American par at the 71st out of a trash bag, we find him on the tee at the 72nd, ready to be only the third pro in history to win three majors in a row, joining Hogan and Tiger Woods on that short list. You had to remember that Phil had won the PGA last August and the Masters last April.

But what have we here? Phil has the driver in his hands. Oh, boy. The same club that's been torturing him all day. He'd been going both ways with it early, hooks first, slices later. Why not a 4-wood or even a long iron?

Something he can steer-job into the fairway?

Hogan-thinking would be in order here. Phil should cinch no worse than a bogey for a tie, but still have a chance at the win. Don't all the pros today—even Phil—have a go-to club in the bag when they need to find the fairway?

Guess not.

Mickelson's tee shot with the ill-chosen driver was a horrible slice off the so-called Champions Pavilion into tromped-down grass. And unluckily it was directly behind a big tree. He had a shot, but it required a huge slice. Phil knew the situation: par to win, bogey to tie. And which guy would you have liked in an 18-hole playoff, Phil Mickelson or What's-His-Name Ogilvy?

But the "over-cut" was Phil's only dead-on shot of the day, striking the tree and going, oh, let's see, what do you think, 25 yards?

Then came an 8-iron into a fried-egg lie in the front-left bunker, a blast across the sloping green into more rough, a chip, and a putt. A double-bogey six for a pitiful 74 to lose by a stroke.

For Mickelson rooters, it was an incomparable catastrophe, but not for historians. Losing in surprising ways has happened to others of note—Arnold Palmer and Jack Nicklaus, to name two.

Arnold did it twice. First at the '61 Masters, when he doubled the last hole to let Gary Player in the door, and again in the '66 Open at Olympic, when he squandered a seven-shot lead over the last nine holes and eventually let Billy Casper in the door.

Nicklaus did it twice. The last day of the '71 Masters was where Jack played 13 and 15, the birdie holes, three over par and let Charles Coody slide into the green jacket. And it was at the U.S. Open on Medinah in '75 that Nicklaus stood on the 70th tee trailing by a stroke, only to bogey the final three holes. Three pars would have beaten Lou Graham and John Mahaffey, and two pars would have tied them.

"It was pretty surreal," Ogilvy said of Mickelson's calamity.

Rick Smith, Phil's swing guru, said it better.

"It was like getting hit by a lightning bolt," he said.

Classy guy that Phil is, he stuck around for interviews, forced some smiles, signed autographs, and remembered to go back into the locker room and increase his tip to the staff.

Meanwhile, if you're wondering what happened to Tiger Woods, the old commodore was hoping to become the first player to win a major while staying on board his ship.

That would be his 155-foot yacht that has the insulting name of *Privacy*. It was anchored in Long Island Sound, not too far from Winged Foot. But after a nine-week layoff, Tiger missed his first 36-hole cut since he became a pro, even though he turned a couple of 82s into a couple of 76s. His cut streak ended at 39.

Tiger simply wasn't ready, and he picked the wrong week, the wrong course, and possibly the wrong lodging not to be ready.

92

NOW YOU'RE COOKING

Tiger Wins 2007 PGA at Southern Hills

THE ONLY rock star in golf did the sport a welcome service when he cooked the field of the 2007 PGA Championship worse than the August heat in Tulsa. They all could have passed for a chicken fried steak.

When Tiger Woods tenderized Southern Hills in the second round with that seven-under-par 63, he left the game's pretenders with nothing to do but wipe the gravy stains off their shirts.

He did tease them a little bit on Sunday, but Tiger's not the kind of guy who's going to wilt. Not against somebody like Woody Austin, anyway. He closed with a 69 and won by two.

Tiger is the third rock star golf has known in the modern era, since the game exploded in popularity on TV and got helped along by the steroid golf ball, the nuclear shaft, and the Abrams tank for a clubhead.

Arnold Palmer was the first one, then came Jack Nicklaus, and now there's Tiger. And just in time, for without him these days the sport might have all the relevance of slalom kayaking.

Other fascinating guys have populated the game and seized the occasional spotlight. Engaging personalities like Lee Trevino, Gary Player, Tom Watson, Greg Norman. But they weren't full-fledged rock stars.

A full-fledged rock star in golf is the consistent ticket-seller, the crowd-pleaser, the purse-increaser, and the dwarfer of all human beings around him. A presence like no other.

Tiger saved the year with the excitement he created at Southern Hills, dogleg capital of the universe. This course may have started late in life, but it was holding its seventh major championship—three U.S. Opens and three PGAs had taken place previously, all of them in ovens like this one.

Woods reclaimed the year from Masters winner Zach Johnson, who might or might not have been channeling Jack Fleck; from Angel Cabrera, the Argentine anti-guru, who struck a blow for self-taught golfers when he won the U.S. Open at Oakmont; and from Padraig Harrington, the Irishman who overcame his Van de Velde moment at Carnoustie to win the British Open in a four-hole playoff with Sergio Garcia.

Tiger's 63 on Friday, the lowest round he's shot in a major, sent TV announcers and a majority of the press-center poets into various states of hysteria and awe, but a few things need to be said about it.

First of all, it might not have been his finest ball-striking round in a major. He mostly did it at Southern Hills with his putter, aside from the fact that he birdied three par-fours after hitting 4- and 5-irons off the tee. Some of us are partial to the 65 he fashioned last year at Hoylake, or his 66 at St. Andrews in 2000.

Second of all, Raymond Floyd once shot a 63 at Southern Hills in the opening round of the 1982 PGA, which Floyd went on to win, and Raymond did it with persimmon and a golf ball that wasn't juiced.

Finally, a 63 is *not* the lowest round in a major, despite what you might have been told on TV. That still belongs to Ben Hogan, who shot a 62—a mere 10-under-par round—on the second day of the 1942 "wartime" U.S. Open at Ridgemoor Country Club in Chicago.

We Hoganistas devotedly count it, and so, I might add, did Ben.

After this PGA was over, we did find out what Woody Austin thought about Tiger's 63.

"I went over his round and over my round, and I outplayed him tee to green," said the incomprehensible, 43-year-old Austin. "I outplayed him, but he beat me seven shots. Does that mean he's that much better than me? I don't get it."

Woody was living proof that four days of 100-degree heat can play with your mind.

The anxious moments on Sunday were provided first by Ernie Els, who fired a 66, a round that could have been lower if he hadn't missed two short birdie putts and bogeyed two other holes.

Then there was Austin. He refused to disappear like Woody Austins normally do, but he also cut into Tiger's five-shot lead, trimming it down to one. His name did have that Rich Beem–Wayne Grady–Shaun Micheel–PGA winner ring to it.

But Tiger showed what he can do when he's pushed. He rammed home a 15-foot birdie putt at the 15th and followed that by launching a massive and dead-straight drive on the 507-yard 16th—a par four, no less—that propelled him to an easy par on the toughest hole.

Tiger did something else by winning at Southern Hills. Heretofore, in all those other majors, it had been an unwelcome layout for the game's dominant player. Hogan, Nicklaus, Watson, Tiger—they'd never done well at Southern Hills. Okay, that's behind us now.

Theories abound as to why Southern Hills could have given us Woody Austin instead of Tiger Woods. August is a furnace, the top pros are tired of grinding, the last major is a letdown, and only the unknowns, the run-of-the-mill players, have something to prove.

What continually saves the PGA, however, are the precious few immortals who have the built-in factors of greed and arrogance going for them and only have to show up to remind the others that they are purely set decoration. Tiger at Southern Hills was the latest example.

Rock star onstage. Everybody take a seat.

93

IMMELMAN'S TURN

Trevor Immelman Wins 2008 Masters

EVERY SHERPA in Nepal knew Tiger Woods was going to win the Grand Slam in 2008, starting with the Masters. Waiters in Budapest and Prague knew it. People still locked in caucuses knew it. Superdelegates. Fry cooks in Waffle Houses. Certainly every sportswriter and blogger in North America had been giving it to him for months. Tiger said so himself: "Easily within reach." So you can only imagine the looks of shock on all those faces when the green jacket wound up on a guy named Immelman.

No, not that Immelman. Not a descendant of Max Immelman, the German ace who invented the Immelman Turn in a biplane—think of a flop shot that flies back at you. He is actually Trevor Immelman, a South African with a sweet swing and some grit. He got a little help from Tiger's out-of-sync game and a cluster of uncertified contenders. They took more lumps than the leader did on a long, windy, lengthened, and toughed-up course that provided the challenges a major is supposed to provide.

Tiger finished runner-up in a major for the fifth time, putting him

14 behind Jack Nicklaus in that department, and he remains stuck on 13 victories in professional majors, five behind Jack.

The world was surely aware that for all of Tiger's wins in the majors, he had yet to come from behind after 54 holes to capture one of them. If it's true that Woods is really playing against Nicklaus, Ben Hogan, and Bobby Jones, then this seems like an opportune time to point out that in winning their bundles of majors, Nicklaus came from behind eight times, and Hogan and Jones did it three times each.

Was this Masters going to be the time Tiger would finally do it? Could he catch and pass not only Immelman but young Brandt Snedeker, whose Vanderbilt degree hadn't helped him find a barbershop; Steve Flesch, who achieves recognition by playing left-handed; and Paul Casey, who'd been hitting golf shots but putting with an anvil? The Masters appeared to be set up for Sunday's traditional chaos.

The day presented a strong and puzzling wind—a glimmer of Ken Venturi wind, if you will, 1956 vintage—and there has rarely been a more amusing day of chaos.

While Tiger was uncharacteristically gunching short putts and would wind up with an even-par 72, three of the lurkers he had to catch went almost as far south as Mobile. Casey banged around with 79, Flesch clobbered himself with 78, and Snedeker wobbled home with 77.

But there was one lurker too many. Immelman. Trevor put a water lock on 11, 12, 13, and 15 while protecting his lead, and was able to afford dunking a ball into 16 and taking a double. It didn't matter in the end that his closing 75 tied for the highest last round for a Masters winner since Arnold Palmer back in 1962.

Immelman said of his day of tremors, "It was the ultimate roller-coaster ride—and I hate roller coasters."

Remember the roars for birdies and eagles at Augusta? They were so noticeably missing this time that one former winner called the place "a morgue." The fans had to give it up for pars, like Tiger's circus act at the 18th hole on Friday.

From the tee he put himself in a prison of pines on the right. One option was to play out backward into the fairway and have 200 yards to the green. This was what Ben Hogan would have done. Take the bogey, be happy. Of course, Hogan would never have driven into the pines in the first place.

But Tiger had, and now he saw another option. An opening about one foot wide into the 10th fairway. The 10th fairway? Was he kidding? Not at all. He punched out there and left himself with a blind, uphill pitch shot of about 80 yards to a tight pin.

All he did was hit it perfectly, land it perfectly, from where it dribbled down to within six feet of the cup after bumping into Stuart Appleby's ball, which was already on the green. The putt might as well have been a gimme. It was a throat deal.

In this department's memory, Tiger's miracle four ranks up there with a par five that Nicklaus made at Firestone's 625-yard 16th hole in the '75 PGA. Jack drove wildly into a creek, took a penalty drop, smashed a 260-yard 6-iron across the course to place himself behind the tallest trees in Ohio, somehow got a 9-iron up and onto the green, and holed a 30-foot putt.

Immortals have a way of doing these things at times.

Now we are left to think about what's going on in this era. Consider that although Tiger played like dogmeat at Augusta, he still finished second. What does that say about his competition?

The fact is that when Tiger Woods doesn't win a major—and on other occasions when Phil Mickelson, the game's other glamour guy, doesn't— what the game gets is Paul Lawrie, Ben Curtis, Todd Hamilton, Shaun Micheel, Rich Beem, Zach Johnson, Michael Campbell, Angel Cabrera, Mike Weir, and say hello to Trevor Immelman.

It's strictly up to future years to determine whether all these guys will be one-timers, which is to say trivia answers, or something more important in the history books.

Well, up to the future and maybe Tiger Woods.

94

TIGER WOODS AND THE KNEE-JERK OPEN

Tiger Beats Rocco at 2008 U.S. Open at Torrey Pines

I**T'S NOT** easy to write about the 2008 U.S. Open with this bad knee.

Not that it hurts as bad as Tiger Woods's knee. I didn't have a head-on with a Greyhound bus like he did, but that's only according to most of the sportswriters out here at Torrey Pines.

I only twisted mine trying to get from Microsoft Word to aol.com, and Internet Explorer kept laughing at me.

In actual fact, Tiger was playing hurt two months after having arthroscopic surgery on his left knee. He limped so often after hitting poor shots that it will probably encourage a lot of recreational golfers to hire a friend of Tonya Harding to whack them across the knee with a pipe.

How to Break 100 with a Busted Knee. New instruction book.

Of course, every golfer on the planet now has a better chance of winning a tournament the rest of this year than Tiger does. After going 91 holes to outlast Rocco Mediate, who was trying to be the Jack Fleck in Tiger's life, and win his third U.S. Open at Torrey Pines, he announced he was going to "shut it down" for the remainder of 2008.

Woods had played in this Open with two stress fractures in his leg and whatever pain that remained from a 10-month-old operation on his anterior cruciate ligament. Never mind that he'd won three tournaments and finished second in the Masters since then.

Wincing, grimacing, retching became the three favorite words of sportswriters covering the Open. They made it sound like Tiger was wincing, grimacing, and retching on every shot when, in fact, he hardly ever winced, grimaced, or retched when he sank monstrous eagle putts, or 20-foot par putts, or now and then located the fairway with his driver, or did that imitation of Mick Jagger on the 72nd green after he holed the bumpy 12-foot putt that got him into the playoff.

However, he did wince, grimace, and retch when he three-putted four times, bladed chip shots, flubbed sand shots, drove hideously, and made four double bogeys.

When was the last time somebody made four double bogeys and still won a U.S. Open? I'll tell you. It was Bobby Jones at Winged Foot in 1929. Counting the playoff, Jones made five double bogeys and two triple bogeys in that championship, which, if you're scoring, was considerably worse.

But not to make too light of Tiger's limp. He was obviously tweaked with pain on occasion, and, all in all, it was a gallant performance.

Tiger might never win a tougher major. Now, at the age of 32 in his pursuit of Jack Nicklaus's record (18 or 20, depending on how you count), he's closing in on Jack. He has 14 professional majors, and 17 if you include the U.S. Amateurs. But the knee thing is an obvious concern. So is the long layoff until he returns to competition. Will something be lost that can never be regained? Have we seen the best of Tiger Woods?

Open playoffs used to be epic. They involved most of the greats of the game and they were exciting. But over the last 25 years they've tended to be dogs. There hadn't been a good one since Lee Trevino and

Jack Nicklaus in 1971 at Merion. Then along came unlikely Torrey Pines, and it gave us grand theater as well as the proper winner.

Woods actually missed a chance to achieve further fame in his play-off with Rocco, which Tiger led by three after 10 holes, suddenly fell behind by one after 15, and then extended it to a 91st hole with a birdie at 18.

Most of the greatest players in the game lost an Open playoff somewhere along the way: Harry Vardon, Bobby Jones (twice), Ben Hogan, Byron Nelson, Sam Snead, Arnold Palmer (three times), and Jack Nicklaus.

Tiger certainly gave himself a chance to join the list against Rocco, who for much of the day was the most popular 45-year-old journeyman with a bad back that golf has known in a while.

"I'm sure I scared him," Rocco said, and he was right. Tiger, on one leg or both, kept clawing for pars, saved by his putter. But that was nothing new. He's been making crucial putts for 15 years—and one reason is because he's the best reader of greens, ever.

In one comeback stretch, Rocco birdied the 13th, 14th, and 15th holes to take the lead. At 15, he did a Tiger thing. He sank a 35-foot putt that broke three feet.

But Rocco couldn't close the deal. He missed an 18-foot putt on the last green that would have won it, and with the 18-hole playoff (they each shot 71) now sudden death, Mediate drove into a terrible lie in a fairway bunker, while Tiger no-limped a huge tee shot into the heart of the fairway. That was pretty much it. Par for Tiger, bogey for Rocco, and Tiger had won another major, one that he said "might be the sweetest of all."

It was in pretty sweet surroundings, by the way. The ocean-bordered southern part of California has always been a place of Hollywood make-believe, casual opulence, suntans, and jewelry. As S. J. Perelman once said, it's the place that gave us the shirt worn outside the pants. So it was time the Open came to the area of sprawling San Diego, where the residents of La Jolla and Rancho Santa Fe have a notion that anyone who earns less than half a million a year probably qualifies for food stamps.

The big surprise was that Torrey Pines, a public course in a State Preserve located on cliffs above the Pacific, presented such a stern challenge for this Open. With too many pros calling it "very fair," it was expected that the layout would be sliced up like barbecue brisket.

That it didn't is something of a tribute to Mike Davis, who took over as the USGA's course preparer two years ago. He's the guy who took the players back to five-over 285 at Winged Foot and Oakmont. He's also the guy who knew the gnarly Kikuya grass bordering Torrey's fairways, the uneven, Poa-infested green speed, and his mixing up of the tee boxes would take their tolls even though the course never played at its advertised length of 7,643 yards. That's how Davis held the winning total to one-under 283.

The USGA quickly decided that Torrey Pines is a keeper for future Opens. The 400 million spectators that poured onto the premises every day had something to do with it. The organization made so much money out of the week—start the guessing at 50 million—it might allow one USGA officer's family to live in a home in Rancho Santa Fe for a whole year, depending on the upkeep and the size of the garage.

In this lush environment, the USGA knew how to entertain the crowds. It offered up a glamour pairing in the first two rounds—Tiger Woods, Phil Mickelson, and Adam Scott.

Tiger the Magnificent Magician, Phil the Deep Thinker (he took the driver out of his bag and carried five wedges), and Scott, the young and single "Babe Magnet," as he has been labeled by Larry Dorman of the *New York Times*.

But then the most interesting incident on Friday had nothing to do with golf being played by the glamour threesome. Tony Navarro, Adam

Scott's caddie, got into it with an unruly fan at the ninth tee. It was thought that the overserved fan lobbed an ethnic slur of some sort. The caddie suggested they meet at the bottom of the hill. They did, and observers declared Tony Navarro the winner on points.

Unfortunately, the seven-year-old son of the unruly fan was in the gallery, as was the unruly fan's own father, who was also apprehended after Adam Scott leaped about hollering, "Security!"

In the end, it struck those of us who appreciate dark humor that the little kid, seeing his dad and granddad being led away by gentlemen in uniforms, would in future years have a fond remembrance of something that occurred within 48 hours of Father's Day, 2008.

There's no doubt that Saturday at Torrey Pines was the most surreal and thrilling day of a U.S. Open since the Open used to end on Saturdays.

Tiger made two eagles—with 66- and 45-foot putts—and holed out for a birdie from the greenside rough, all in the last six holes. It was jaw-dropping stuff.

But Phil provided something more amusing with the way he ended his chances on the par-five 13th hole. That day he put the driver back in the bag and removed one wedge. Which could have been the one he needed to pitch the ball onto the green in less than four tries on his way to a quadruple nine.

Up the ball would go to the front of the green, and back down to Mickelson's feet in the hollow it would roll. Once. Twice. Three times. It brought to mind the lament of Seve Ballesteros four-putting that time: "I miss, I miss, I miss . . . I make."

It also begged the question of whether Phil's head needed more rehabilitating than Tiger's knee.

Speaking of which, Tiger in his post-playoff press conference had a word for all of the sportswriters who'd worn out their laptop keys on wincing, grimacing, retching. It was when someone asked him if he thought his performance ranked up there with Ben Hogan's comeback at Merion in 1950.

With a look, Tiger said, "Hogan didn't know if he was even going to *walk* again, much less play golf."

Couldn't have said it better myself.

EPILOGUE

ONE WAY TO look at it is that six decades of covering majors and hanging out with the game's elite is a lot of air travel, typing, and late-night bar food. But I wouldn't trade any of it, especially all the quaint moments that never made print.

I suppose earning Ben Hogan's friendship, cooperation, and, to some degree, his respect has been the greatest treasure of this journey. Obviously, it didn't hurt anything in the 1950s in Fort Worth that I was the local writer covering most of his big stuff, and a decent enough golfer not to be too embarrassed in all the rounds I played with him at Colonial.

Ben was a mythological figure even then, and believe me, I was grateful for the privilege of knowing him, appreciative of the access to him, and quite aware of my good luck at being in that place at that time.

A true story. After a round with Hogan at Colonial in the spring of 1956, I was sitting in the grill room with Ben and Marvin Leonard, his best friend. Leonard was the man who built Colonial, helped bring the 1941 U.S. Open to town, introduced the first bent greens to the South-west, and started the annual Colonial event in 1946 that's still a part of the PGA Tour.

I hadn't thought much of the golf that afternoon. Ben had shot his usual 67. I had shot my usual 75. But suddenly I found Hogan staring at me and saying, "You have length, you see, and you can *putt.* Nobody can teach that . . . but the rest of your game can use some improvement."

I nodded, shrugged. It was no news to me that the rest of my game was pure guesswork.

A moment later, I was stunned to hear him say, "If you'll work with me three or four days a week for the next three months . . . do everything I tell you to do . . . I think we can develop your game to where you can compete in the National Amateur."

Flattery will usually get you everywhere with me, but I could only be honest with him. I smiled and said, "Thanks, Ben, but I just play golf for fun, you know . . . and sometimes a $2 Nassau. All I've ever wanted to be is a sportswriter."

Hogan looked at me like I'd stabbed him in the heart. How could anyone in his right mind turn down an offer like that? I had no idea what to expect from him. Finally, he said:

"Well. Keep working at it."

•

BYRON NELSON WAS as lovely a gentleman and as great a champion as ever played the game. He was much help to me over the years, allowing his brain to be picked.

Watching him play at his peak is still a vivid memory, although I was yet to emerge from high school at the time. I don't believe anyone ever hit the ball as consistently close to the pins as Byron did—with whatever iron might be in his hands.

I always looked forward to the pleasure of spending time with him at the majors, forcing him back into the old days. One morning at Augusta he said, "You know, it's a funny thing, but Ben and Sam, two of the greatest players in the world, never could beat me. I don't know why that was, or how it worked out that way. It was just the funniest thing."

That sent me scurrying to the record books. And sure enough . . .

Byron did indeed beat Ben Hogan the three times they went head-to-head. First, in a playoff for the Texas Open in 1940 at Brackenridge Park in San Antonio, 70 to 71. Second, by 3 and 1 in a quarterfinal match of the PGA at Cherry Hills in Denver. Last, by 69 to 70 in their epic playoff for the Masters in 1942.

Nelson also held an edge of 18 to 9 in victories over Hogan in tournaments in which they both competed between 1940, when Ben was becoming Ben, and 1946, when Nelson retired.

Where Snead was concerned, Byron beat Sam one-up in the finals of the 1940 PGA at Hershey Country Club, and again in a 36-hole playoff for the Charlotte Open (69–69 to 69–73) in 1945.

Moreover, Byron won 28 tournaments to Sam's 18 at stops where they both competed between 1937 and 1946.

It was just the funniest thing.

●

FELLOW TEXANS HAVE always been reliable for quotes, even if the remarks were unprintable at times. Jimmy Demaret was top banana.

Demaret once said to Lloyd Mangrum, who was wounded in the Battle of the Bulge and came home with two Purple Hearts, "Man, I'm tired of reading about 'Purple Heart Veteran Lloyd Mangrum' in the newspapers. I know how you got one of your Purple Hearts, Lloyd. You stepped on a broken beer bottle running out of a Paris whorehouse."

Demaret went into the Navy in '43 as an apprentice seaman, and many other pros were in uniform during World War II. Among them:

Capt. Jay Hebert, a Marine who hit the beach at Iwo Jima, Lt. Ben Hogan, Lt. Horton Smith, Lt. j. g. Lawson Little, Sgt. E. J. (Dutch) Harrison, Sgt. Vic Ghezzi, Sgt. Clayton Heafner, Sgt. Jimmy Turnesa, Sgt. Skip Alexander, Cpl. Paul Runyan, Pvt. Chick Harbert, and Pvt. Thomas Henry Bolt.

Jimmy liked to joke that his effort did more to win the war than Mangrum's or Hebert's or anyone else's. It ranked up there with the patriotic slogan "Remember Pearl Harbor."

Demaret's primary duty in the Navy was to play golf with the brass, and his major contribution to the war effort was a statement he said he frequently uttered in the line of duty:

"That'll play, Admiral."

•

MY CLOSE PAL Dave Marr was runner-up to Demaret for quick wit.

The night before the final round of the '72 U.S. Open at Pebble Beach, we were having dinner together in the Lodge with our wives.

My mind was trying to prepare for the story I'd have to write the next evening. Jack Nicklaus was leading by one after 54 holes. I was always prepared for a Nicklaus victory, and I was even prepared for all of the serious contenders who were within striking distance, except for one—the Australian Bruce Crampton. He was only a shot behind Jack.

I knew Crampton wasn't the most popular guy on the tour with the other players or the press. He wasn't very friendly. But that's about all I knew. So I asked Dave if he could think of the three worst things Bruce had ever done, that Marr was aware of. Maybe I could work it into the piece if Crampton won the Open.

Dave only took a second to reply. He said:

"Got born . . . came to America . . . stayed."

•

IF I HAVE a favorite deadline moment, it's the one at the U.S. Open in '75 at hot, muggy, miserable Medinah.

Lou Graham had finally won it in an 18-hole playoff over John Mahaffey on Monday—a playoff that may not have been dull to them but was utterly boring to the rest of us—and I was pounding away on the manual Olivetti in the hot, muggy press tent.

My employer at the time, *Sports Illustrated*, was holding the issue open for my story, and I'd been told that if it wasn't filed by 2 o'clock that afternoon, it was going to cost the magazine 700 million dollars a minute, or something like that.

It wasn't my money, of course, but I was a team player, so there I was floorboarding the old Olivetti when I felt a tap on my shoulder.

"What, *what?*" I said, more like a snarl, turning around to see who'd interrupted me. It was this pretty blond chick, Patsy Graham. Lou Graham's wife. And in a soft Southern drawl, she said:

"Be nice, Dan. He's really a good guy."

•

OKAY, I'M NOT getting out of here without picking my All-Time All-Star Golf Team. It's based on experience and observations over the years, the probing of history, and is probably not without prejudice.

Here goes, with the backups in parentheses:

Driver: Ben Hogan (Jack Nicklaus)

Fairway Woods: Gene Sarazen (Sam Snead)

Long Irons: Jack Nicklaus (Byron Nelson)

Middle Irons: Jimmy Demaret (Tommy Bolt)

Short Irons: Byron Nelson (Johnny Miller)

Pitching: Ben Hogan (Sam Snead)

Chipping: Lee Trevino (Raymond Floyd)

Sand: Gary Player (Julius Boros)

Putting: Tiger Woods (Ben Crenshaw)

Trouble: Tiger Woods (Seve Ballesteros)

Swing: Sam Snead (Ben Hogan)

Charisma: Arnold Palmer (Bobby Jones)

Interview: Jack Nicklaus (Nobody else even close)

Let's see if I can defend my team.

You want a man to put a drive in the fairway for your *life*? It has to be Hogan. Who ever hit more fairways? Nicklaus was the first player to be long *and* straight—on those occasions when he was long and straight.

Tee ball in fairway. That's mainly how Hogan and Nicklaus won all those U.S. Opens.

Hard to go up against Sarazen's double eagle at Augusta with the 4-wood, the shot that made the Masters. Sarazen hit a few other good ones along the way or he wouldn't have won six other majors.

Snead in his best years between 1937 and 1954 tried to hit more par fives in two—and did—than anybody else in the game. Sam was fairly adept with the spoon.

Nicklaus with the long irons is a no-brainer. Jack was the first guy to get them up and keep them on the greens. Byron Nelson in the thirties and forties was recognized as the game's finest with the long irons.

With the 4-, 5-, and 6-iron Demaret was automatic to get it on the green. His go-to clubs. "I won three Masters with the 5-iron," he said.

Hard to recall anybody ever knocking down more flags than Byron with the short irons. Miller came close. So did Lanny Wadkins.

Hogan usually laid up at the par fives but still birdied. He owned the pitching wedge. Snead was murder on the short par fours.

Trevino's chipping won him a famous British Open and a few other titles. It was a strong part of Floyd's game as well as Bob Rosburg's.

Gary Player at his peak was a magician in the sand. Boros won two of his three majors out of the sand.

Nobody has ever made more incredible putts than Tiger, and nobody has ever read greens better. He heads a list of brilliant putters—Crenshaw, Billy Casper, Jackie Burke Jr., Dave Stockton.

When he wasn't holing crucial putts for 15 years, Tiger was getting himself out of trouble with creative shots like no other. Ballesteros in his prime was stunning. The press didn't label Seve "the car park champion" for nothing.

Snead had the most beautiful natural swing God ever gave a human. Hogan's was the finest manufactured swing, stemming from years of hard work, experimentation, and practice.

If Arnold Palmer didn't have charisma in his day, the purses on the PGA Tour wouldn't be what they are today. Bobby Jones obviously popularized golf in the twenties, not just by winning but by being handsome, intelligent, and charming along with it.

Jack Nicklaus remains the most interesting, cooperative, and informative athlete I've ever interviewed in any sport, ever.

Maybe he knew that all I ever wanted to be was a sportswriter.

APPENDIX

THE TOP TENS

THE 1951 U.S. OPEN
Oakland Hills C.C. (South Course)
Detroit, Michigan, June 14–16
6,917 yards, Par 70

1.	Ben Hogan	76 -73 -71 -67 –287
2.	Clayton Heafner	72 -75 -73 -69 –289
3.	Bobby Locke	73 -71 -74 -73 –291
4.	Julius Boros	74 -74 -71 -74 –293
	Lloyd Mangrum	75 -74 -74 -70 –293
6.	Paul Runyan	73 -74 -72 -75 –294
	Al Besselink	72 -77 -72 -73 –294
	Dave Douglas	75 -70 -75 -74 –294
	Fred Hawkins	76 -72 -75 -71 –294
10.	Sam Snead	71 -78 -72 -74 –295
	(with three others)	

THE 1952 MASTERS
Augusta National G.C.
Augusta, Georgia, April 3–6
6,925 yards, Par 72

1.	Sam Snead	70 -67 -77 -72 –286
2.	Jack Burke Jr.	76 -67 -78 -69 –290
3.	Tommy Bolt	71 -71 -75 -74 –291
	Al Besselink	70 -76 -71 -74 –291
	Jim Ferrier	72 -70 -77 -72 –291
6.	Lloyd Mangrum	71 -74 -75 -72 –292
7.	Ben Hogan	70 -70 -74 -79 –293
	Julius Boros	73 -73 -76 -71 –293
	Lew Worsham	71 -75 -73 -74 –293
	Fred Hawkins	71 -73 -78 -71 –293

THE 1952 U.S. OPEN
Northwood G.C.
Dallas, Texas, June 12–14
6,782 yards, Par 70

1.	Julius Boros	71 -71 -68 -71 –281
2.	Porky Oliver	71 -72 -70 -72 –285
3.	Ben Hogan	69 -69 -74 -74 –286
4.	Johnny Bulla	73 -68 -73 -73 –287
5.	George Fazio	71 -69 -75 -75 –290
6.	Dick Metz	70 -74 -76 -71 –291
7.	Tommy Bolt	72 -76 -71 -73 –292
	Ted Kroll	71 -75 -76 -70 –292
	Lew Worsham	72 -71 -74 -75 –292
10.	Sam Snead	70 -75 -76 -72 –293
	(with two others)	

THE 1953 U.S. OPEN
Oakmont C.C.
Pittsburgh, Pennsylvania, June 11–13
6,916 yards, Par 72

1.	Ben Hogan	67 -72 -73 -71 –283
2.	Sam Snead	72 -69 -72 -76 –289
3.	Lloyd Mangrum	73 -70 -74 -75 –292
4.	Jimmy Demaret	71 -76 -71 -76 –294
	George Fazio	70 -71 -77 -76 –294
	Pete Cooper	78 -75 -71 -70 –294
7.	Dick Metz	75 -70 -74 -76 –295
	Ted Kroll	76 -71 -74 -74 –295
9.	Jay Hebert	72 -72 -74 -78 –296
	Frank Souchak (a)*	70 -76 -76 -74 –296
	Marty Furgol	73 -74 -76 -73 –296

---

*(a) means that the player was an amateur at the time.

THE 1954 MASTERS
Augusta National G.C.
Augusta, Georgia, April 8–12
6,925 yards, Par 72

1.	Sam Snead	74-73-70-72 –289
	Ben Hogan	72-73-69-75 –289
3.	Billy Joe Patton (a)	70-74-75-71 –290
4.	Lloyd Mangrum	71-75-76-69 –291
	Dutch Harrison	70-79-74-68 –291
6.	Jack Burke Jr.	71-77-73-71 –292
	Bob Rosburg	73-73-76-70 –292
	Jerry Barber	74-76-71-71 –292
9.	Cary Middlecoff	73-76-70-70 –294
	Al Besselink	74-74-74-72 –294

Snead (70) beat Hogan (71) in playoff.

THE 1955 MASTERS
Augusta National G.C.
Augusta, Georgia, April 7–10
6,925 yards, Par 72

1.	Cary Middlecoff	72-65-72-70 –279
2.	Ben Hogan	73-68-72-73 –286
3.	Sam Snead	72-71-74-70 –287
4.	Julius Boros	71-75-72-71 –289
	Bob Rosburg	72-72-72-73 –289
	Mike Souchak	71-74-72-72 –289
7.	Lloyd Mangrum	74-73-72-72 –291
8.	Harvie Ward (a)	77-69-75-71 –292
	Stan Leonard	77-73-68-74 –292
10.	Byron Nelson	72-75-74-72 –293
	Arnold Palmer	76-76-72-69 –293
	Dick Mayer	78-72-72-71 –293

THE 1955 U.S. OPEN
Olympic C.C. (Lake Course)
San Francisco, California, June 16–19
6,700 yards, Par 70

1.	Jack Fleck	76-69-75-67 –287
	Ben Hogan	72-73-72-70 –287
3.	Sam Snead	79-69-70-74 –292
	Tommy Bolt	67-77-75-73 –292
5.	Bob Rosburg	78-74-67-76 –295
	Julius Boros	76-69-73-77 –295
7.	Harvie Ward (a)	74-70-76-76 –296
	Doug Ford	74-77-74-71 –296
	Bud Holscher	77-75-71-73 –296
10.	Jack Burke Jr.	71-77-72-77 –297
	Mike Souchak	73-79-72-73 –297

Fleck (69) beat Hogan (72) in playoff.

THE 1956 MASTERS
Augusta National G.C.
Augusta, Georgia, April 5–8
6,925 yards, Par 72

1.	Jack Burke Jr.	72-71-75-71 –289
2.	Ken Venturi (a)	66-69-75-80 –290
3.	Cary Middlecoff	67-72-75-77 –291
4.	Sam Snead	73-76-72-71 –292
	Lloyd Mangrum	72-74-72-74 –292
6.	Jerry Barber	71-72-76-75 –294
	Doug Ford	70-72-75-77 –294
8.	Ben Hogan	69-78-74-75 –296
	Tommy Bolt	68-74-78-76 –296
	Shelley Mayfield	68-74-80-74 –296

THE 1958 U.S. OPEN
Southern Hills C.C.
Tulsa, Oklahoma, June 12–14
6,907 yards, Par 70

1.	Tommy Bolt	71-71-69-72 –283
2.	Gary Player	75-69-73-71 –287
3.	Julius Boros	71-75-72-71 –289
4.	Gene Littler	74-73-67-76 –290
5.	Bob Rosburg	75-74-72-70 –291
	Walter Burkemo	75-74-70-72 –291
7.	Don January	79-73-68-73 –293
	Dick Metz	71-78-73-71 –293
	Jay Hebert	77-76-71-69 –293
10.	Ben Hogan	75-73-75-71 –294
	(with two others)	

THE 1959 U.S. OPEN
Winged Foot G.C. (West Course)
Mamaroneck, New York, June 11–13
6,873 yards, Par 70

1.	Billy Casper	71-68-69-74 –282
2.	Bob Rosburg	75-70-67-71 –283
3.	Mike Souchak	71-70-72-71 –284
	Claude Harmon	72-71-70-71 –284
5.	Arnold Palmer	71-69-72-74 –286
	Ernie Vossler	72-70-72-72 –286
	Doug Ford	72-69-72-73 –286
8.	Ben Hogan	69-71-71-76 –287
	Sam Snead	73-72-67-75 –287
10.	Dick Knight	69-75-73-73 –290

THE 1960 MASTERS
Augusta National G.C.
Augusta, Georgia, April 7–10
6,925 yards, Par 72

1. Arnold Palmer	67-73-72-70	–282
2. Ken Venturi	73-69-71-70	–283
3. Dow Finsterwald	71-70-72-71	–284
4. Billy Casper	71-71-71-74	–287
5. Julius Boros	72-71-70-75	–288
6. Ben Hogan	73-68-72-76	–289
Gary Player	72-71-72-74	–289
Walter Burkemo	72-69-75-73	–289
9. Lionel Hebert	74-70-73-73	–290
Stan Leonard	72-72-72-74	–290

THE 1960 U.S. OPEN
Cherry Hills, C.C.
Denver, Colorado, June 16–18
7,004 yards, Par 71

1. Arnold Palmer	72-71-72-65	–280
2. Jack Nicklaus (a)	71-71-69-71	–282
3. Julius Boros	73-69-68-73	–283
Mike Souchak	68-67-73-75	–283
Dow Finsterwald	71-69-70-73	–283
Dutch Harrison	74-70-70-69	–283
Ted Kroll	72-69-75-67	–283
Jack Fleck	70-70-72-71	–283
9. Ben Hogan	75-67-69-73	–284
Don Cherry (a)	70-71-71-72	–284
Jerry Barber	69-71-70-74	–284

THE 1961 MASTERS
Augusta National G.C.
Augusta, Georgia, April 6–10
6,925 yards, Par 72

1. Gary Player	69-68-69-74	–280
2. Arnold Palmer	68-69-73-71	–281
Charlie Coe (a)	72-71-69-69	–281
4. Tommy Bolt	72-71-74-68	–285
Don January	74-68-72-71	–285
6. Paul Harney	71-73-68-74	–286
7. Jack Nicklaus (a)	70-75-70-72	–287
Jack Burke Jr.	76-70-68-73	–287
Billy Casper	72-77-69-69	–287
Bill Collins	74-72-67-74	–287

THE 1961 U.S. OPEN
Oakland Hills C.C. (South Course)
Detroit, Michigan, June 15–17
6,907 yards, Par 70

1. Gene Littler	73-68-72-68	–281
2. Bob Goalby	70-72-69-71	–282
Doug Sanders	72-67-71-72	–282
4. Jack Nicklaus (a)	75-69-70-70	–284
Mike Souchak	73-70-68-73	–284
6. Dow Finsterwald	72-71-71-72	–286
Doug Ford	72-69-71-74	–286
Eric Monti	74-67-72-73	–286
9. Gary Player	75-72-69-71	–287
Jacky Cupit	72-72-67-76	–287
Gardner Dickinson	72-69-71-75	–287

THE 1961 PGA
Olympia Fields C.C. (North Course)
Chicago, Illinois, July 27–31
6,722 yards, Par 70

1. Jerry Barber	69-67-71-70	–277
Don January	72-66-67-72	–277
3. Doug Sanders	70-68-74-68	–280
4. Ted Kroll	72-68-70-71	–281
5. Arnold Palmer	73-72-69-68	–282
Gene Littler	71-70-72-69	–282
Doug Ford	69-73-74-66	–282
Art Wall Jr.	67-72-73-70	–282
Johnny Pott	71-73-67-71	–282
Wes Ellis Jr.	71-71-68-72	–282

Barber (67) beat January (68) in playoff.

THE 1962 MASTERS
Augusta National G.C.
Augusta, Georgia, April 5–9
6,925 yards, Par 72

1. Arnold Palmer	70-66-69-75	–280
Gary Player	67-71-71-71	–280
Dow Finsterwald	74-68-65-73	–280
4. Gene Littler	71-68-71-72	–282
5. Jimmy Demaret	73-73-71-70	–287
Billy Maxwell	71-73-72-71	–287
Mike Souchak	70-72-74-71	–287
Jerry Barber	72-72-69-74	–287
9. Ken Venturi	75-70-71-72	–288
Charlie Coe (a)	72-74-71-71	–288

Palmer (68) beat Player (71) and Finsterwald (77) in playoff.

THE 1962 U.S. OPEN
Oakmont C.C.
Pittsburgh, Pennsylvania, June 14–17
6,894 yards, Par 72

1.	Jack Nicklaus	72-70-72-69–283
	Arnold Palmer	71-68-73-71–283
3.	Phil Rodgers	74-70-69-72–285
	Bobby Nichols	70-72-70-73–285
5.	Gay Brewer	73-72-73-69–287
6.	Gary Player	71-71-72-74–288
	Tommy Jacobs	74-71-73-70–288
8.	Gene Littler	69-74-72-75–290
	Billy Maxwell	71-70-75-74–290
	Doug Ford	74-75-71-70–290

Nicklaus (71) beat Palmer (74) in playoff.

THE 1962 BRITISH OPEN
Royal Troon G.C.
Ayrshire, Scotland, July 11–13
6,583 yards, Par 72

1.	Arnold Palmer	71-69-67-69–276
2.	Kel Nagle	71-71-70-70–282
3.	Phil Rodgers	75-70-72-72–289
	Brian Huggett	75-71-74-69–289
5.	Bob Charles	75-70-70-75–290
6.	Sam Snead	76-73-72-71–292
	Peter Thomson	70-77-75-70–292
8.	Peter Alliss	77-69-74-73–293
	Dave Thomas	77-70-71-75–293
10.	Syd Scott	77-74-75-68–294

THE 1964 U.S. OPEN
Congressional C.C. (Blue Course)
Bethesda, Maryland, June 18–20
7,053 yards, Par 70

1.	Ken Venturi	72-70-66-70–278
2.	Tommy Jacobs	72-64-70-76–282
3.	Bob Charles	72-72-71-68–283
4.	Billy Casper	71-74-69-71–285
5.	Arnold Palmer	68-69-75-74–286
	Gay Brewer	76-69-73-68–286
7.	Bill Collins	70-71-74-72–287
8.	Dow Finsterwald	73-72-71-72–288
9.	Bob Rosburg	73-73-70-73–289
	Johnny Pott	71-73-73-72–289

THE 1966 U.S. OPEN
Olympic C.C. (Lake Course)
San Francisco, California, June 16–20
6,719 yards, Par 70

1.	Billy Casper	69-68-73-68–278
	Arnold Palmer	71-66-70-71–278
3.	Jack Nicklaus	71-71-69-74–285
4.	Dave Marr	71-74-68-73–286
	Tony Lema	71-74-70-71–286
6.	Phil Rodgers	70-70-73-74–287
7.	Bobby Nichols	74-72-71-72–289
8.	Johnny Miller (a)	70-72-74-74–290
	Doug Sanders	70-75-74-71–290
	Wes Ellis Jr.	71-75-74-70–290

Casper (69) beat Palmer (73) in playoff.

THE 1967 MASTERS
Augusta National G.C.
Augusta, Georgia, April 6–9
6,925 yards, Par 72

1.	Gay Brewer	73-68-72-67–280
2.	Bobby Nichols	72-69-70-70–281
3.	Bert Yancey	67-73-71-73–284
4.	Arnold Palmer	73-73-70-69–285
5.	Julius Boros	71-70-70-75–286
6.	Gary Player	75-69-72-71–287
	Paul Harney	73-71-74-69–287
8.	Lionel Hebert	77-71-67-73–288
	Tommy Aaron	75-68-74-71–288
10.	Ben Hogan	74-73-66-77–290
	(with four others)	

THE 1968 U.S. OPEN
Oak Hill C.C. (East Course)
Rochester, New York, June 13–16
6,962 yards, Par 70

1.	Lee Trevino	69-68-69-69–275
2.	Jack Nicklaus	72-70-70-67–279
3.	Bert Yancey	67-68-70-76–281
4.	Bobby Nichols	74-71-68-69–282
5.	Don Bies	70-70-75-69–284
	Steve Spray	73-75-71-65–284
7.	Bob Charles	73-69-72-71–285
	Jerry Pittman	73-67-74-71–285
9.	Sam Snead	73-71-74-68–286
	(with five others)	

THE 1968 PGA
Pecan Valley C.C.
San Antonio, Texas, July 10–13
7,252 yards, Par 72

1.	Julius Boros	71 -71 -70 -69 –281
2.	Arnold Palmer	71 -69 -72 -70 –282
	Bob Charles	72 -70 -70 -70 –282
4.	Marty Fleckman	66 -72 -72 -73 –283
	George Archer	71 -69 -74 -69 –283
6.	Billy Casper	74 -70 -70 -70 –284
	Frank Beard	68 -70 -72 -74 –284
8.	Charles Coody	70 -77 -70 -68 –285
	(with eight others)	

THE 1969 MASTERS
Augusta National G.C.
Augusta, Georgia, April 10–13
6,925 yards, Par 72

1.	George Archer	67 -73 -69 -72 –281
2.	Billy Casper	66 -71 -71 -74 –282
	Tom Weiskopf	71 -71 -69 -71 –282
	George Knudson	70 -73 -69 -70 –282
5.	Charles Coody	74 -68 -69 -72 –283
	Don January	74 -73 -70 -66 –283
7.	Miller Barber	71 -71 -68 -74 –284
8.	Gene Littler	69 -75 -70 -71 –285
	Lionel Hebert	69 -73 -70 -73 –285
	Tommy Aaron	71 -71 -73 -70 –285

THE 1969 U.S. OPEN
Champions G.C. (Cypress Creek Course)
Houston, Texas, June 12–15
6,967 yards, Par 70

1.	Orville Moody	71 -70 -68 -72 –281
2.	Bob Rosburg	70 -69 -72 -71 –282
	Al Geiberger	68 -72 -72 -70 –282
	Deane Beman	68 -69 -73 -72 –282
5.	Bob Murphy	66 -74 -72 -71 –283
6.	Arnold Palmer	70 -73 -69 -72 –284
	Miller Barber	67 -71 -68 -78 –284
	Bruce Crampton	73 -72 -68 -71 –284
9.	Bunky Henry	70 -72 -68 -75 –285
10.	Dave Marr	75 -69 -71 -71 –286
	(with two others)	

THE 1970 U.S. OPEN
Hazeltine National G.C.
Minneapolis, Minnesota, June 18–21
7,151 yards, Par 72

1.	Tony Jacklin	71 -70 -70 -70 –281
2.	Dave Hill	75 -69 -71 -73 –288
3.	Bob Charles	76 -71 -75 -67 –289
	Bob Lunn	77 -72 -70 -70 –289
5.	Ken Still	78 -71 -71 -71 –291
6.	Miller Barber	75 -75 -72 -70 –292
7.	Gay Brewer	75 -71 -71 -76 –293
8.	Lee Trevino	77 -73 -74 -70 –294
	(with three others)	

THE 1970 BRITISH OPEN
Royal and Ancient G.C. (Old Course)
St. Andrews, Scotland, July 8–12
6,951 yards, Par 72

1.	Jack Nicklaus	68 -69 -73 -73 –283
	Doug Sanders	68 -71 -71 -73 –283
3.	Lee Trevino	68 -68 -72 -77 –285
	Harold Henning	67 -72 -73 -73 –285
5.	Tony Jacklin	67 -70 -73 -76 –286
6.	Neil Coles	65 -74 -72 -76 –287
	Peter Oosterhuis	73 -69 -69 -76 –287
8.	Hugh Jackson	69 -72 -73 -74 –288
9.	Peter Thomson	68 -74 -73 -74 –289
	(with two others)	

Nicklaus (72) beat Sanders (73) in playoff.

THE 1970 PGA
Southern Hills C.C.
Tulsa, Oklahoma, August 13–16
6,962 yards, Par 70

1.	Dave Stockton	70 -70 -66 -73 –279
2.	Arnold Palmer	70 -72 -69 -70 –281
	Bob Murphy	71 -73 -71 -66 –281
4.	Gene Littler	72 -71 -69 -70 –282
	Larry Hinson	69 -71 -74 -68 –282
6.	Jack Nicklaus	68 -76 -73 -66 –283
	Bruce Crampton	73 -75 -68 -67 –283
8.	Raymond Floyd	71 -73 -65 -75 –284
	Dick Lotz	72 -70 -75 -67 –284
10.	Billy Maxwell	72 -71 -73 -69 –285
	Mason Rudolph	71 -70 -73 -71 –285

THE 1971 MASTERS
Augusta National G.C.
Augusta, Georgia, April 8–11
6,925 yards, Par 72

1.	Charles Coody	66-73-70-70-279
2.	Jack Nicklaus	70-71-68-72-281
	Johnny Miller	72-73-68-68-281
4.	Gene Littler	72-69-73-69-283
	Don January	69-69-73-72-283
6.	Gary Player	72-72-71-69-284
	Tom Weiskopf	71-69-72-72-284
	Ken Still	72-71-72-69-284
9.	Frank Beard	74-73-69-70-286
	(with two others)	

THE 1972 MASTERS
Augusta National G.C.
Augusta, Georgia, April 6–9
6,925 yards, Par 72

1.	Jack Nicklaus	68-71-73-74-286
2.	Tom Weiskopf	74-71-70-74-289
	Bruce Crampton	72-75-69-73-289
	Bobby Mitchell	73-72-71-73-289
5.	Homero Blancas	76-71-69-74-290
	Bruce Devlin	74-75-70-71-290
	Jerry McGee	73-74-71-72-290
	Jim Jamieson	72-70-71-77-290
	Jerry Heard	73-71-72-74-290
10.	Gary Player	73-75-72-71-291
	Dave Stockton	76-70-74-71-291

THE 1971 U.S. OPEN
Merion G.C. (East Course)
Philadelphia, Pennsylvania, June 17–21
6,544 yards, Par 70

1.	Lee Trevino	70-72-69-69-280
	Jack Nicklaus	69-72-68-71-280
3.	Bob Rosburg	71-72-70-69-282
	Jim Colbert	69-69-73-71-282
5.	Jim Simons (a)	71-71-65-76-283
	Johnny Miller	70-73-70-70-283
	George Archer	71-70-70-72-283
8.	Raymond Floyd	71-75-67-71-284
9.	Bert Yancey	75-69-69-72-285
	(with three others)	

Trevino (68) beat Nicklaus (71) in playoff.

THE 1972 U.S. OPEN
Pebble Beach Golf Links
Carmel, California, June 15–18
6,812 yards, Par 72

1.	Jack Nicklaus	71-73-72-74-290
2.	Bruce Crampton	74-70-73-76-293
3.	Arnold Palmer	77-68-73-76-294
4.	Lee Trevino	74-72-71-78-295
	Homero Blancas	74-70-76-75-295
6.	Kermit Zarley	71-73-73-79-296
7.	Johnny Miller	74-73-71-79-297
8.	Tom Weiskopf	73-74-73-78-298
9.	Chi Chi Rodriguez	71-75-78-75-299
	Cesar Sanudo	72-72-78-77-299

THE 1971 BRITISH OPEN
Royal Birkdale G.C.
Southport, England, July 7–10
7,080 yards, Par 73

1.	Lee Trevino	69-70-69-70-278
2.	Lu Liang-Huan	70-70-69-70-279
3.	Tony Jacklin	69-70-70-71-280
4.	Craig Defoy	72-72-68-69-281
5.	Jack Nicklaus	71-71-72-69-283
	Charles Coody	74-71-70-68-283
7.	Gary Player	71-70-71-72-284
8.	Billy Casper	73-71-74-67-285
	Peter Thomson	70-73-73-69-285
	Doug Sanders	73-71-74-67-285

THE 1972 BRITISH OPEN
Hon. Co. of Edinburgh Golfers
Muirfield, Scotland, July 12–15
6,892 yards, Par 71

1.	Lee Trevino	71-70-66-71-278
2.	Jack Nicklaus	70-72-71-66-279
3.	Tony Jacklin	69-72-67-72-280
4.	Doug Sanders	71-71-69-70-281
5.	Brian Barnes	71-72-69-71-283
6.	Gary Player	71-71-76-67-285
7.	Arnold Palmer	73-73-69-71-286
	Tom Weiskopf	73-74-70-69-286
	Guy Hunt	75-72-67-72-286
	David Vaughan	74-73-70-69-286

THE 1973 U.S. OPEN
Oakmont C.C.
Pittsburgh, Pennsylvania, June 14–17
6,921 yards, Par 71

1.	Johnny Miller	71-69-76-63 –279
2.	John Schlee	73-70-67-70 –280
3.	Tom Weiskopf	73-69-69-70 –281
4.	Jack Nicklaus	71-69-74-68 –282
	Arnold Palmer	71-71-68-72 –282
	Lee Trevino	70-72-70-70 –282
7.	Lanny Wadkins	74-69-75-65 –283
	Julius Boros	73-69-68-73 –283
	Jerry Heard	74-70-66-73 –283
10.	Jim Colbert	70-68-74-72 –284

THE 1973 BRITISH OPEN
Royal Troon G.C.
Ayrshire, Scotland, July 11–14
7,064 yards, Par 72

1.	Tom Weiskopf	68-67-71-70 –276
2.	Johnny Miller	70-68-69-72 –279
	Neil Coles	71-72-70-66 –279
4.	Jack Nicklaus	69-70-76-65 –280
5.	Bert Yancey	69-69-73-70 –281
6.	Peter Butler	71-72-74-69 –286
7.	Lanny Wadkins	71-73-70-74 –288
	Bob Charles	73-71-73-71 –288
	Christy O'Connor	73-68-74-73 –288
10.	Lee Trevino	75-73-73-68 –289
	(with three others)	

THE 1973 PGA
Canterbury G.C.
Cleveland, Ohio, August 9–12
6,852 yards, Par 71

1.	Jack Nicklaus	72-68-68-69 –277
2.	Bruce Crampton	71-73-67-70 –281
3.	Lanny Wadkins	73-69-71-69 –282
	J. C. Snead	71-74-68-69 –282
	Mason Rudolph	69-70-70-73 –282
6.	Tom Weiskopf	70-71-71-71 –283
	Dan Sikes	72-68-72-71 –283
	Don Iverson	67-72-70-74 –283
9.	Sam Snead	71-71-71-71 –284
	(with two others)	

THE 1975 MASTERS
Augusta National G.C.
Augusta, Georgia, April 10–13
6,925 yards, Par 72

1.	Jack Nicklaus	68-67-73-68 –276
2.	Johnny Miller	75-71-65-66 –277
	Tom Weiskopf	69-72-66-70 –277
4.	Hale Irwin	73-74-71-64 –282
	Bobby Nichols	67-74-72-69 –282
6.	Billy Casper	70-70-73-70 –283
7.	Dave Hill	75-71-70-68 –284
8.	Tom Watson	70-70-72-73 –285
	Hubert Green	74-71-70-70 –285
10.	Lee Trevino	71-70-74-71 –286
	(with two others)	

THE 1975 U.S. OPEN
Medinah C.C. (No. 3 Course)
Chicago, Illinois, June 19–23
7,032 yards, Par 71

1.	Lou Graham	74-72-68-73 –287
	John Mahaffey	73-71-72-71 –287
3.	Ben Crenshaw	70-68-76-74 –288
	Frank Beard	74-69-67-78 –288
	Hale Irwin	74-71-73-70 –288
	Bob Murphy	74-73-72-69 –288
7.	Jack Nicklaus	72-70-75-72 –289
	Peter Oosterhuis	69-73-72-75 –289
9.	Arnold Palmer	69-75-73-73 –290
	Tom Watson	67-68-78-77 –290
	Pat Fitzsimons	67-73-73-77 –290

Graham (71) beat Mahaffey (73) in 18-hole playoff.

THE 1975 PGA
Firestone C.C. (South Course)
Akron, Ohio, August 7–10
7,180 yards, Par 70

1.	Jack Nicklaus	70-68-67-71 –276
2.	Bruce Crampton	71-63-75-69 –278
3.	Tom Weiskopf	70-71-70-68 –279
4.	Andy North	72-74-70-65 –281
5.	Hale Irwin	72-65-73-73 –283
	Billy Casper	69-72-72-70 –283
7.	Gene Littler	76-71-66-71 –284
	Dave Hill	71-71-74-68 –284
9.	Tom Watson	70-71-71-73 –285
10.	Ben Crenshaw	73-72-71-70 –286
	(with six others)	

THE 1976 U.S. OPEN
Atlanta Athletic Club (Highlands Course)
Atlanta, Georgia, June 17–20
7,015 yards, Par 70

1.	Jerry Pate	71 -69-69-68 –277
2.	Tom Weiskopf	73 -70-68-68 –279
	Al Geiberger	70-69-71 -69 –279
4.	John Mahaffey	70-68-69-73 –280
	Butch Baird	71 -71 -71 -67 –280
6.	Hubert Green	72 -70-71 -69 –282
7.	Tom Watson	74 -72-68-70 –284
8.	Ben Crenshaw	72 -68-72-73 –285
	Lyn Lott	71 -71 -70-73 –285
10.	Johnny Miller	74 -72 -69-71 –286

THE 1977 BRITISH OPEN
Turnberry G.C. (Ailsa Course)
Ayrshire, Scotland, July 6–9
6,875 yards, Par 70

1.	Tom Watson	68-70-65 -65 –268
2.	Jack Nicklaus	68-70-65 -66 –269
3.	Hubert Green	72 -66-74 -67 –279
4.	Lee Trevino	68-70-72 -70 –280
5.	Ben Crenshaw	71 -69-66-75 –281
	George Burns	70-70-72 -69 –281
7.	Arnold Palmer	73 -73 -67 -69 –282
8.	Raymond Floyd	70-73 -68-72 –283
9.	Johnny Miller	69-74 -67 -74 –284
	(with three others)	

THE 1977 PGA
Pebble Beach Golf Links
Carmel, California, August 11–14
6,804 yards, Par 72

1.	Lanny Wadkins	69-71 -72 -70 –282
	Gene Littler	67-69-70-76 –282
3.	Jack Nicklaus	69-71 -70-73 –283
4.	Charles Coody	70-71 -70-73 –284
5.	Jerry Pate	73 -70-69-73 –285
6.	Tom Watson	68-73 -71 -74 –286
	Don January	75 -69-70-72 –286
	Al Geiberger	71 -70-73 -72 –286
	Lou Graham	71 -73 -71 -71 –286
	Jerry McGee	68-70-77 -71 –286

*Wadkins beat Littler on third hole of sudden-
death playoff.*

THE 1978 MASTERS
Augusta National G.C.
Augusta, Georgia, April 6–9
6,925 yards, Par 72

1.	Gary Player	72 -72 -69-64 –277
2.	Tom Watson	73 -68-58 -69 –278
	Hubert Green	72 -69-65 -72 –278
	Rod Funseth	73 -66-70-69 –278
5.	Bill Kratzert	70-74 -67 -69 –280
	Wally Armstrong	72 -70-70-68 –280
7.	Jack Nicklaus	72 -73 -69-67 –281
8.	Hale Irwin	73 -67 -71 -71 –282
9.	David Graham	75 -69-67 -72 –283
	Joe Inman	69-73 -72 -69 –283

THE 1979 MASTERS
Augusta National G.C.
Augusta, Georgia, April 12–15
6,925 yards, Par 72

1.	Fuzzy Zoeller	70-71 -69-70 –280
	Ed Sneed	68-67 -69-76 –280
	Tom Watson	68-71 -70-71 –280
4.	Jack Nicklaus	69-71 -72 -69 –281
5.	Tom Kite	71 -72 -68-72 –283
6.	Bruce Lietzke	67-75 -68-74 –284
7.	Lanny Wadkins	73 -69-70-73 –285
	Craig Stadler	69-66-74 -76 –285
	Len Thompson	68-70-73 -74 –285
10.	Gene Littler	74 -71 -69-72 –286
	Hubert Green	74 -69-72 -71 –286

*Zoeller beat Sneed and Watson on second hole of
sudden-death playoff.*

THE 1979 U.S. OPEN
Inverness Club
Toledo, Ohio, June 14–17
6,982 yards, Par 71

1.	Hale Irwin	74 -68-67 -75 –284
2.	Gary Player	73 -73 -72 -68 –286
	Jerry Pate	71 -74 -69-72 –286
4.	Tom Weiskopf	71 -74 -67 -76 –288
	Bill Rogers	71 -72 -73 -72 –288
	Larry Nelson	71 -68-76-73 –288
7.	David Graham	73 -73 -70-73 –289
8.	Tom Purtzer	70-69-75 -76 –290
9.	Jack Nicklaus	74 -77 -72 -68 –291
	Keith Fergus	70-77 -72 -72 –291

THE 1979 BRITISH OPEN
Royal Lytham & St. Anne's G.C.
Lancashire, England, July 18–21
6,822 yards, Par 71

1.	Seve Ballesteros	73 -65 -75 -70 –283
2.	Jack Nicklaus	72 -69 -73 -72 –286
	Ben Crenshaw	72 -71 -72 -71 –286
4.	Mark James	76 -69 -69 -73 –287
5.	Rodger Davis	75 -70 -70 -73 –288
6.	Hale Irwin	68 -68 -75 -78 –289
7.	Isao Aoki	70 -74 -72 -75 –291
	Graham Marsh	74 -68 -75 -74 –291
	Bob Byman	73 -70 -72 -76 –291
10.	Greg Norman	73 -71 -72 -76 –292
	(with two others)	

THE 1980 PGA
Oak Hill C.C. (East Course)
Rochester, New York, August 7–10
6,964 yards, Par 70

1.	Jack Nicklaus	70 -69 -66 -69 –274
2.	Andy Bean	72 -71 -68 -70 –281
3.	Lon Hinkle	70 -69 -69 -75 –283
	Gil Morgan	68 -70 -73 -72 –283
5.	Curtis Strange	68 -72 -72 -72 –284
	Howard Twitty	68 -74 -71 -71 –284
7.	Lee Trevino	74 -71 -71 -69 –285
8.	Bill Rogers	71 -71 -72 -72 –286
	Bobby Walzel	68 -76 -71 -71 –286
10.	Tom Watson	75 -74 -72 -67 –288
	Tom Weiskopf	71 -73 -72 -72 –288
	Jerry Pate	72 -73 -70 -73 –288
	Peter Jacobsen	71 -73 -74 -70 –288
	Terry Diehl	72 -72 -68 -76 –288

THE 1980 MASTERS
Augusta National G.C.
Augusta, Georgia, April 10–13
6,925 yards, Par 72

1.	Seve Ballesteros	66 -69 -68 -72 –275
2.	Gibby Gilbert	70 -74 -68 -67 –279
	Jack Newton	68 -74 -69 -68 –279
4.	Hubert Green	68 -74 -71 -67 –280
5.	David Graham	66 -73 -72 -70 –281
6.	Ben Crenshaw	76 -70 -68 -69 –283
	Gary Player	71 -71 -71 -70 –283
	Jerry Pate	72 -68 -76 -67 –283
	Tom Kite	69 -71 -74 -69 –283
	Larry Nelson	69 -72 -73 -69 –283
	Ed Fiori	71 -70 -69 -73 –283

THE 1981 PGA
Atlanta Athletic Club (Highlands Course)
Atlanta, Georgia, August 6–9
7,070 yards, Par 70

1.	Larry Nelson	70 -66 -66 -71 –273
2.	Fuzzy Zoeller	70 -68 -68 -71 –277
3.	Dan Pohl	69 -67 -73 -69 –278
4.	Jack Nicklaus	71 -68 -71 -69 –279
	Greg Norman	73 -67 -68 -71 –279
	Tom Kite	71 -67 -69 -72 –279
	Isao Aoki	75 -68 -66 -70 –279
	Bruce Lietzke	70 -70 -71 -68 –279
	Keith Fergus	71 -71 -69 -68 –279
	Bob Gilder	74 -69 -70 -66 –279

THE 1980 U.S. OPEN
Baltusrol G.C. (Lower Course)
Springfield, New Jersey, June 12–15
7,076 yards, Par 70

1.	Jack Nicklaus	63 -71 -70 -68 –272
2.	Isao Aoki	68 -68 -68 -70 –274
3.	Tom Watson	71 -68 -67 -70 –276
	Lon Hinkle	66 -70 -69 -71 –276
	Keith Fergus	66 -70 -70 -70 –276
6.	Mark Hayes	66 -71 -69 -74 –280
	Mike Reid	69 -67 -75 -69 –280
8.	Ed Sneed	72 -70 -70 -70 –282
	Hale Irwin	70 -70 -73 -69 –282
	Andy North	68 -75 -72 -67 –282
	Mike Morley	73 -68 -69 -72 –282

THE 1982 U.S. OPEN
Pebble Beach Golf Links
Carmel, California, June 17–20
6,815 yards, Par 72

1.	Tom Watson	72 -72 -68 -70 –282
2.	Jack Nicklaus	74 -70 -71 -69 –283
3.	Bill Rogers	70 -73 -69 -74 –286
	Bobby Clampett	71 -73 -72 -70 –286
	Dan Pohl	72 -74 -70 -70 –286
6.	Lanny Wadkins	73 -76 -67 -71 –287
	David Graham	73 -72 -69 -73 –287
	Jay Haas	75 -74 -70 -68 –287
	Gary Koch	78 -73 -69 -67 –287
10.	Bruce Devlin	70 -69 -75 -74 –288
	Calvin Peete	71 -72 -72 -73 –288

THE 1984 MASTERS
Augusta National G.C.
Augusta, Georgia, April 12–15
6,925 yards, Par 72

1.	Ben Crenshaw	67 -72 -70 -68 – 277
2.	Tom Watson	74 -67 -69 -69 – 279
3.	Gil Morgan	73 -71 -69 -67 – 280
	David Edwards	71 -70 -72 -67 – 280
5.	Larry Nelson	76 -69 -66 -70 – 281
6.	Tom Kite	70 -68 -69 -75 – 282
	David Graham	69 -70 -70 -73 – 282
	Mark Lye	69 -66 -73 -74 – 282
	Ronnie Black	71 -74 -69 -68 – 282
10.	Fred Couples	71 -73 -67 -72 – 283

THE 1984 U.S. OPEN
Winged Foot G.C. (West Course)
Mamaroneck, New York, June 14–18
6,930 yards, Par 70

1.	Fuzzy Zoeller	71 -66 -69 -70 – 276
	Greg Norman	70 -68 -69 -69 – 276
3.	Curtis Strange	69 -70 -74 -68 – 281
4.	Johnny Miller	74 -68 -70 -70 – 282
	Jim Thorpe	68 -71 -70 -73 – 282
6.	Hale Irwin	68 -68 -69 -79 – 284
7.	Peter Jacobsen	72 -73 -73 -67 – 285
	Mark O'Meara	71 -74 -71 -69 – 285
9.	Lee Trevino	71 -72 -69 -74 – 286
	Fred Couples	69 -71 -74 -72 – 286

Zoeller (67) beat Norman (75) in playoff.

THE 1985 MASTERS
Augusta National G.C.
Augusta, Georgia, April 11–14
6,925 yards, Par 72

1.	Bernhard Langer	72 -74 -68 -68 – 282
2.	Seve Ballesteros	72 -71 -71 -70 – 284
	Raymond Floyd	70 -73 -69 -72 – 284
	Curtis Strange	80 -65 -68 -71 – 284
5.	Jay Haas	73 -73 -72 -67 – 285
6.	Jack Nicklaus	71 -74 -72 -69 – 286
	Craig Stadler	73 -67 -76 -70 – 286
	Bruce Lietzke	72 -71 -73 -70 – 286
	Gary Hallberg	68 -73 -75 -70 – 286
10.	Lee Trevino	70 -73 -72 -72 – 287
	Tom Watson	69 -71 -75 -72 – 287
	Fred Couples	75 -73 -69 -70 – 287
	David Graham	74 -71 -71 -71 – 287

THE 1985 U.S. OPEN
Oakland Hills C.C. (South Course)
Detroit, Michigan, June 13–16
6,966 yards, Par 70

1.	Andy North	70 -65 -70 -74 – 279
2.	Tze-Chung Chen	65 -69 -69 -77 – 280
	Dave Barr	70 -68 -70 -72 – 280
	Denis Watson	72 -65 -73 -70 – 280
5.	Lanny Wadkins	70 -72 -69 -70 – 281
	Seve Ballesteros	71 -70 -69 -71 – 281
	Payne Stewart	70 -70 -71 -70 – 281
8.	Johnny Miller	74 -71 -68 -69 – 282
9.	Fuzzy Zoeller	71 -69 -72 -71 – 283
	(with three others)	

THE 1986 MASTERS
Augusta National G.C.
Augusta, Georgia, April 10–13
6,925 yards, Par 72

1.	Jack Nicklaus	74 -71 -69 -65 – 279
2.	Greg Norman	70 -72 -68 -70 – 280
	Tom Kite	70 -74 -68 -68 – 280
4.	Seve Ballesteros	71 -68 -72 -70 – 281
5.	Nick Price	79 -69 -63 -71 – 282
6.	Tom Watson	70 -74 -68 -71 – 283
	Jay Haas	76 -69 -71 -67 – 283
8.	Payne Stewart	75 -71 -69 -69 – 284
	Bob Tway	70 -73 -71 -70 – 284
	T. Nakajima	70 -71 -71 -72 – 284

THE 1986 U.S. OPEN
Shinnecock Hills G.C.
Southampton, New York, June 12–15
6,912 yards, Par 70

1.	Raymond Floyd	75 -68 -70 -66 – 279
2.	Lanny Wadkins	74 -70 -72 -65 – 281
	Chip Beck	75 -73 -68 -65 – 281
4.	Lee Trevino	74 -68 -69 -71 – 282
	Hal Sutton	75 -70 -66 -71 – 282
6.	Ben Crenshaw	76 -69 -69 -69 – 283
	Payne Stewart	76 -68 -69 -70 – 283
8.	Jack Nicklaus	77 -72 -67 -68 – 284
	(with three others)	

THE 1986 BRITISH OPEN
Turnberry G.C. (Ailsa Course)
Ayrshire, Scotland, July 17–20
6,957 yards, Par 70

1.	Greg Norman	74 -63 -74 -69 –280
2.	Gordon J. Brand	71 -68 -75 -71 –285
3.	Bernhard Langer	72 -70 -76 -68 –286
	Ian Woosnam	70 -74 -70 -72 –286
5.	Nick Faldo	71 -70 -76 -70 –287
6.	Seve Ballesteros	76 -75 -73 -64 –288
	Gary Koch	73 -72 -72 -71 –288
8.	Fuzzy Zoeller	75 -73 -72 -69 –289
	Brian Marchbank	78 -70 -72 -69 –289
	T. Nakajima	74 -67 -71 -77 –289

THE 1987 U.S. OPEN
Olympic G.C. (Lake Course)
San Francisco, California, June 16–19
6,709 yards, Par 70

1.	Scott Simpson	71 -68 -70 -68 –277
2.	Tom Watson	72 -65 -71 -70 –278
3.	Seve Ballesteros	68 -75 -68 -71 –282
4.	Ben Crenshaw	67 -72 -72 -72 –283
	Curtis Strange	71 -72 -69 -71 –283
	Bernhard Langer	69 -69 -73 -72 –283
	Larry Mize	71 -68 -72 -72 –283
	Bobby Wadkins	71 -71 -70 -71 –283
9.	Mac O'Grady	71 -69 -72 -72 –284
	(with four others)	

THE 1988 U.S. OPEN
The Country Club
Boston, Massachusetts, June 16–20
7,010 yards, Par 71

1.	Curtis Strange	70 -67 -69 -72 –278
	Nick Faldo	72 -67 -68 -71 –278
3.	Mark O'Meara	71 -72 -66 -71 –280
	D. A. Weibring	71 -69 -68 -72 –280
	Steve Pate	72 -69 -72 -67 –280
6.	Paul Azinger	69 -70 -76 -66 –281
	Scott Simpson	69 -66 -72 -74 –281
8.	Fuzzy Zoeller	73 -72 -71 -66 –282
	Bob Gilder	68 -69 -70 -75 –282
10.	Fred Couples	72 -67 -71 -73 –283
	Payne Stewart	73 -73 -70 -67 –283

Strange (71) beat Faldo (75) in playoff.

1989 U.S. OPEN
Oak Hill C.C. (East Course)
Rochester, New York, June 15–18
6,902 yards, Par 70

1.	Curtis Strange	71 -64 -73 -70 –278
2.	Ian Woosnam	70 -68 -73 -68 –279
	Chip Beck	71 -69 -71 -68 –279
	Mark McCumber	70 -68 -72 -69 –279
5.	Brian Claar	71 -72 -68 -69 –280
6.	Scott Simpson	67 -70 -69 -75 –281
	Jumbo Ozaki	70 -71 -68 -72 –281
8.	Peter Jacobsen	71 -70 -71 -70 –282
9.	Tom Kite	67 -69 -69 -78 –283
	(with three others)	

1990 U.S. OPEN
Medinah C.C. (No. 3 Course)
Chicago, Illinois, June 14–18
7,195 yards, Par 72

1.	Hale Irwin	69 -70 -74 -67 –280
	Mike Donald	67 -70 -72 -71 –280
3.	Nick Faldo	72 -72 -68 -69 –281
	Billy Ray Brown	69 -71 -69 -72 –281
5.	Greg Norman	72 -73 -69 -69 –283
	Mark Brooks	68 -70 -72 -73 –283
	Tim Simpson	66 -69 -75 -73 –283
8.	Fuzzy Zoeller	73 -70 -68 -73 –284
	(with five others)	

Irwin (74) beat Donald (74) on first sudden-death hole after playoff tied.

THE 1991 BRITISH OPEN
Royal Birkdale G.C.
Southport, England, July 10–13
6,940 yards, Par 70

1.	Ian Baker-Finch	71 -71 -64 -66 –272
2.	Mike Harwood	68 -70 -69 -67 –274
3.	Fred Couples	72 -69 -70 -64 –275
	Mark O'Meara	71 -68 -67 -69 –275
5.	Jodie Mudd	72 -70 -72 -63 –277
	Bob Tway	75 -66 -70 -66 –277
	Eamonn Darcy	73 -68 -66 -70 –277
8.	Craig Parry	71 -70 -69 -68 –278
9.	Seve Ballesteros	66 -73 -69 -71 –279
	Greg Norman	74 -68 -71 -66 –279
	Bernhard Langer	71 -71 -70 -67 –279

THE 1991 PGA
Crooked Stick G.C.
Indianapolis, Indiana, August 8–11
7,295 yards, Par 72

1.	John Daly	69-67-69-71 –276
2.	Bruce Lietzke	68-69-72-70 –279
3.	Jim Gallagher Jr.	70-72-72-67 –281
4.	Kenny Knox	67-71 -70-74 –282
5.	Bob Gilder	73 -70-67-74 –283
	Steven Richardson	70-72-72-69 –283
7.	Raymond Floyd	69-74 -72-69 –284
	Hal Sutton	74 -67-72-71 –284
	Craig Stadler	68-71 -69-76 –284
	David Feherty	71 -74 -71 -68 –284
	Steve Pate	70-75 -70-69 –284
	John Huston	70-72 -70-72 –284

THE 1992 MASTERS
Augusta National G.C.
Augusta, Georgia, April 9–12
6,925 yards, Par 72

1.	Fred Couples	69-67-69-70 –275
2.	Raymond Floyd	69-68-69-71 –277
3.	Corey Pavin	72 -71 -68-67 –278
4.	Mark O'Meara	74 -67-69-70 –280
	Jeff Sluman	65-74 -70-71 –280
6.	Greg Norman	70-70-73 -68 –281
	Nick Price	70-71 -67-73 –281
	Larry Mize	73 -69-71 -68 –281
	Ian Baker-Finch	70-69-68-74 –281
	Steve Pate	73 -71 -70-67 –281
	Nolan Henke	70-71 -70-70 –281
	Ted Schultz	68-69-72 -72 –281

THE 1992 U.S. OPEN
Pebble Beach Golf Links
Carmel, California, June 18–21
6,809 yards, Par 72

1.	Tom Kite	71 -72 -70-72 –285
2.	Jeff Sluman	73 -74 -69-71 –287
3.	Colin Montgomerie	70-71 -77 -70 –288
4.	Nick Faldo	70-76 -68-77 –291
	Nick Price	71 -72 -77 -71 –291
6.	Ian Woosnam	72 -72 -69-79 –292
	Tom Lehman	69-74 -72 -77 –292
	Billy Andrade	72 -74 -72 -74 –292
	Jay Don Blake	70-74 -75 -73 –292
	Bob Gilder	73 -70-75 -74 –292
	Mike Hulbert	74 -73 -70-75 –292
	Joey Sindelar	74 -72 -68-78 –292

THE 1993 BRITISH OPEN
Royal St. George's Golf Club
Sandwich, England, July 15–18
6,860 yards, Par 72

1.	Greg Norman	66-68-69-64 –267
2.	Nick Faldo	69-63 -70-67 –269
3.	Bernhard Langer	67-66-70-67 –270
4.	Corey Pavin	68-66-68-79 –272
	Peter Senior	66-69-70-67 –272
6.	Ernie Els	68-69-69-68 –274
	Nick Price	68-70-67-69 –274
	Paul Lawrie	72 -68-69-65 –274
9.	Fred Couples	68-66-72 -69 –275
	(with two others)	

THE 1994 PGA
Southern Hills C.C.
Tulsa, Oklahoma, August 11–14
6,824 yards, Par 70

1.	Nick Price	67-65 -70-67 –269
2.	Corey Pavin	70-67-69-69 –275
3.	Phil Mickelson	68-71 -67-70 –276
4.	Greg Norman	71 -69-67-70 –277
	Nick Faldo	73 -67-71 -66 –277
	John Cook	71 -67-69-70 –277
7.	José María Olazabal	72 -66-70-70 –278
	Steve Elkington	73 -70-66-69 –278
9.	Ben Crenshaw	70-67-70-72 –279
	(with four others)	

THE 1995 MASTERS
Augusta National G.C.
Augusta, Georgia, April 6–9
6,925 yards, Par 72

1.	Ben Crenshaw	70-67-69-68 –274
2.	Davis Love III	69-69-71 -66 –275
3.	Greg Norman	73 -68-68-68 –277
	Jay Haas	71 -64-72 -70 –277
5.	Steve Elkington	73 -67-67-72 –279
	David Frost	66-71 -71 -71 –279
7.	Phil Mickelson	66-71 -70-73 –280
	Scott Hoch	69-67-71 -73 –280
9.	Curtis Strange	72 -71 -65 -73 –281
10.	Fred Couples	71 -69-67-75 –282
	Brian Henninger	70-68-68-76 –282

THE 1996 MASTERS
Augusta National G.C.
Augusta, Georgia, April 11–14
6,925 yards, Par 72

1.	Nick Faldo	69-67-73-67 –276
2.	Greg Norman	63-69-71-78 –281
3.	Phil Mickelson	65-73-72-72 –282
4.	Frank Nobilo	71-71-72-69 –283
5.	Scott Hoch	67-73-73-71 –284
	Duffy Waldorf	72-71-69-72 –284
7.	Davis Love III	72-71-74-68 –285
	Corey Pavin	75-66-73-71 –285
	Jeff Maggert	71-73-74-74 –285
10.	David Frost	70-68-74-74 –286
	Scott McCarron	70-70-72-74 –286

THE 1996 PGA
Valhalla Golf Club
Louisville, Kentucky, August 8–11
7,144 yards, Par 72

1.	Mark Brooks	68-70-69-70 –277
	Kenny Perry	66-72-71-68 –277
3.	Steve Elkington	67-74-67-70 –278
	Tommy Tolles	69-71-71-67 –278
5.	Justin Leonard	71-66-72-70 –279
	Vijay Singh	69-69-69-72 –279
	Jesper Parnevik	73-67-69-70 –279
8.	Phil Mickelson	67-67-74-72 –280
	(with five others)	

*Brooks beat Perry on first hole of sudden-death
playoff.*

THE 1997 MASTERS
Augusta National G.C.
Augusta, Georgia, April 10–13
6,925 yards, Par 72

1.	Tiger Woods	79-66-65-69 –270
2.	Tom Kite	77-69-66-70 –282
3.	Tommy Tolles	72-72-72-67 –283
4.	Tom Watson	75-68-69-72 –284
5.	Constantino Rocca	71-69-70-75 –285
	Paul Stankowski	68-74-79-74 –285
7.	Davis Love III	72-71-72-71 –286
	Fred Couples	72-69-73-72 –286
	Bernhard Langer	72-72-74-68 –286
	Justin Leonard	76-60-71-70 –286
	Jeff Sluman	74-67-72-73 –286

THE 1997 PGA
Winged Foot G.C. (West Course)
Mamaroneck, New York, August 14–17
6,987 yards, Par 70

1.	Davis Love III	66-71-66-66 –269
2.	Justin Leonard	68-70-65-71 –274
3.	Jeff Maggert	69-69-73-65 –276
4.	Lee Janzen	69-67-74-69 –279
5.	Tom Kite	68-71-71-70 –280
6.	Jim Furyk	69-72-72-68 –281
	Scott Hoch	71-72-68-70 –281
	Phil Blackmar	70-68-74-69 –281
9.	Tom Byrum	69-73-70-70 –282
10.	Tom Lehman	69-72-72-70 –283
	(with two others)	

THE 1998 BRITISH OPEN
Royal Birkdale G.C.
Southport, England, July 16–19
7,018 yards, Par 70

1.	Mark O'Meara	72-68-72-68 –280
	Brian Watts	68-69-73-70 –280
3.	Tiger Woods	65-73-77-66 –281
4.	Jim Furyk	70-70-72-70 –282
	Jesper Parnevik	68-72-72-70 –282
	Raymond Russell	68-73-75-66 –282
	Justin Rose (a)	72-66-75-69 –282
8.	Davis Love III	67-73-77-68 –285
9.	Thomas Bjørn	68-71-76-71 –286
	Constantino Rocca	72-74-70-70 –286

O'Meara beat Watts in 4-hole playoff.

THE 1999 U.S. OPEN
Pinehurst Resort C.C. (No. 2 Course)
Pinehurst, North Carolina, June 17–20
7,175 yards, Par 70

1.	Payne Stewart	68-69-72-70 –279
2.	Phil Mickelson	67-70-73-70 –280
3.	Tiger Woods	68-71-72-70 –281
	Vijay Singh	69-70-73-69 –281
5.	Steve Stricker	70-73-69-73 –285
6.	Tim Herron	69-72-70-75 –286
7.	David Duval	67-70-75-75 –287
	Hal Sutton	69-70-76-72 –287
	Jeff Maggert	71-69-74-73 –287
10.	Darren Clarke	73-70-74-71 –288
	Billy Mayfair	67-72-74-75 –288

THE 1999 BRITISH OPEN
Carnoustie Golf Club
Angus, Scotland, July 15–18
7,381 yards, Par 71

1.	Paul Lawrie	73 -74 -76 -67 –290
	Justin Leonard	73 -74 -71 -72 –290
	Jean Van de Velde	75 -68 -70 -77 –290
4.	Angel Cabrera	75 -69 -77 -70 –291
	Craig Parry	76 -75 -67 -73 –291
6.	Greg Norman	76 -70 -75 -72 –293
7.	Tiger Woods	74 -72 -74 -74 –294
	Davis Love III	74 -74 -77 -69 –294
	David Frost	80-69-71 -74 –294
10.	Jim Furyk	78 -71 -76 -70 –295
	(with four others)	

Lawrie (5-4-3-3) beat Leonard (5-4-4-5) and Van de Velde (6-4-3-5) in four-hole playoff.

THE 1999 PGA
Medinah C.C. (No. 3 Course)
Chicago, Illinois, August 12–15
7,398 yards, Par 72

1.	Tiger Woods	70 -67 -68 -72 –277
2.	Sergio Garcia	66 -73 -68 -71 –278
3.	Stewart Cink	69 -70 -68 -73 –280
	Jay Haas	68 -67 -75 -70 –280
5.	Nick Price	70 -71 -69 -71 –281
6.	Colin Montgomerie	72 -70 -70 -70 –282
	Bob Estes	71 -70 -72 -69 –282
8.	Jim Furyk	71 -70 -69 -74 –284
	Steve Pate	72 -70 -73 -69 –284
10.	David Duval	70 -71 -72 -72 –285
	(with five others)	

THE 2000 U.S. OPEN
Pebble Beach Golf Links
Carmel, California, June 15–18
6,828 yards, Par 72

1.	Tiger Woods	65 -69 -71 -67 –272
2.	Ernie Els	74 -73 -68 -72 –287
	Miguel Ángel Jiménez	66 -74 -76 -71 –287
4.	John Huston	67 -75 -76 -70 –288
5.	Padraig Harrington	73 -71 -72 -73 –289
	Lee Westwood	71 -71 -76 -71 –289
7.	Nick Faldo	69 -74 -76 -71 –290
8.	Vijay Singh	70 -73 -80-68 –291
	David Duval	75 -71 -74 -71 –291
	Stewart Cink	77 -72 -72 -70 –291
	Loren Roberts	68 -78 -73 -72 –291

THE 2000 BRITISH OPEN
Royal and Ancient G.C. (Old Course)
St. Andrews, Scotland, July 20–23
7,115 yards, Par 72

1.	Tiger Woods	67-66-67 -60–269
2.	Ernie Els	66 -72 -70 -69 –277
	Thomas Bjørn	69-69-68 -71 –277
4.	Tom Lehman	68 -70 -70 -70 –278
	David Toms	69-67 -71 -71 –278
6.	Fred Couples	70 -68 -72 -69 –279
7.	Paul Azinger	69 -72 -72 -67 –280
	Loren Roberts	69 -68 -70 -73 –280
	Darren Clarke	70 -69 -68 -73 –280
	Pierre Fulke	69 -72 -70 -69 –280

THE 2000 PGA
Valhalla Golf Club
Louisville, Kentucky, August 17–20
7,167 yards, Par 72

1.	Tiger Woods	66 -67 -70 -67 –270
	Bob May	72 -66-66 -66 –270
3.	Thomas Bjørn	72 -68 -67 -68 –275
4.	José María Olazabal	76 -68 -63 -69 –276
	Stuart Appleby	70 -69 -68 -69 –276
	Greg Chalmers	71 -69-66 -70 –276
7.	Franklin Langham	72 -71 -65 -69 –277
8.	Notah Begay III	72 -66 -70 -70 –278
9.	Phil Mickelson	70 -70 -69 -70 –279
	(with five others)	

Woods beat May in three-hole playoff.

THE 2001 MASTERS
Augusta National G.C.
Augusta, Georgia, April 6–9
6,985 yards, Par 72

1.	Tiger Woods	70 -66 -68 -68 –272
2.	David Duval	71 -66 -70 -67 –274
3.	Phil Mickelson	67 -69 -69 -70 –275
4.	Mark Calcavecchia	72 -66 -68 -72 –278
	Toshi Izawa	71 -66 -74 -67 –278
6.	Ernie Els	71 -68 -68 -72 –279
	Jim Furyk	69 -71 -70 -69 –279
	Bernhard Langer	73 -69 -68 -69 –279
	Kirk Triplett	68 -70 -70 -71 –279
10.	Angel Cabrera	66 -71 -70 -73 –280
	(with four others)	

THE 2001 U.S. OPEN
Southern Hills C.C.
Tulsa, Oklahoma, June 14–18
6,973 yards, Par 70

1.	Retief Goosen	66-70-69-71 –276
	Mark Brooks	72-64-70-70 –276
3.	Stewart Cink	69-69-67-72 –277
4.	Rocco Mediate	71 -68-67-72 –278
5.	Tom Kite	73 -72-72-64 –281
	Paul Azinger	74 -67-69-71 –281
7.	Phil Mickelson	70-69-68-75 –282
	Vijay Singh	74 -70-74-64 –282
	Angel Cabrera	70-71 -72-69 –282
	Davis Love III	72-69-71 -70 –282
	Kirk Triplett	72 -69-71 -70 –282

Goosen (70) beat Brooks (72) in playoff.

THE 2002 U.S. OPEN
Bethpage G.C. (Black Course)
Farmingdale, New York, June 13–16
7,214 yards, Par 70

1.	Tiger Woods	67-68-70-72 –277
2.	Phil Mickelson	70-73 -67-70 –280
3.	Jeff Maggert	69-73 -68-72 –282
4.	Sergio Garcia	68-74 -67-74 –283
5.	Nick Faldo	70-76-66-73 –285
	Scott Hoch	71 -75-70-69 –285
	Billy Mayfair	69-74 -68-74 –285
8.	Nick Price	72 -75 -69-70 –286
	Padraig Harrington	70-68-73 -75 –286
	Tom Byrum	72 -72-70-72 –286

THE 2002 BRITISH OPEN
Hon. Co. of Edinburgh Golfers
Muirfield, Scotland, July 18–21
7,034 yards, Par 71

1.	Ernie Els	70 -66-72 -70 –278
	Steve Elkington	71 -73 -68-66 –278
	Stuart Appleby	73 -70-70-65 –278
	Thomas Levet	72 -66-72 -66 –278
5.	Padraig Harrington	69-67-76-67 –279
	Shigeki Maruyama	68-68-75 -68 –279
	Gary Evans	72 -68-74 -65 –279
8.	Sergio Garcia	71 -69-71 -69 –280
	(with five others)	

Els beat Levet on first sudden-death hole after four-hole playoff eliminated Elkington and Appleby.

THE 2003 BRITISH OPEN
Royal St. George's G.C.
Sandwich, England, July 17–20
7,106 yards, Par 71

1.	Ben Curtis	72 -72 -70-69 –283
2.	Thomas Bjørn	73 -70-69-72 –284
	Vijay Singh	75 -70-69-70 –284
4.	Tiger Woods	73 -72 -69-71 –285
	Davis Love III	69-72 -72 -72 –285
6.	Brian Davis	77 -73 -68-68 –286
	Freddie Jacobson	70-76-70-70 –286
8.	Nick Faldo	76-74 -67-70 –287
	Kenny Perry	74 -70-70-73 –287
10.	Sergio Garcia	73 -71 -70-74 –288
	(with four others)	

THE 2004 MASTERS
Augusta National G.C.
Augusta, Georgia, April 8–11
7,285 yards, Par 72

1.	Phil Mickelson	72 -69-69-69 –279
2.	Ernie Els	70-72 -71 -67 –280
3.	K. J. Choi	71 -72 -72 -69 –282
4.	Sergio Garcia	72 -72 -75 -66 –285
	Bernhard Langer	71 -73 -69-72 –285
6.	Nick Price	72 -73 -71 -70 –286
	Davis Love III	75 -67-74 -70 –286
	Fred Couples	73 -69-74 -70 –286
	Chris DiMarco	69-73 -68-76 –286
	Vijay Singh	75 -73 -69-69 –286
	Paul Casey	75 -69-68-74 –286
	Kirk Triplett	71 -74 -69-72 –286

THE 2004 BRITISH OPEN
Royal Troon G.C.
Ayrshire, Scotland, July 15–18
7,175 yards, Par 71

1.	Todd Hamilton	71 -67-67-69 –274
	Ernie Els	69-69-68-68 –274
3.	Phil Mickelson	73 -66-68-68 –275
4.	Lee Westwood	72 -71 -68-67 –278
5.	Davis Love III	72 -69-71 -67 –279
	Thomas Levet	66-70-71 -72 –279
7.	Scott Verplank	69-70-70-71 –280
	Retief Goosen	69-70-68-73 –280
9.	Tiger Woods	70-71 -68-72 –281
	Mike Weir	71 -68-71 -71 –281

Hamilton beat Els in four-hole playoff.

THE 2004 PGA
Whistling Straits G.C.
Kohler, Wisconsin, August 12–15
7,514 yards, Par 72

1.	Vijay Singh	67-68-69-76 –280
	Justin Leonard	66-69-70-75 –280
	Chris DiMarco	68-70-71 -71 –280
4.	Ernie Els	66-70-72 -73 –281
	Chris Riley	69-70-69-73 –281
6.	Phil Mickelson	69-72-67-74 –282
	K. J. Choi	68-71 -73 -70 –282
	Paul McGinley	69-74-70-69 –282
9.	Adam Scott	71 -71 -69-72 –283
	(with three others)	

Singh beat Leonard and DiMarco in three-hole playoff.

THE 2005 PGA
Baltusrol C.C. (Lower Course)
Springfield, New Jersey, August 11–15
7,392 yards, Par 70

1.	Phil Mickelson	67-65 -72 -72 –276
2.	Steve Elkington	68-70-68-71 –277
	Thomas Bjørn	71 -71 -63 -72 –277
4.	Tiger Woods	75 -69-66-68 –278
	Davis Love III	68-68-68-74 –278
6.	Retief Goosen	68-70-69-72 –279
	Geoff Ogilvy	69-69-72-69 –279
	Michael Campbell	73 -68-69-69 –279
	Pat Perez	68-71 -67-73 –279
10.	Vijay Singh	70-67-69-74 –280
	(with four others)	

THE 2006 U.S. OPEN
Winged Foot G.C. (West Course)
Mamaroneck, New York, June 15–18
7,264 yards, Par 70

1.	Geoff Ogilvy	71 -70-72-72 –285
2.	Phil Mickelson	70-73 -69-74 –286
	Colin Montgomerie	69-71 -75 -71 –286
	Jim Furyk	70-72-74-70 –286
5.	Padraig Harrington	73 -69-74-71 –287
6.	Vijay Singh	71 -74-70-73 –288
	Mike Weir	71 -74-71 -72 –288
	Steve Stricker	70-69-76-73 –288
	Jeff Sluman	74 -73 -72 -69 –288
	Nick O'Hern	75 -70-74-69 –288
	Kenneth Ferrie	71 -70-71 -76 –288

THE 2007 PGA
Southern Hills C.C.
Tulsa, Oklahoma, August 9–12
7,131 yards, Par 70

1.	Tiger Woods	71 -63 -69-69 –272
2.	Woody Austin	68-70-69-67 –274
3.	Ernie Els	72 -68-69-66 –275
4.	Aaron Oberholser	68-72-70-69 –279
	John Senden	69-70-69-71 –279
6.	Geoff Ogilvy	69-68-74-69 –280
	Trevor Immelman	75 -70-66-69 –280
	Simon Dyson	73 -71 -72 -64 –280
9.	Scott Verplank	70-66-74-71 –281
	Boo Weekley	76 -69-65 -71 –281
	Kevin Sutherland	73 -69-68-71 –281

THE 2008 MASTERS
Augusta National G.C.
Augusta, Georgia, April 9–12
7,445 yards, Par 72

1.	Trevor Immelman	68-68-69-75 –280
2.	Tiger Woods	72 -71 -68-72 –283
3.	Stewart Cink	72 -69-71 -72 –284
	Brandt Snedeker	69-68-70-77 –284
5.	Phil Mickelson	71 -68-75 -72 –286
	Padraig Harrington	74 -71 -69-72 –286
	Steve Flesch	72 -67-69-78 –286
8.	Miguel Ángel Jiménez	77 -70-72 -68 –287
	Andres Romero	72 -72-70-73 –287
	Robert Karlsson	70-73 -71 -73 –287

THE 2008 U.S. OPEN
Torrey Pines G.C. (South Course)
San Diego, California, June 12–16
7,643 yards, Par 71

1.	Tiger Woods	72 -68-70-73 –283
	Rocco Mediate	69-71 -72 -71 –283
3.	Lee Westwood	70-71 -70-73 –284
4.	Robert Karlsson	70-70-75 -71 –286
	D. J. Trahan	72 -69-73 -72 –286
6.	Carl Pettersson	71 -71 -77-68 –287
	John Merrick	73 -72-71 -71 –287
	Miguel Ángel Jiménez	75 -66-74 -71 –287
9.	Geoff Ogilvy	69-73 -72 -74 –288
	Brandt Snedeker	76 -73 -68-71 –288
	Heath Slocum	75 -74 -74 -65 –288
	Eric Axley	69-79-71 -69 –288
	Camillo Villegas	73 -71 -71 -73 –288

Woods beat Mediate with par on first sudden-death hole after they tied at 71 in 18-hole playoff.

INDEX